With EDWARDS *in the* GOVERNOR'S MANSION

With
EDWARDS
in the
GOVERNOR'S
MANSION
FROM ANGOLA TO FREE MAN

By Forest C. Hammond-Martin, Sr. • Edited by Tom Aswell

PELICAN PUBLISHING COMPANY
GRETNA 2012

The word "Pelican" and the depiction of a pelican
are trademarks of Pelican Publishing Company, Inc.,
and are registered in the U.S. Patent and Trademark Office.

Library of Congress Cataloging-in-Publication Data

Hammond-Martin, Forest C.
  With Edwards in the Governor's mansion : from Angola to free man / by
Forest C. Hammond-Martin, Sr. ; edited by Tom Aswell.
    p. cm.
  ISBN 978-1-4556-1625-1 (hbk : alk. paper) — ISBN 978-1-4556-1626-
8 (e-book) 1. Hammond-Martin, Forest C. 2. Edwards, Edwin W. 3. Ex-
convicts—Louisiana—Baton Rouge—Biography. 4. African American
prisoners—Louisiana—Baton Rouge—Biography. 5. Criminal justice,
Administration of—Corrupt practices—Louisiana—Baton Rouge. 6.
Convict labor—Louisiana—Baton Rouge. 7. Governors—Louisiana—
Conduct of life. 8. Political corruption—Louisiana—Baton Rouge. I.
Aswell, Tom. II. Title.
  HV9468.H225A3 2012
  976.3'063092—dc23
  [B]
                                        2012006975

Printed in the United States of America
Published by Pelican Publishing Company, Inc.
1000 Burmaster Street, Gretna, Louisiana 70053

All the world's a stage,
And all the men and women merely players;
They have their exits and their entrances,
And one man in his time plays many parts,
His acts being seven ages.

—Shakespeare

Contents

Acknowledgments

There are so many people to acknowledge for their help and moral support. I wish to thank all my friends who assisted me in one way or another. Special thanks to my lovely wife, Karen, and my children, Angela, Bryan Keith, Misty, Forest, Jr., Neal Nassor, and Miranda, for their patience and understanding while I relived many bad memories during the process of writing this book. Thanks to Cynthia Jardon, feature journalist for the *Alexandria Town Talk*. Thanks to Brenda Kaiser of KALB-TV in Alexandria and her daughters Krystal, Kari, and Kasee. Finally, thanks to Robert Harris, MD, DD, PhD, international vice president and dean of the Institute of Divine Metaphysical Research, who seemed to read my mind when I was ready to quit and always had the right words of encouragement to convince me to soldier on.

Prologue

This is the story of a young man who made a mistake—a grave error in judgment. He was black, he lived in Louisiana, he was a star athlete, and he was a first offender, but he was involved in a crime in which a well-known white businessman was killed.

This is a true story where you will see state and federal criminal justice systems still immersed in the politics of the Civil War, still swimming in the corruption of the Carpetbaggers, and still so divided by bigotry that Lady Justice's blindfold is permanently askew so she might peek at the color of a man's skin before dispensing justice—a justice handed down with the mentality of a plantation overseer.

Corruption in Louisiana isn't news; it's business as usual. It was the early 1970s, and times were tumultuous. Most historians mark this era, which started a decade earlier with the assassinations of John F. Kennedy, Malcolm X, Martin Luther King, Bobby Kennedy, and Medgar Evers and ended with Vietnam and Watergate, as the end of America's innocence. The ground was shifting like quicksand under our feet as we found we could no longer trust the government, that we were unbeatable in war, and that we were always right.

Television brought the Vietnam War into our living rooms and then returned us to the fantasy worlds of *Adam-12* and *The Brady Bunch*. Television and movies were only beginning to reflect society with *The Godfather* and *All in the Family*. *The Deer Hunter*, *Platoon*, and *Apocalypse Now* were still years away from showing us the darker side of the Vietnam War.

In June 1972, the U.S. Supreme Court ruled Louisiana's death penalty unconstitutional, although it would be reinstated four years later. In July 1972, Gov. Edwin W. Edwards signed a bill to strike down the infamous Jim Crow laws that had succeeded for generations in keeping blacks in their place, with separate schools, toilets, drinking fountains, and seats in the back of the bus.

The *Baton Rouge Advocate* newspaper devoted a headline and a mere five paragraphs to the governor's historic action. It quoted one black legislator. The white legislators were silent, because in reality, only outward appearances had changed.

To many Southern whites, a nigger was still a nigger. The color of his skin meant that he was somehow genetically beneath whites as well as inherently evil. Louisiana jails and prisons were overcrowded with these "evil" black men—and still are. The entire country still battles the stereotypical prejudice that would have us all see in a young black man not the potential of a contributor to society but of a criminal, a commodity to be used to till the soil of the fields in the state penitentiary.

Louisiana has the highest prison-sentence rate in the nation. At Angola, the largest and bloodiest of all the nation's penitentiaries, the truth could be viewed, but not by the outside world. Angola's 18,000 acres of farmland are the site of an old plantation where, more than a century after Abraham Lincoln freed slaves, judicial slaves still toil in the fields from sunup to sundown. The original slaves who lived there and worked the land were purchased from the African country of Angola during the eighteenth century, thus the inspiration for the name. Then and now, the stakes are high: the crop is cash. The commodity is still human bondage and black athleticism.

This story shows how our system of justice was allowed to break down for one man and can fail us all, regardless of our guilt or innocence.

With
EDWARDS
in the
GOVERNOR'S
MANSION

PART I

Chapter 1

Krewe of da Mansion

Dense exhaust billowed from the tailpipe, almost engulfing the white fifteen-seat passenger van parked at the gate of the Louisiana State Police inmate barracks, and then quietly disappeared, its gray wisps swallowed up in the pitch-blackness of the predawn hours. Parked on white seashells and facing an open storm-fence gate, the van had on its running lights. The driver was Slim, a tall, thirty-something black man with a round, small head. He nervously stared down a lighted walkway between a half-dome-shaped military barracks on the left and an eighty-foot trailer office on the right. Slim's right hand rested uneasily on the gear lever. He revved the engine, signaling he was ready to go. A purple, green, and gold Mardi Gras emblem on the driver's door read, *KREWE OF DA MANSION*. Below it in fine print appeared: State of Louisiana—Department of Public Safety and Corrections—Executive Department.

A disc jockey howled over WXOK, a local black radio station, "It's the last day of the last month of the last year of the seventies decade; you figure out the date. It's twenty-six degrees here in the capital city. For those of you who have to work today, I'm sorry, but happy New Year anyway. If you were due to clock in at five, you're already ten minutes late. People, dress warm and drink your hot chocolate because it's freezing outside."

Two black males, one tall and one short, rushed through the gate, opened the double side doors of the van, and jumped inside to escape the cold. Slim looked in his rearview mirror and counted heads. On the rear seat and to the far right sat Bobby. Forty-eight, husky, and of average height, he was the executive chef at the governor's mansion, currently occupied by Edwin Edwards and family. He had worked there for nearly eight years. A huge pair of sunglasses covered Bobby's face despite the darkness of the hour. Draped on his head was an oversized colorful knit hat—a fashionable piece of the early-1970s Sly Stone era. Two orange puffy knit balls dangled on strings and rested on his shoulders like pillows about his neck. His eyes kept moving behind the dark lenses, watching everyone, though no one could tell. For all anyone knew, Bobby was asleep.

Sally sat on the seat in front of Bobby. The stern, solid frame of the fifty-five-year-old mansion dishwasher was coal black with snow-white teeth and red eyes. A white sailor's cap complemented the heavy, dark-blue jacket, giving the appearance that he was in the navy. A French-speaking native of Opelousas, Sally had his customary toothpick hanging out of the left side of his mouth. He looked around shaking his head in disgust at the younger men asleep in their seats. They had staggered into the van as if by instinct alone. Heads covered with caps, they leaned against each other or the cold windows. They were exhausted, unable to open their eyes. They had just gotten out of the van two hours earlier from a forty-eight-hours-straight shift. Next to Sally was Francis, the quiet assistant chef who always had a neatly folded clean towel on his shoulder.

Ross, a short black man in his forties, worked alone in the mansion's basement laundry. He dry-cleaned the executive family's entire wardrobe, including the clothes of the first couple's children, Anna, Stephen, Victoria, and big David, the youngest. Ross also dry-cleaned the three-piece suits and blue state-police uniforms of nine mansion security intelligence officers (MSIOs) and the governor's four drivers, who were also his bodyguards.

Ross's eyes were always red, as if he'd been drinking, but that was strictly prohibited. Ross worked from sunup to sundown and never damaged one piece of laundry. He was a New Orleans thug/dropout turned street hustler. He was destined by fate and a felony murder charge to be a member of the Krewe of da Mansion. Ross knew the governor's favorite suits and the order in which he wore them. "Pops never wears the same suit twice in a month," Ross would declare, flaunting his knowledge of the governor's habits that the others didn't possess.

Ellis, whom everyone called BigOne, sat in the front passenger seat with his feet propped up against the dashboard. He was asleep. He and Slim helped park cars and directed mansion-guest traffic during huge luncheons, a daily occurrence when the legislature was in session. He washed all executive vehicles and the first couple's family cars, vans, and trucks, including those of the governor's children, and of mansion employees. He, Slim, Vic, and Ross wore dark-green uniforms indicative of their positions at the mansion as *field niggers*—not allowed in the house. If they were ever caught on the first floor by the first lady, it was back to Africa for them, as she so eloquently alluded to the Louisiana State Penitentiary at Angola during her initial interview with each convict. At lunch and dinnertime, the field niggers' meals were sent down on the dumbwaiter. They ate in the basement, sitting on milk crates.

Frank LeBlanc, or "Jughead," a butler, was forty-five and a former drug dealer and hustler from New Orleans. He was extremely nervous, repeatedly brushing his face with his palm. Jughead cleaned all the state's silverware daily. When he had been arrested, a New Orleans policeman fired his .357 magnum next to his ear, damaging his hearing. Because of that, Jughead talked in a loud voice and always double-checked instructions from mansion personnel. He was called "Two Times" because everything had to be said to him twice.

"All right, wake up in here!" Slim said, raising his voice a bit and disturbing his sleeping passengers. "I got fourteen and I need fifteen. Whoever's not in here, speak up." The sleeping passengers, most of whom were in their late twenties, refused to open their eyes, because to do so would interrupt precious seconds of sleep they needed to make it through the day.

Roy Lee, a butler who was also a baseball coach in Angola, was from Baton Rouge. His assigned area was the entrance foyer and sitting and drawing rooms. He had reserved the only vacant seat for his homeboy, who had not come in yet.

Larry "Sugar Bear" Allen, a butler from New Orleans, sat in the first seat behind Slim, with big, tall, baritone-voiced Vic. Sugar Bear was Anna's babysitter. Watching the governor's grandson, John Todd, during the food-service rush hours got him out of lots of menial housework in his assigned area of the state dining room and guest restrooms off the entrance foyer. The other butlers were always angry with him.

Butler Tommy Mason was short, dark skinned, clean cut, and articulate. He was the assistant editor of the *Angolite*, the nationally renowned prison magazine whose editor, Wilbert Rideau, was a high-profile, ex-death-row convict from Lake Charles. Tommy was assigned to the first couple's bedroom and bathrooms.

The sneakiest butler in the mansion was Phillip. Barely six feet tall, he was skinny and of a color that made him appear to be of Asian extraction. He had curly hair and a baritone voice. Also from New Orleans, he aspired to be a ladies' man. His assigned area was the governor's office and elevator foyer, where the governor's appointments waited to see him.

Devold, the oldest butler, was forty-six. He was from Eunice, near Opelousas. Devold spoke French fluently. He was nervous and paranoid and consumed coffee all day. Keeping fresh Community coffee for the governor and making sure drinks were in the cooler in the butler's station were his primary duties.

Everyone except Bobby and Sally was insecure in his hopes of being pardoned by the governor. Their fears, for the most part, were groundless but sufficient to make them paranoid about any mansion transgressions. The Krewe of da Mansion was comprised of fifteen felons who ran the governor's mansion and made it all happen. All of them had been Angola inmates serving life sentences for murder before being transferred to the state police barracks to work at the mansion. All except Bobby and Sally had been working at the mansion for nearly four years. If they lasted until the governor finished his term in office on March 20, 1980, without getting into trouble, they would be pardoned by the governor.

"Whoever ain't in here yet, speak up!" Slim yelled. Bobby chuckled. Sally uttered words in French, shaking his head. Devold replied in French without opening his eyes.

"What was that, Sally?" Bobby asked, chuckling.

Mr. Williams, a correctional officer in plain clothes, burst out of the main barracks door and walked swiftly towards the van, wearing his big parka and blowing in his hands to keep them warm. Slim waited until he arrived at the driver's-side door before lowering the window an inch so he could hear him.

"Y'all better come quick! It's Hammond! He said he's not going today. He said he's off!" Williams shouted. Slim closed the window. He stared at the dashboard clock. It was five twenty.

"Man, I got a five-mile drive to make in ten minutes!" Slim shouted. "Mrs. Elaine gonna be looking out her window upstairs at that driveway at five thirty. I ain't gonna be late. Y'all better go get that niggah." Slim put the van in reverse and backed into the street headed north, revving the engine as he did so. The name "Elaine" had the power to raise the dead, prompting those sleeping to open their eyes and look around, fully conscious as if they had eight hours worth of sleep.

Sally finally answered Bobby's question, in English. "I said I never seen such a sorry-a-- bunch of young niggahs in all my life,

I swear before God. You young niggahs is suppose to look out for one another."

Bobby, Francis, Sally, and Roy Lee exited the van. "Close the door, niggah! It's cold!" Sugar Bear exclaimed. Roy Lee kept walking, ignoring him, but looked back and rolled his eyes as Sugar Bear closed the doors. Slim watched the four convicts follow Williams down the walkway and back inside the barracks.

Once past the office, Williams turned his flashlight on and entered the dark, warm dormitory through double doors, the other four men following close behind. At the first top bunk in the left corner, the light was shone towards Saint's head. Saint was naked except for a worn and faded pair of red and gold Capitol High Lions gym shorts. An array of legal documents was strewn amidst the blanket and sheets on his bunk. Other documents were torn or balled up on the floor.

"Damn!" Roy Lee exclaimed, shaking his head.

Where You At, God?

Roy Lee, Francis, and Sally stood waiting for Bobby's orders. Bobby observed the paperwork and breadbox at the foot of Saint's bunk. He chuckled again. "Say, Saint, come on, man—let's go. You know what you gotta do. Let's go get it over with, Champ," Bobby said with the tone of a compassionate counselor.

"I'm off today," Saint mumbled from under a pillow. "The good white folks said I could take the day off. I ain't gotta go in. I got to fight tonight." Bobby smiled, having experienced years of what Saint was going through for the first time.

Saint had come to the mansion in February 1979—eleven months earlier. This was his first holiday season. Bobby knew he just needed to hold out for less than three months and he'd be freed. Bobby, who often read his little New Testament half-a-Bible, likened Saint's situation to the parable about the laborers who early one morning agreed to work all day for a penny. Then a laborer came in at the eleventh hour, worked only one hour, and got the same penny. Saint hadn't worked at the mansion a full year and was about to get the same penny for which Bobby and others had labored hard for years: freedom.

Saint had been a special, highly volatile case from the first day Bobby saw him. In less than a year, Saint was just as valuable to the governor as Bobby was as executive chef. He was twenty-four and the youngest of the Krewe of da Mansion. The other convicts were expendable, but Bobby and Saint were viable commodities. Saint was a boxer, but not just any boxer; otherwise Edwards would never have sent for Detective Joe Whitmore to bring Saint from Angola to the mansion. Edwards and some wealthy businessmen had taken a serious interest in Saint's fighting abilities. Saint was the light-heavyweight champion in Angola. News of how he dominated the boxing ring reached Edwards through a former pro boxer and trainer named Billy Roth. Roth had taken his boxing team from the Baton Rouge Police Training Academy to Angola to fight exhibitions against prison fight clubs, to tune up his young team for the upcoming National A.A.U. Championship Tournament in the free world. A recent federal suit had resulted in a federal court order banning inmates from A.A.U. competitions.

Tom Landry from Lake Charles, the ninth-ranked U.S. Golden Gloves light heavyweight, was present to get a tune-up fight, but at 197 pounds, he was overweight. His trainer didn't want him to fight an Angola heavyweight. Saint, who weighed in perfectly at 173 pounds, had been unmatched for months because no one would get in the ring with him, not even for a workout. Cheyenne, Saint's boxing trainer and the best fight trainer in Angola, offered him to fight five three-minute rounds with Landry. When Roth saw the speed with which Saint fought, his Muhammad Ali dance and boxing style, and his devastating combinations, combined with the fact that Landry never landed one punch to Saint's head, he visualized lots of money. He spoke with Saint after the fight. When Saint told Roth of his criminal charges, Roth said, "I knew Billy Middleton. He was a good friend of mine. I also know Governor Edwards. He's a good friend of mine, too."

"You know, Mr. Roth, when I got in trouble, I had a football scholarship," Saint said. "I lost that. Now, I'm the light-heavyweight champion, and I haven't had a fight in eight months. No one will get in the ring with me. With the right food, rest, and Cheyenne in my corner, no professional fighter out there in my weight class can beat me." Saint spoke with so much confidence that Roth believed him. He'd witnessed the proof in the ring.

"I'll see what I can do, okay?" Roth shook Saint's hand.

"Grab his legs," Bobby ordered. Roy Lee and Sally grabbed Saint's legs while Bobby grabbed his left wrist. Saint jerked away and held the iron rail of the bed.

"Come on, Saint, man. Let's get it over with, man," Bobby repeated.

"Leave me alone, Bobby. I'm telling you. Leave me alone."

Bobby was unable to pull Saint's handgrip free. A white inmate named Coleman in the bunk below Saint awakened and yelled in fear of being attacked. Not knowing what was happening, he fled the dorm.

"Say, Roy Lee, he must t'ink somebody was after that a--," Sally said in his French accent and chuckled.

Roy Lee grinned as he pulled the mattress from under Saint, causing the breadbox containing clothes and files to fall and scatter on the floor. Williams kept his flashlight on Saint's face. Inmates in the immediate area sat up, watching.

"Come on, Saint! Let's go, man," Roy Lee pleaded. "You know what this means? Mrs. Elaine gonna send your a-- back to Africa, boy. Now get up!"

After jerking him free, the four men carried Saint by his four limbs. Shouting obscenities, he twisted and struggled to get loose but couldn't. They carried him out through the double doors and the activity room. Williams stood in the cold, holding the door open.

"I ain't going!" Saint screamed. "Let me go! Turn me loose, Bobby! Roy Lee, let me go! I don't care no more! Send me back! I object! I need some rest! I can't fight like this. I'm tired. I need a typewriter, law books. This a setup. They set me up. This ain't 'bout boxing. That b---- Polozola dismissed my case."

Saint yielded to fatigue and fell asleep cursing. He was delirious and dead tired. Even the freezing weather had no effect upon him.

"Y'all hurry. I'll put all his stuff back in his box," Williams said.

"All right, Mr. Williams. Thanks," Roy Lee said.

They carried Saint down the walkway. Slim revved the engine, creating another cloud of exhaust.

"Put him down," Bobby ordered. Sally and Roy Lee gently lowered Saint's bare feet as Bobby and Francis lowered his head and arms onto the cold street.

"Ain't this niggah gonna freeze, Bobby?" Roy Lee asked, mildly protesting.

Bobby opened the van door and got in, saying nothing. The others followed.

Slim pulled off slowly, observing the five-mile-per-hour speed-limit signs posted every twenty feet in the Department of Public Safety and Corrections complex.

Inside the dormitory, Williams reset the mattress on the bunk with the blanket, sheets, and pillow. He unwrapped a bundle of foil and found it full of delicious pecan brownies from the mansion. He stuck one halfway in his mouth, holding it with his lips, while closing the foil and placing it under Saint's pillow. He put all of Saint's papers in the breadbox, with his clothes and red Bible on top.

"He usually keeps his box slid right here under my head on the floor," said Coleman, who had by now returned to his bunk and saw that Williams was about to place the box on top of the bunk. He slid the breadbox where Coleman suggested. Williams noticed a huge ball of several sheets of paper on the floor at the edge of the light coming through the windows of the double door from the activity room. When he opened them, he saw the papers were from the United States District Court, Middle District of Louisiana, and signed by U.S. District Judge E. Gordon West. Ten pages consisted of the magistrate's report, signed by Magistrate Frank J. Polozola. Another sheet contained the heading, "Judgment and Order." The document read: "IT IS ORDERED that petitioner's application for a writ of habeas corpus be, and it is hereby DENIED, and this suit is hereby DISMISSED. Baton Rouge, Louisiana, November 26, 1979."

Saint, meanwhile, eyes wide open, was lying on his back in the freezing street, still clad only in his old red Capitol High gym shorts. He stared into the clear winter sky at millions of stars. Shivering uncontrollably, he finally lifted his head. He saw the van 400 feet down the street. "What the f---?" Saint sprang to his feet and began sprinting. *Come on, Saint. You got to do it,* he thought. "Aw, damn!" he exclaimed aloud. A white seashell had cut into his foot. He limped a few steps before stopping. He raised his foot and pulled out a blood-covered shell.

"*Where you at, God?*" Saint shouted as he stood in the cold. *How in the world did I ever get in this s---?* he thought again, as he had done every day that he'd been locked up. This question had been his daily companion for nearly seven years.

Thanks to a good memory, answers had always come to him in the form of flashbacks. *Where is this one coming from? What will it show? What does it want me know?*

If the State violates your constitutional rights, you can appeal to the State Supreme Court. If they deny you, you can appeal to the federal court. If the federal court denies you, you have to appeal to the good Lord. He was desperate. Listening within, he waited for a response through his conscience, but none came forth. Behind bars and inside Angola, he felt reprobated by the world. It had been a long time since he'd heard from his friend.

The latest duplicity by the Louisiana criminal-justice system had Saint running in pitch-black darkness through the woods with a tiny keychain flashlight. He felt that Mr. Anding, his federal-court-appointed lawyer, had sold him out, or the federal clerk of court did not send him notice so that an objection could be filed in his case. Either way, his case was now dead. He was stuck with serving a life sentence for a crime of which he was never convicted and to which he did not plead guilty. He now struggled with the realization that he might be working at the mansion for four additional years, serving Republican governor-elect David C. Treen.

"If they think I'm gonna work four years for Treen, they got another thought coming."

In nanoseconds, a phantasmagoria of Saint's days of growing up in Baton Rouge's Zion City neighborhood through his last days in high school culminated on April 10, 1973.

Chapter 2
Run, Forest, Run!

Around the spacious patio in front of Capitol Senior High's cafeteria were concrete bench seats that students occupied during lunch period. They sat talking in small groups. Early arrivals claimed the shaded area under a few trees. Some worked on writing assignments or studied textbooks before their next class. On this particular day, Saint reclined on the patio steps, resting his head on his mesh book sack. He adjusted his authentic camouflage bush hat that a Vietnam-veteran friend, Hindu Spurlock, had given him. It covered his face, blocking the noonday sun. Next to Saint, in the same posture, was his longtime friend, Raymond Valentine. Raymond and Saint's long legs were stretched over two platform steps, with their feet resting on the patio floor. The two had just come from smoking Kools in a recess near the door to the band department in front of the school. It was in the open but safer than smoking in the restroom, where coaches usually caught athlete smokers and punished them with extra practices.

The Capitol High track team. Raymond Valentine is in the front row, far right. Saint is in the back row, center, wearing a wristband.

The Capitol Lions' mile-relay track team had not lost a race all year. Saint, as the third leg, could run a 47.5-second quarter, bringing the baton to Raymond, who could finish the last 400-meter sprint in 48 seconds. The two teenagers had grown up together in Easy Town since 1965. Their mothers had been friends and were both deceased, a commonality the teens shared as brothers.

Nearly five years after the suicide, Saint still had questions lingering in his mind that he never got a chance to ask his mother as he was growing up. *Who am I?* he wondered. *How did I get*

Saint's mother, Edna, as a Red Cross nurse in the 1940s.

here? Why am I here? Why do people die? Where will I go after I die? Who is God? How does He exist? Saint often asked himself these perplexing questions. *Do I not believe because God let my best friend in the world die? Why do I live on the edge of death?*

In Zion City, it was a hot summer noonday in the mid-1960s. Eight-year-old Forest left the store carrying a brown paper grocery bag of bread, eggs, lemons, butter, and a pack of Salem cigarettes. Ignoring a voice in his conscience, he stopped at his favorite spot next to a little red church on Ford Street—the crawfish hole. Forest was barefoot, wearing cutoff jeans and no shirt. Sensing a creeping presence in a bushy area, he grabbed the grocery bag and took off running through the crawfish hole. John Henry exploded out of the bush, jumping over the hole in his track sneakers. Jesse James barely cleared it with his leap. Fat Bo-Bo jumped, landing in the middle of the puddle and getting stuck. As Forest followed a bending dirt trail through the woods, he grabbed a leaning branch. When John Henry saw the branch coming back, he ducked. Jesse James caught the branch in the face, flattening him to the ground. By the time Forest made it to the gravel road at Kissel Street a block and a half from home, John Henry was ten yards behind. Forest, covered with mud but still holding the grocery bag, ran across the hot thick bed of gravel. He prayed silently for help: *Good Lord, help me. Where you at?* At the corner of Kissel and Packard, Forest turned at Bea's Café. He ran through hedges and John Henry followed. Forest began zigzagging. John Henry zigzagged in close pursuit.

Where all the old people at? Forest wondered, since God hadn't helped yet. *They usually be sitting on the porch. If they was sitting in they chairs and saw John Henry, they'd say, "Leave that boy alone! I'm a whip your a--, boy! Take your bad a-- home!"*

As they ran past old wood-framed shotgun houses on the dusty dirt homestretch, it was quiet like a desert silence—with only the sounds of the rustling paper bag, bare feet slapping the dry ground, and grunts and deep breathing echoing each boy's determination and refusal to give up. Then, something happened. Voices started talking to Forest again.

Stop running. He's not behind you anymore. You're just running for nothing. Stop! Turn around and see. Don't be scared. Just turn. Aren't you tired of running? one voice asked.

He's behind you, warned the other. *No need to turn around. You don't need to see. You hear him. Just know that he's back there and keep running.* Both voices sounded like his own.

With his arm extended, John Henry reached, clawed, scratched, and grabbed with each step—his fingers slipping off Forest's sweaty right shoulder as his prey stayed one step ahead. Forest jumped over a raised water meter. John Henry tripped over it and fell headfirst into an algae-filled ditch. Forest passed his younger brother Paul as he turned at the corner of the house and ran to the back and up the steps. He burst through the screen door, falling with the bag onto the floor. Lemons exploded out of the bag and scattered everywhere.

Edna was repeatedly striking the telephone receiver on the base. Just prior to her son's dramatic entrance, she was serving lunch to her children when the phone rang. "Hello, Edna Bernitha speaking," she said.

"Is this the white half-breed b---- whose man I had last night? Half-breed, last night your man was hunting and shooting his two-legged coon," a black woman's voice uttered.

Now, Edna was gazing at her mud-covered, breathless son.

"Mommy! John Henry and them was chasing after me. You shoulda seen me running! Boy, I was running so faaaast. You shoulda seen me, Mommy! He couldn't catch me neither. He was breathing in my ears. I could hear him. His finger was scratching my shoulder. I wasn't tired neither! I ain't dropped your bag neither, Mommy."

Edna took her mashed bread and egg-covered pack of Salems out of the bag.

"I'm so proud of you, darling. We have an old Indian saying," Edna said as she bandaged the soles of her son's feet. "'He that fights or runs away shall live to fight another day.' Now, don't forget that, you hear? Because you ran doesn't mean you're scared. A lot of people who didn't run are in graveyards."

Edna was born on September 1, 1921, in Lawrenceville, Illinois. Her father, Elmer Hammond, was Jewish and her mother, Olivia Lyles, was Blackfoot Indian. Edna was raised on a farm and finished twelfth grade. She then moved to Los Angeles to study nursing and took a job with the Red Cross. In late 1949, she was sent to attend to injured veterans in Shreveport, where she met Forest Martin.

me & my beloved daddy.

Edna and her father on the Fourth of July 1948 in Lawrenceville.

I Call myself dressed up. Huh!

Edna in 1948.

Edna lived in Hollywood.

Horseback riding in the Hollywood hills.

Forest Martin in the 1940s in New Roads, Louisiana.

Martin was born on February 27, 1915, in Tolbert, Louisiana, about five miles south of New Roads. At the age of fourteen, he quit school and went to work on a log camp to help his mother take care of the family. He earned fifty cents a day. He became a hustler and streetwise businessman. When he met Edna, he owned a fleet of dump trucks in Baton Rouge and sold dirt to housing and commercial building contractors. The two moved in together. Fern Lorraine was first to be born to Edna and Forest, in 1951. Then Edna left Forest and lived in Indianapolis for over a year. When she returned, she did so with a second child, Vincent. Forest rejected Vincent, and Edna sent him to Los Angeles to live with her sister, Fern. In 1955, Forest Hammond was born, followed by his brother Paul in 1958. Their parents got married in 1959, and three more children were born: Teresa, Daisy, and Michael.

Forest was watching his mother as she tended to him. "Mommy, something told me not to go to that crawfish hole," he admitted.

"See, that's the still small voice of your guardian angel, Yahweh Eloah, talking to you. If you listen and obey his voice, it'll keep you out of trouble. I told you to go to the store and come straight back—not go to the crawfish hole. You didn't listen; now look at your soles. You better start obeying what he tells you. One of these days, you'll wish you had listened," Edna admonished. She walked to the mantel and lit jar candles and incense. Above the mantel was a board with sketches of baby faces of her seven children. Normally she burned the candles and incense after she and her husband argued.

"You saying another prayer for me? Who them people is on those candles?" Forest asked.

Forest, Aunt Fern, Fern Lorraine, and Vincent in 1956.

Edna pointed at the images painted on the jars and called their names. "St. Michael, St. Paul, St. Teresa, and St. Vincent. These are saints I named your brothers and sister after," she answered.

He searched the mantel in vain for his namesake candle jar. "Well, where St. Forest at, then?" he asked.

Edna laughed and hugged her son. "You're so crazy. You always make me laugh. There is no . . . Aw, you're my special amazing Saint, just like your Amazing Spiderman."

The 1954 *Brown vs. Board of Education* desegregation decision by the United States Supreme Court was finally being implemented in Baton Rouge. The family moved from 5035 Packard Street to 3113 Newton Street in Easy Town. There Martin got out of the dirt-selling business and started a janitorial service. He bought a white van to haul his equipment in. Then the family moved to 205 North Twenty-Fifth Street, at the corner of Convention Street. Edna registered Saint at Westdale Junior High on Claycut Road. She convinced him to take certain courses, including music and French. Little did he know he would experience a side of life in this world he never knew existed—full-blown racism at the hands of white students and white teachers. In the hallway on the first day of school, as twelve-year-old Saint and other black students changed classes or went to their lockers, they heard, "Nigger, nigger, nigger," "Look at that nigger," "Darky," "There's goes another coon," or "Look at that spook." It was as if the white

Saint, Paul, Teresa, and Daisy, Easter Sunday 1966. A Martin's Janitorial van is visible behind them.

students were trying to make black students feel inferior for being black—as if anyone had a choice in the matter of what color they would be born.

Saint's last class that day was American history. His teacher was a Sergeant Carter lookalike. His name was Mr. Chambers. He had the traditional military haircut, khaki pants, a plaid shirt, and a loud, baritone voice. A yellow pencil stayed perched on one of his large ears. The class was held in a metal building on the backside of the main school building. Saint, the only black student in that class, claimed the last seat on the end row nearest the door. He wanted to be the first to run out when the bell sounded and the first on the school bus. After Mr. Chambers issued textbooks, he gave the first assignment to his class.

"Learn the preamble to the United States Constitution and know it by heart tomorrow. You're going to be graded on this assignment," Chambers said.

That night, Edna had Saint recite the preamble over and over until he began complaining and making excuses. "Mommy, in all my classes, them white children know stuff I ain't never heard of in all my life. They know what Mrs. Eubanks be talking about in

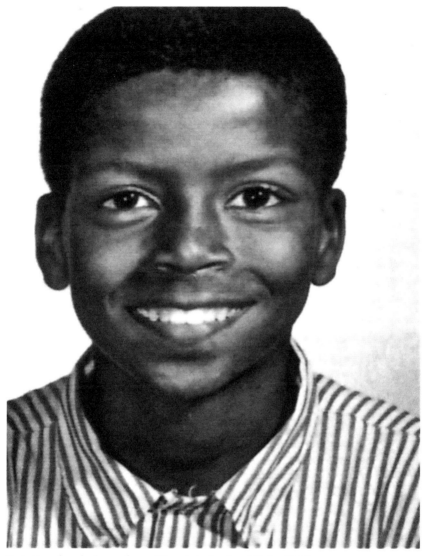

Saint's school photo from Westdale Junior High, 1967.

math. I ain't never heard none of them words before. Fractions! Them white students know everything she been talking about. They must have learned that in sixth grade wherever they went. I don't know nothing, Mommy. Mr. Woods and Mr. White never taught us none of that stuff," Saint said. "The preamble is too long. I can't remember all of that."

"You remembered the universe assignment from the encyclopedias

I bought you all for Christmas in Zion City. You knew it by heart. You can remember this," Edna replied.

The next day, after getting past wanting to fight any white student who called anybody "nigger," Saint couldn't wait to get to his American history class. He raised his hand each time Chambers asked, "Who wants to try it next?" Saint knew that the teacher had to see his only black arm in the class that was raised high—even lifting himself out of his seat to be recognized. Finally, when not one of the twenty-seven white students could recite the preamble without making mistakes, Chambers moved on to giving out assignments for the next day. This class had obviously come to an end.

"Mr. Chambers!" Saint called.

The teacher looked around the class as though he couldn't determine from which direction the voice came.

"It's the nigger," a white boy said. The class roared with laughter, but Chambers cut it short.

"Now, stop that. We're not going to have that in this class. Don't say that," Chambers instructed mildly. "Ah, yes, ah, Hammond, what is it?"

"I know it. I want to say it—the preamble. I can say it."

"Ah, I didn't get you? I didn't see you back there. Ah, go ahead, Hammond. Stand," Chambers, said looking in his roll book.

When Saint stood, the entire class became silent.

"'We the People of the United States, in order to form a more perfect union, establish justice, insure domestic tranquility, provide for the common defense, promote the general welfare, and secure the blessings of liberty to ourselves and our posterity, do ordain and establish this Constitution for the United States of America.' Ah, that's it. It's just fifty-two words," Saint added before sitting down.

"Very good, Hammond. That's a 100 percent grade for you. Well done," Chambers said. Then he moved Saint's desk to the first row, directly in front of his own desk.

When Saint got home, he found Edna in the washroom and told her everything.

"That bastard!" she said. "He's got me so mad I can chew arrowheads. He was just trying to show the white kids there was no need in calling on a Negro, because they can't learn anything anyhow so why waste the time. I'm so proud of you, darling. You're not as ignorant as they want you to be. One day you're going to college and get a good education and be a lawyer like your grandpa.

The more you know makes it hard for people to control you." Edna gave her son a long hug.

Edna Bernitha was in tears in the same washroom on Saint's last day of school. She stood reading her son's final report card, which said: *RETAIN SEVENTH GRADE.* "Lord, I've been a failure," she cried, unable to look her son in the eyes. "The good Lord will make a way somehow. You're going to a Negro school next year. These Southern hypocrite bastards."

Saint had never seen his mother so hurt. His father only made her angry. Seeing her children stripped of their dignity and made to believe they were stupid devastated her. The only classes Saint had passed were reading, music, and physical education.

Edna registered Saint at Valley Park Junior High in 1968.

On the hot and muggy Friday night of October 4, 1968, Saint was awakened by the sound of the television two rooms away. The station had gone off the air but the volume was all the way up, so the static noise was very loud. Saint heard Vincent crying hysterically. "I'm sorry, Lord! Take me! Please don't take her! When you made her you threw away the mold! You threw away the mold! You threw away the *mold!*" He was on his knees praying.

"Vincent, what's wrong? *Why you crying?*" Saint asked, almost shouting to be heard over the television. Vincent's eyes remained closed. He didn't acknowledge that he heard his brother. He seemed to search for words to penetrate some invisible realm where he could find help for the problem for which he was praying. Saint passed him and entered the living room/bedroom. Approaching the bed, he saw that Edna's left arm hung lifelessly over the side. Her right arm was draped limply over her forehead. Her glassy eyes stared at the ceiling without blinking.

"Mommy. What's wrong? Why you looking like that?" Saint asked. He then saw it: a small bloodstain on Edna's pink nightgown in the area of her heart. Next, he saw a piece of wood partially covered by the bedspread in the middle of the bed. He walked around to the foot and pulled the cover slightly back. It was the butt of his father's hunting rifle. He pulled the cover further and saw the barrel lying on Edna's chest in a puddle of blood.

"Oh, no, Mommy! I love you! Why you did this? I love you, Mommy!" Saint cried frantically. He ran to Vincent. "Vincent! What happened? What happened? Mommy's shot!" he shouted but got no response. Vincent continued his crying. Saint grabbed the keys to the old Chevy station wagon and ran through the back-porch screen door. Jumping over the four steps, he fell in the gravel in the back driveway. He got up quickly and started the Chevy. He didn't know how to drive, but Baton Rouge General Hospital was a straight shot up Convention Street. He could keep the car in the middle of the road, he felt, and hit the brakes when necessary. Saint ran back inside and tried to get Vincent to help him lift Edna from the bed, carry her through the house, and place her in the car. She was too heavy for both of them. Vincent continued to pray with his eyes closed, tears running down his cheeks. He didn't hear Saint or feel him jerking him. He appeared oblivious to the turmoil around him, almost as though he were in a trance. Saint turned the television off, ran to the phone, and dialed zero. It took forever for the zero to complete the full dial.

"Operator! Send an ambulance to 205 North Twenty-Fifth Street. My mama's shot! She's bleeding all over the bed!"

"I've already done that!" Vincent yelled from the other room, apparently jolted back to reality. "The police and the ambulance are on the way!"

"Look at all these children in here," a detective said after the ambulance had taken Edna to Baton Rouge General. As Saint sat on the green sofa with his hands rolled in his T-shirt, a detective stuck his head out the front door to speak to detectives on the porch. "What was the name of the doctor that pronounced the death?" he asked. Those were the cruelest words Saint had ever heard.

Later, Saint's father came home and stood beside the bloodstained mattress. He held his stomach with his bad right hand and covered his face with his left hand as he cried into it. White detectives surrounded him. They questioned Vincent about the location of others in the house. He had been the only one awake when Edna committed suicide. They were trying to determine how she could shoot herself with a long rifle.

After Edna's funeral, Vincent and Fern Lorraine moved to Los Angeles. Saint assumed the responsibility of rearing his younger siblings.

By the fall of 1969, Martin's success with his janitorial business enabled him to buy a new house. Fairfields was an emerging black middle-class subdivision in Baton Rouge. Capitol Senior High was within walking distance. The house at 2929 Washington Avenue was a mansion compared to the other places they had lived, but

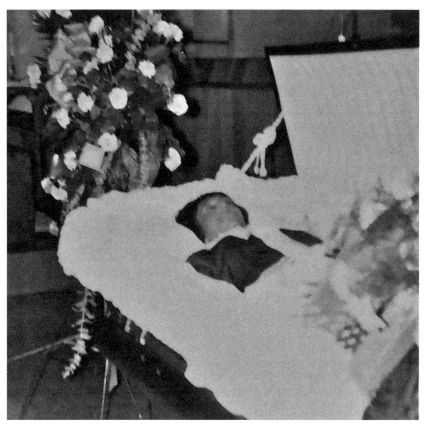

Edna's body lay at rest at Elm Grove Baptist Church, 1069 North Thirty-Eighth Street, October 6, 1968.

without Edna's presence, everyone, even Martin, felt a sense of emptiness. Because Saint was older than the others, his memories of the night Edna killed herself were vivid and longer lasting. His emptiness was deep.

Martin's business continued to grow. He hired employees. One spring day in 1971, when Saint and Paul came home from school, there was a 1963 red and white Ford station wagon parked at the curb in front of the house. It drove well, but it was ugly. It had no wide rear tires and no dual exhaust, and when Saint drove it, it felt as if he was steering a ship. He named it the fire wagon. Martin bought the car so Saint and Paul would have transportation to the offices they cleaned on weekdays and Saturdays.

Vincent, Saint wearing his Westdale Junior High track medal that made Edna proud, and Michael, in the living room the day of Edna's funeral.

Saint and Paul had worked with Martin each day after school since 1965. Martin groused at his two sons about everything: "Use that hand scraper like I showed you! Scrape all the paint drops off them windows! Get down on your hands and knees and scrape all that old dead wax out them corners off the flo'! That's too much water on the flo'!" Martin raised his voice about everything. "I said damp-mop the flo', not soak it! What you trying to do, flood the damn building?" He drove his boys so hard on cleaning jobs that one thing was for certain: they would know how to work and do a job right the first time. By the end of summer workweeks, Saint's and Paul's arms were so sore and heavy and they were so tired that they would sleep all day on Sundays. The two boys worked and waxed so many buildings over the years that they were young professionals. The constant working in the cleaning business, vacuuming and using his arms, gave Saint fast hands that would serve him well one day.

Fern Lorraine after moving to Los Angeles.

For the long-awaited matchup between the Capitol Lions and McKinley Panthers basketball teams in the early spring of 1972, the Capitol High gym was packed. Spectators stood in the area behind each goal. Saint spotted a beautiful light-skinned girl, with long silky hair like his mother's. He had never seen her at Capitol and figured she went to McKinley from the blue she wore. She entered the Lions' side of the gym with an armful of drinks, popcorn, and hotdogs and searched the stands for her friends.

"Right there! Right there!" Saint yelled. She saw him and looked in the direction he was pointing. She then saw his arm extended, but his index finger was curled back, pointing at himself. "You're looking for me?" he yelled, smiling. When she gave him the most beautiful smile he'd ever seen, Saint stepped down, took the drinks out of her hand, helped her up, and gave her his spot, the last one available. He sat on the floor near the doorway and watched the game. Throughout the game they were caught watching each other. When the game was over, Saint waited until she exited and introduced himself. She told him her name was Daisy Marie Bessix. "For real?" he asked. "I got a sister and aunt named Daisy. Is it okay if I call you DMB, and can I call you tonight?" Saint asked, smiling. He got her phone number and called her later that night.

East Baton Rouge Parish schools were dismissed early for those who wanted to attend the inauguration of the new Louisiana governor, Edwin W. Edwards, on the steps of the State Capitol. Saint picked DMB up in the fire wagon and together they attended the inauguration. Governor Edwards spoke English and French, thoroughly pleasing the crowd.

"On the campus of LSU, I have personally cooked, with my mama's own Cajun recipe, tubs of shrimp, sausage, and chicken jambalaya! I have wagons pulled by horses all across the campus. I'm hungry. I hope you are! Everybody is invited to come eat. The food is good, and *it's free!*" he yelled.

Once DMB located the wagon where Governor Edwards was serving, she and Saint got in line. She wanted the new governor to serve her. Saint was already eating with his head down when he bumped into DMB, knocking her into Edwards' arms. Edwards caught her with one arm and held a bowl of jambalaya in the other.

"Beautiful women just fall in my arms," the governor said. The huge crowd around him laughed.

"Oh my goodness, Mr. Governor Edwards, I'm so sorry. I didn't mean to. Good Lord, look at me," DMB said shyly. "I'm so embarrassed." The governor gave her a bowl of jambalaya and served Saint another bowl as well.

On February 7, 1973, Saint accepted an offer of a full four-year football scholarship from Southern Illinois University at Carbondale. When head coach Dick Towers and Capitol High coach Roman Bates, Jr., visited him in his living room, Martin beamed with pride. "I never miss a game," he said.

"I've never seen anyone play football like he does, with the speed he has," Coach Towers declared. "In one game on film, we counted nine fumbles he caused playing nose guard, and he's just 168 pounds. He's unbelievably fast. He almost got handoffs from the quarterback several games. He was offside twice for ten yards. I'll take ten yards of penalties on any game day in return for nine fumble recoveries. Playing intercollegiate football, we'll move him to running back."

Saint tackles East Ascension High quarterback Guidry, at Memorial Stadium, Baton Rouge, 1972.

"Forest is the best defensive end Capitol has ever had," Coach Bates told Towers. "He never caused us any problems. He makes good grades. He's disciplined and he respects all his teachers. I think he's going to do real good at SIU, Coach."

"I own Martin's Personal Janitorial Service," Martin chimed in. "He cleans eleven offices for me every night. He strips and waxes floors every Saturday, but I knew one day I was gonna lose him to some college. Coach Bates called me one day and told me colleges all over the nation was calling him about my boy. They can't stop him."

Saint signed and dated the letter of intent. He looked back at siblings Paul, Teresa, Daisy, and Michael standing in the hall door-way, sad at the prospect of his moving away.

It was now less than two months before high-school graduation as Saint and Raymond lounged on the patio steps. Near the end of lunch period, Michael "Dike" Ingram and Curtis "Bones" Addison joined them. David, who sometimes worked with Saint for Martin, sat down too, along with Steve Ingram. Steve played left defensive end opposite Saint. Thanks to Saint giving Steve a good recommendation, Coach Towers awarded Steve a scholarship when Saint visited the SIU campus two weeks earlier. The four were dressed in their Army ROTC uniforms. After his first-hour ROTC class, Saint had gone home, changed out of his uniform, and returned wearing his favorite clothes.

When the bell rang ending the first half of the lunch period, everyone had a class to go to except Saint. He remained stretched out on the patio steps enjoying the sun, his hat still covering his face. Suddenly, someone kicked his feet. He looked up, shielding his face from the sun with his hand.

"Say, Forest Hammond, I got a proposition for you," Alton "Boodie" Ramsey declared as he sat down beside him. Eighteen-year-old Boodie was second string on the football team, playing on special teams. He had just come to Capitol a year before, and his nickname was appropriate for his big butt. He only knew Saint from watching him at football and track practice; their relationship was merely casual.

"Now, where did you hear that big word? I know you can't spell it."

"I'm serious, man. Look, I heard you got some fireworks. If you let me borrow them for a week, I'll make it worth your while. I'll give you a thousand dollars."

The streets were hazardous for young black males, and Saint had been shot at on occasion by street thugs, so he had purchased a 9mm and .38 for protection. He considered a teen named Skookie, who hung out in his Fairfields neighborhood, to be particularly dangerous. Saint wanted to be sure he had his "fireworks" if he attended any parties that spring.

"I don't know where you heard that at, but I don't pop firecrackers no more. Besides, it's against the law to pop them in the city limits," Saint replied.

"Man, I'm serious. Pee Wee hooked us up with a good job where we gonna make thousands," Boodie continued. "I'll give you two thousand dollars."

The sound of the money was enticing, especially since Saint had a new girlfriend and his father wasn't paying him a penny.

"You know where I live?" Saint asked. After giving Boodie instructions for the pickup, Saint added, "You get 'em; they're yours. You never got 'em from me. I don't know nothing about 'em, you understand?"

"Okay, I got you covered," Boodie said, then got up and walked away.

Mrs. Stelly, a beautiful and fine white teacher, stood in the middle of Typing II with her stopwatch, timing the double classroom filled with students as they took their test. Saint's fingers were flying. His hands were so strong and fast that, while the best students were typing 40 and

50 words per minute, he was producing 97. His goal was to reach 100.

"Time. Hands off the home-row keys!" Mrs. Stelly shouted. All typing ceased except for the quick strikes coming from Saint's typewriter. "That'll cost you five words, Forest Hammond. You need to follow the rules," she said.

"Aaaah, Mrs. Stelly. I reached 100. Look!"

"This isn't Hollywood," she said. "'Stop' means stop."

The girls around Saint taunted him by pretending to brush lint off their shoulders. Saint often used the same gesture, to indicate a small thing that did not bother him.

As the class was leaving, a girl named Brenda begged, "Forest Hammond, please tell me you'll come to my birthday party tonight."

"You sound desperate," he answered, smiling.

"I know, but it's just every football or basketball player I ask, they turn me down. I know it's because of my brother and his friend Skookie. They know he'll be there with his gang. I want somebody to come that everybody knows, and you and Chase are the most well known," Brenda explained.

Saint looked at his watch and rushed off, ducking and dodging students. He turned back before running out of sight and called to Brenda, "I gotta go! I'll be there—promise."

That night, Baton Rouge police detectives Bob and Jimmy sat in their unmarked unit nearly a block away from Brenda's house party, at the corner of Fairfields and Twenty-Eighth. Concealed by trees and shrubbery, they were staking out the party because confidential informants told them that drug dealers and those responsible for committing several armed robberies in the area would be there. Police were sure that Fairfields was the right place to look for suspects in the robberies.

Detective Jimmy read a nature magazine. "Did you know that a cockroach is the fastest-running creature on the planet earth, pound for pound? When threatened by danger it can run up to a hundred miles per hour. That's amazing," he said.

Watching through binoculars, Detective Bob saw several black teens on the porch, smoking what appeared to be marijuana. "No, I didn't know that," he said.

At home, Michael followed Saint around as his older brother was getting dressed. Michael was seven years old. "I think I'm gonna get that kiss tonight," Saint said, teasing Michael. "Granny is supposed to meet me over where I'm going." Michael cringed.

Saint dressed for a weekend party.

Earlier that night, before cleaning the last office, Paul, David, and Michael sat in the fire wagon waiting for Saint while he visited DMB at her home. Her grandfather dozed in a rocking chair in the living room. A double-barrel shotgun leaned within arm's reach against a chinaware cabinet. Grandpa was skinny, black as tar, and neatly dressed in a black suit and bowtie. He'd been a preacher years before. DMB'S mother was folding clothes. DMB sat at the dining-room table, doing homework. Grandpa's wife, Big Mama, stood in front of her husband interrogating Saint, who was perched on a stool facing Grandpa. Big Mama had no teeth and chewed her tongue with her gums.

"Do you work, boy? You got a job?"

"Ah, yes ma'am," Saint answered.

"You aren't fooling 'round with them drugs, are you?"

"No ma'am."

"Them drugs will kill you, boy, you know that? Let me see your hands," she said, grabbing Saint's hands as she looked at and felt the palms. "Yeah, you a worker. You can work in my garden and flowerbeds with theses hands."

Through the French doors, Michael could see Big Mama questioning Saint as he sat on the stool, with her holding his hands.

Big Mama turned both of Saint's hands over and saw shiny nail hardener on his fingernails. "Oooo, Lord Jesus, have mercy!" she yelled. Grandpa awoke, reaching for the shotgun out of reflex, but when he saw Saint, he stopped short of grabbing it. Saint looked at Grandpa, then at the shotgun, then at the door to his right. "Boy, tell me this isn't fingernail gloss I'm looking at!" Big Mama screamed. "Boy, tell me. I needs to know! Are you a fruitcake? Huh? Are you? Are you a fruitcake? Tell me, boy, now!" Big Mama's frown over her toothless gums formed an oval that looked like an abyss from where a command could come that would end Saint's life.

"Yes ma'am," Saint answered. "I mean, no ma'am." Daisy and her mother were nearly crying from laughter.

"Big Mama, Big Mama!" Daisy shouted. "That's fingernail hardener. He's a football player. He has to reach and grab football peoples. He wears that so his nails don't break. He's not a fruitcake, Big Mama. He's a football player."

Later, as the fire wagon pulled away from DMB's home, the right low-beam blew out as Michael began questioning Saint.

"Hey, Saint."

"Hey, Michael."

"I want to ask you a question," Michael said. "How Daisy look?"

"You been living with her all your life."

"I'm talking about your Daisy, DMB," Michael said, laughing. "You know?"

Saint had been so busy cleaning offices since he met DMB that he had not brought her around the house yet. He had not even kissed her yet.

"Oh, Daisy Marie Bessix. I call her DMB to not get her mixed up with Daisy and Aunt Daisy. Well, she's about 101 years old. She's old. She wears these knee-high brown stocking socks that's rolled up. Her hair is silver and white. She got a whole lot of wrinkles all over her body. Even her eyeballs have wrinkles. She chews on her tongue with her gums because she doesn't have any teeth, and, let me see, sometimes she chews tobacco, and, ah, yeah, that's about it. Oh, she wears an old white cap and a gown."

With each detail described, Michael grimaced. "I think you better go back to Darlene or Joan, or Linda, or Shirley," he advised. "It sounds like Daisy is an old granny. Well, I'm not going to ask if you, ah . . . "

"Kissed her yet?" Saint inquired quickly.

"Yeah," Michael said, nodding, unsure if he wanted to know.

"I wanted to, but she was too busy chewing her tongue. But she did grab both my hands and was holding and feeling them before I left. Old people like to feel hands first," Saint explained. Michael had seen that and made another face.

"But, but, why you choose to go with an old granny, Saint? I mean, she's 101 years old! Isn't she about to die?" Michael asked. David and Paul erupted with laughter.

"Well, we're just going together right now. We aren't getting married yet. I haven't finished school." Saint was biting his tongue to keep a straight face. Michael was leaning forward from the backseat with his chin resting on the middle of the front seat, studying his big brother. He struggled to understand his older brother's decision to date an old lady and not the beautiful young girls he had previously seen him with.

"Smokin' Joe, look. You got to realize, she's old-fashion, and them old-fashion peoples don't kiss on the first date."

"You ain't never lied," David said, laughing.

At 9:30 that night, Saint was in the bathroom brushing his teeth. He put his bush hat on and admired himself in the mirror. Michael crept up on him, with his hands behind his back.

"Saint, don't look. Close your eyes and turn to me. I got a surprise for you," Michael said. Saint complied.

"Ooh! Michael! Why you did that?" Saint chased him around the living room, the kitchen twice, and caught him in his bedroom, throwing him on his bed.

"I was trying to bust your lip so you couldn't kiss old Granny tonight," Michael said, laughing. He had his Smokin' Joe kids' boxing gloves on and had punched Saint in the mouth.

"So you wanna play Smokin' Joe, huh? Ali's on the ropes; he throws Smokin' Joe on the bed and tickles him. Smokin' Joe laughs and laughs." Saint quickly grabbed his leather jacket and ran out of the house. Michael got up, raced to the window, and tapped on it. He waved at Saint, who turned and waved back. Michael watched Saint's hat, jacket, bleach-stained jeans, and white Converses go out of sight.

As Saint neared the party, he could hear "It's a Family Affair," by Sly & and the Family Stone. Brenda's porch was crowded with hoodlums. Skookie's huge Afro made him easy to spot. Saint stepped onto Brenda's lawn. B.C., a recently expelled student from Capitol, saw him. "Say, Skookie, look at that niggah Saint coming to the party. I ain't never liked that niggah," B.C. declared. Skookie stared at Saint. Buddy, Dent, Deadeye, Foots, and others were on the porch smoking joints.

"Saint! Niggah, you ain't invited to the party! Who told you to come?" Skookie shouted.

"Brenda, niggah! Who else? She's in my typing class," Saint answered after he drew closer. He made eye contact with everyone as he walked up to the steps. Skookie moved and stood blocking Saint from the porch. Saint reached the third step, then jumped, pivoting around a porch pillar. The door was opened by someone coming outside, and Saint slipped in.

Inside, psychedelic lights flashed and music blasted. The house was populated mostly by girls. A few guys were dancing, but Saint knew none of them. He found his way to the long food table set up across the open kitchen door. Saint got a party plate and piled it alternately with miniature meatballs, tuna bites, birthday cake, and mixed nuts. He washed it down with a glass of spiked punch. The next song was slow. Brenda stood on the dance floor with a huge smile, beckoning for Saint to dance. Saint was dancing with Brenda when Skookie came in with his friends and stood with their backs against the wall, staring. Skookie liked Brenda, but she only gave him the time of day because her brother Mike was his best friend. This was their first time meeting each other, but Saint knew Skookie was dangerous. Saint did a series of gorilla grinds, where his and Brenda's bodies touched below the waist. It brought Skookie out.

"Brenda, why you dancing with that ol' punk-a—niggah?" he yelled.

A new song started and Skookie began dancing with Brenda. Saint went back to the food table. Buddy, Dent, Deadeye, Foots, and B.C. surrounded Saint as he reached across the table for food. Saint pretended not to see the pistols in their waistbands, but seeing them caused him to feel a sudden need to be somewhere else. As Saint walked past Skookie and Brenda, Skookie grabbed Saint's leather jacket sleeve, balling it in his fist and popping a button off as he jerked Saint back.

"Niggah, why you bumped into my bush?" Skookie yelled. He stopped dancing. The thugs put their plates on the table and rushed up, flanking Saint. They stood watching him, but Saint knew he had not touched Skookie's hair. That was the only way Skookie could stop him from leaving. Saint jerked his arm free.

"Niggah, put your bush in your pocket," he answered.

"Put your pussy in your pocket, ol' punk-a-- niggah!" Skookie shot back.

Saint stared at them all, then turned and continued through the crowd of dancers. The thugs went back to get their food about eight feet away. Skookie, however, never took his eyes off Saint and saw when he stopped, turned around, and came rushing back towards him with his fist balled. Skookie held his chin out, daring Saint to hit him. Saint hesitated, as if something told him not to punch him. He instead spread his open right hand over Skookie's face and shoved him. The thrust sent him airborne—falling on the floor on his butt and sliding past B.C. B.C. saw two legs sticking out from under the table. He raised the tablecloth and Skookie sat looking up at him in shock. Blood oozed from his nose. The thugs turned around to see Saint standing and pointing at Skookie.

"Get off your a-- and put that in your pocket, ol' jive-a-- niggah," Saint sneered.

Skookie opened the right side of his black leather jacket. When Saint saw the pearl handle of a pistol, he disappeared into the crowd.

Skookie burst out the front door, screaming and wielding his .38 special. "Where that niggah Saint at? Which way did he go?"

The porch crowd was too busy smoking marijuana and didn't see Saint dart out and disappear across the street. "Who all got they s---?" Skookie asked. Each thug pulled out a gun. They searched the area around the house, looking like ants on a disturbed mound. "Buddy, show me where that niggah lives. We gonna go shoot that niggah's house up. I don't give a f--- who I kill inside. I'm 'a body bag somebody tonight."

Skookie led the pack towards Washington Avenue, two blocks away.

Hearing the thugs as he squatted nearby behind huge leaves in an exotic flower garden, Saint feared for his siblings. "Damn. What have I got my family into now?" he whispered. Multiple thoughts darted through his mind as to what he should do, but mulling his options was taking too much time, so he simply took off running.

Roots from a giant oak tree made the broken sidewalk perilous for a runner at night. Saint took long, leaping strides into dark areas, knowing the hazards of landing on a piece of uneven pavement and snapping his ankle. Fate was on his side, however, and he ran faster.

"Something's definitely going down," Detective Bob said to his partner, Jimmy. "Pull up a bit. I can't see for all the trees. A gang of 'em just crossed the street."

Jimmy slowly nudged the brown Plymouth Fury forward. Bob held the binoculars to his eyes. The front tires crossed the sidewalk.

"Keep going, a little more," Bob said.

"If I go any further, we'll be going—*aw, s----!*" Jimmy shouted. "What was that?"

"Damn!" Bob exclaimed.

Saint leapt over the hood, never touching the car. Bob looked through the binoculars at the bush hat plastered back on the runner's head under the streetlamp as he disappeared from sight. The runner never broke stride as he cut across the lawn of the house on the corner.

Jimmy sped into the street and to the corner of North Twenty-Sixth. The street was empty. He accelerated a block to Jackson Street and stopped. The officers looked both ways.

"Which way did he go?" Jimmy asked.

Through the binoculars, Bob saw the crowd a block away, passing through the intersection. "There goes our gang," he said. "They're in a hurry. Something's up."

On the far side of Jackson Street, on the shadowy sidewalk, Saint was now running towards the gang. A Pontiac GTO two houses from the corner of North Twenty-Eighth Street blocked his path, forcing him to run out into Jackson Street.

"There he is," Bob said, peering through his binoculars.

"I see him," Jimmy confirmed.

Saint arrived at the intersection, skipping laterally. *"Skookieeee!"* he screamed. The crowd stopped. *"Nanny nanny pooh pooh—you can't get me."*

"Hold up. That's my niggah!" Skookie shouted. He didn't want anyone to shoot Saint except him. Saint began taunting and flipping them off until they came within sixty yards.

Skookie shot at Saint, but he was gone. The bullets struck a stop sign as Saint passed it. Upon turning the corner, B.C. fired into the trees where he thought he might have been. Skookie fired once. Their bullets struck tree limbs and a metal chair on a porch and shattered a front window of a house. A woman screamed.

"Oh, s---! Gunfire! Get down there quick!" Bob barked.

The Plymouth Fury roared down the street with the lights still off. The bulk of the gang arrived at the corner as Jimmy slid sideways into the intersection. Both detectives got out with shotguns drawn. Bob fired a shot in the air and everyone suddenly realized it was an unmarked police unit. Three ran the opposite way, but the detectives held nearly a dozen at gunpoint.

"Drop your godd--- guns!" Detective Bob shouted, as Jimmy called for backup.

Skookie and B.C. followed behind Saint even though they didn't see him. They jogged along opposite sides of the street. A pickup truck was parked by a huge tree on the corner. The house on the right stood five feet away, and smaller trees obstructed the view. Papa, Saint's crippled neighbor, hobbled through the intersection going home towards Washington. B.C. and Skookie both aimed at him but quickly lowered their guns. "That's Papa," B.C. said.

Suddenly, they realized it was Saint, now halfway through the intersection. He had put his hat and jacket under his left armpit and was limping like Papa. *"That's that niggah!"* B.C. yelled and started firing. Saint bolted as B.C. chased him, shooting as he ran. Bullets struck the truck's driver's-side door mirror and window and the rear window before his gun was emptied.

Skookie aimed ahead of Saint, between the tree and house. His first shot hit the side window of a car parked on the side of North Thirtieth, just behind and to Saint's left. The second shot extinguished a light on a house above Saint's head. The third and fourth shots hit the edge of the corner house on Saint's right as he leaned forward out of sight.

"Drop your god--- weapons. I got a shotgun aimed at who don't!" Detective Jimmy shouted. Skookie and B.C. turned slowly to see police-car lights turning in from Plank Road three blocks away. Both were arrested along with the others.

Saint hid for hours in the darkness outside his house, to be sure the coast was clear. Finally he sprinkled sand from a milk carton on the paved steps around the backdoor and climbed halfway into the house through his bedroom window. His right leg was hanging out the window when his father turned the light on.

"If you move, I'll pop a cap in your a--," Martin said, holding a gun in his left hand. Saint looked up, grinning at the gun, then pulled his leg in and stood up. "You gonna get your a-- shot climbing through my window this time of morning!" Martin bellowed.

"What? You're going kill me like you killed Mommy?" His words stunned Martin.

"Boy, what's wrong with you? You sound like you've been out there in them streets smoking that damn dope with them no good-a-- niggahs you hang out with. Go ahead and lie and say you wasn't. What's that, blood you getting on my curtains?"

Skookie's last bullets had broken the skin on the back of Saint's neck, but the adrenaline surging through his body had left him oblivious to the wound. He looked at the curtain, felt the back of his neck, and saw blood on his fingertips. "I wasn't," Saint protested.

Martin lowered his gun. "Your a-- needs to go to church, boy! Something's wrong with you. I didn't kill your mama! I loved Edna! That's why I never got remarried. Why you say I killed your mama?"

"Go to church for what? You and all your women need to go to church. I'm talking about you and all your women killed her. She got tired of you spending money buying all your women jewelry and clothes and she didn't have but three dresses she had to wear and wash out all the time! I remember. Mommy took care of you! You didn't take care of her. You never gave her any money. You don't even want to pay me and Paul for all the work we do! We need clothes and stuff. Everything in my closet I got by my own self—you know how?" Saint was mad now, so it didn't matter. "I stole them! Like, shoplifting. What did you expect?" Saint asked, seeing Martin looking surprised. Tears began rolling down Martin's face. He laid the gun on Saint's bed, took his glasses off, and wiped his eyes with his undershirt. His sons had grown up and he had never realized it.

Saint said, "Before I went to bed that night, Mommy was telling Aunt Daisy you was gone hunting two-legged coons, but then Vincent showed her that your hunting rifle was still in the closet. I didn't know that on those nights you never killed any coons because you really didn't go hunting. When she killed herself, you forgot your rifle and when you came home, you were all dressed up. I remember everything! All you want us for is to work like slaves for you. You didn't even believe I would get a football scholarship, but I got one! I can't wait to graduate next month, because I'm going to Southern Illinois."

Teresa, Daisy, and Michael had crept into the hall behind Martin. Only their heads could be seen as they peered around the doorframe. Paul had turned facing Saint, pretending to be asleep. His mouth moved, telling Saint to shut up for fear of his being shot.

"Boy, you don't even know what it is to be a man yet," Martin said. "When I was fourteen, I was working on a log camp making fifty cents a day. I had to quit school and go to work. I tries to teach y'all the right way. I got a good name in this city. Everybody respects me. I can be a deputy sheriff if I want to. I got good credit. I can buy anything I want. Right is right, and wrong is wrong. When you're right, you're right, and when you're wrong, you're wrong. I am right, and you are wrong. Am I right?" Martin asked for the one-thousandth time.

"No, ya dig?" Saint replied.

"Listen at how you talk to me. Talk to me right! I don't dig s---!" Martin roared. He took the pistol off the bed as if to shoot Saint but slapped him with his bad right hand instead. He'd shot himself when he was nineteen, trying to knock a rabbit out with the butt of his shotgun in order to save a shell. The shotgun discharged, shooting him in his right arm. He was on the side of the road when a white man picked him up and took him to the hospital. Instead of severing his right hand, doctors saved it as best they could, placing steel plates in it. His right hand was shaped like a claw. As he grew older, Martin was known to shoot dice with his left hand and rake the money in with his right claw. Many people feared him and gave him the nickname Iron Claw.

"I don't care what you don't dig!" Saint said, holding the left side of his face.

Martin slowly turned and dragged himself towards his room. He heard Teresa, Daisy, and Michael bumping into furniture. Michael bounced off his door that had closed and fell on his butt. He got up, opened it, and dove into his bed. Martin's thoughts were elsewhere. In the hall he stopped and came back, looking at Saint. He slowly raised his left hand and pointed his finger at Saint, as if casting a spell. "Boy, at the rate you going, you gonna be in penitentiary before you twenty years old. Mark my words."

Saint rolled his eyes as Martin turned, went to his room, and locked his door. Saint turned off the light and sat on the side of his bed. He reached under him, dug in his breadbox beneath the bed, and came out with half a fifth of wine. He took a long swallow and gasped and coughed as he stared in the dimness at the wall at newspaper clippings of his football heroics. He got a rubber band, twisted a paperclip, and shot it at one of his clippings. The paperclip tore the article and bounced off the wall. The face of his picture was ripped and hung down. Saint felt bad for talking to Martin that way, but he didn't know how else to fight back.

Chapter 3
The Middleton Drug Store Shootout

April 10, 1973, started out like any other day on Washington Avenue.

A mockingbird perched atop an electric pole across the street from Papa's house, singing a catalog of deceptive tunes. Aware of the sunrise predator above, a camouflaged stick insect stealthily carried its young on its back on a red rosebush in front of 2929. A school bus stopped at one end of the block to pick up students. A garbage truck compacted trash at the other end. Papa rolled a trashcan to the curb and waited for the truck. Inside 2929, pictures of Edna sat on the television, next to her red Bible. A table laden with trophies, plaques, medals, and ribbons for football and track was stationed in the far-right front corner. The telephone cord ran from the living room to Saint's bedroom. He was asleep, holding the phone to his ear.

"Forest!"

"Huh? DMB, what'cha said, baby?"

"Them garbage cans better be set out!" Martin yelled from his bedroom.

Saint sat up looking at his wristwatch, then sprang to his feet. He wore only a new pair of bright red and gold Capitol High Lions gym shorts. Moving through the washroom, he saw the top up on the washing machine. The clothes were submerged in water. He closed the lid. The wash cycle started. He took dry clothes out of the dryer, dumped in a wet basket, and started the dryer. Outside, he pulled two full garbage cans down the driveway.

"Hey, man! Wait! Wait! Come back!" he yelled. *You should have brought the trashcans out first,* something seemed to tell him. The two sanitation workers hung on the back of the truck saluting Saint, grinning as the truck rounded the corner and drove out of sight. Papa was laughing. Saint mocked his cripple walk, then saw the school-bus lights flashing up the street, and he ran up the driveway.

"Them kids better not miss the bus!" Martin roared. "Is anybody up in this house? I don't hear no noise! Y'all need to wake up in here. It's time to get up!"

Saint tiptoed past Martin's door and woke Teresa and Daisy. "Y'all hurry up. The bus is coming," he whispered frantically. He rushed into Michael's room. Kids' boxing gloves hung on his bedpost. Posters of Joe Frazier knocking Muhammad Ali down were on the wall.

"Smokin' Joe, get up." Michael, as always, sat up quickly.

"Saint, you said last night we was gonna play Smokin' Joe," Michael remarked.

"We don't have time. We late for school," Saint said. Then he figured he could do a thirty-second drill, since they were going to be late anyway. While impersonating ABC Sports announcer Howard Cosell, Saint raised his hands to protect his face, like boxers do when trapped on the ropes by another fighter. "Ali's on the ropes. Smokin' Joe is pounding away at his head, hook after hook, trying to find an opening." Saint pretended to let a hook hit his jaw and fell to the floor.

"What's all that noise in there? You making too much noise in my house!" Martin yelled. "I works at night. I needs my rest. Cut all that noise out in there!"

Saint scrambled to his feet, mocking Martin. Michael loved it and laughed.

Outside, the school bus stopped, and the driver opened its door and blew the horn.

"Them kids better not miss the bus. I hear the school bus!" Martin yelled. All the siblings were in the bathroom brushing their teeth.

"Daddy, I'm taking them today. I have to sign some papers in the office."

"You taking them again? Gasoline thirty-five cent a gallon! You just signed papers the other week. What kind of papers is that you keep signing? You act like you buying a house. They got a free bus ride, boy. You burning my gas! What's wrong with you?"

Saint was fully clad in his Army ROTC uniform. He was ironing Michael's shirt when Daisy rushed into the room, holding two dresses. Saint tilted his head towards the dress on the right.

"I like this one, too. You always pick the one I like," Daisy said, smiling. Saint gave her an affectionate smile as she rushed away. He looked at his watch and yelled. "Teresa Ann! Get out the mirror. That's enough. The curl won't curl!"

"Can I wear your windbreaker?" Paul yelled from the bedroom.

When Martin walked into the living room half-dressed, he was wearing two pistols. He opened the curtains and got mad all over again. "Look at that! I look like a fool living here. You supposed to set the garbage cans out before they pick up the trash, not afterwards! If you go to bed at night and stop talking to them little fast, hot-a-- gulls, you could set the trash out on time."

"Daddy, can I take the fire wagon to school after I drop them off? This is our long night, and we can go to work straight from track practice."

"Hell no. Bring my automobile back home and park it," Martin replied.

"By the way, I got another traffic ticket."

"*Ticket, ticket, ticket!* Every time I look around you got another damn ticket."

"Daddy, the policeman said I ran a red light and I know I didn't run it. It was over by McDonald's on Florida and Foster. It was two cars of them. They got on their loudspeaker and said, 'Make that soldier boy take that hat off and get on his knees and beg for mercy.' Asked me was I in Vietnam. They was messing with me," Saint explained.

Martin listened and calmed down for a second. "I never had a ticket in all my life."

As Saint drove the others to school, a simple question by Michael turned into a full-scale interrogation over his decision to go to Southern Illinois.

"Saint, are you ever coming back home when you go to college?" Michael asked.

"Yeah, I was thinking the same thing. Who's going to take care of us?" Daisy asked.

"Yeah, I'll come back, but y'all are going to have to take care of yourselves. Y'all know how to do that. Y'all know how to clean the house, cook, and wash. Just keep doing what we been doing, that's all. It's easy. That's how you make it. Mommy taught me. I taught y'all. Help each other," Saint instructed.

"Well, Forest, why you have to go all the way up to Illinois?" Teresa asked. "Why don't you stay here and go to Southern University? We are going to miss you. Daddy said he talked to the coach at Southern University and he wants you to play for the Jaguars really bad."

"No, no," Saint replied. "Daddy just wants me here in town to work and slave in his business. I want to get as far away from the old man as possible. I can't stand him."

"Well, why you leaving us to be with him?" Paul asked.

"Daddy gonna shoot you, Paul," Michael said. Paul didn't like that and looked at Michael angrily. Michael glared back and brushed off his shoulders, like brushing off lint.

"Look, I gotta go. I gotta go," Saint said, ending the conversation.

Saint returned the fire wagon and arrived at Capitol High at five minutes to eight. The first-hour class bell was already ringing. He saw Boodie at his locker. "Say, Boodie, you lied to me. Your time's up. I want my fireworks today, you understand?"

Boodie shook his head and grinned. "I'm'a get them to you today, I promise, I promise," he said.

At the 330 track distance marker at the top of the homestretch, a long train of hundreds of students exited the back gate, headed for Eden Park by way of Bogan Walk. Raymond and Saint sprinted together step for step during track practice.

"Hey, Farez!" a male voice shouted. Saint slowed down and saw Boodie walking with his left arm around a girl and using his right hand as a visor to block the sun from his eyes. "Meet me on the basketball court at Fairfields at six o'clock," he yelled.

Returning from work, Saint slowly brought the fire wagon to a stop at the curb at 2929 at 6:05. "Teresa, fix me a plate of red beans and rice, cornbread, and a glass of milk while I wash up, would you please?" Saint asked as he stepped into the house. She was watching the news.

"Forest, this is a live firefight in Vietnam," Teresa said. "A soldier and newsman just got killed."

When Teresa set the steaming hot plate on his stereo, Saint was lying back on his bed, listening to "Room Full of Mirrors" by Jimi Hendrix. He sat up, stirred the beans and bit a piece of cornbread, blew on the hot dish, then lay back again, waiting for it to cool. Michael entered from the hall, crawling on his knees and wearing his boxing gloves. He rose suddenly and punched Saint in the stomach.

"*Ohhhh!*" Saint groaned. He stood and grabbed Michael, to keep him from attacking him. Saint began narrating: "Ali was laying down, ladies and gentlemen. He wasn't on the ropes and Smokin' Joe hit him in the stomach." He let go of Michael. "Ali covers up. Smokin' Joe looks like he's getting tired."

Michael threw blow after blow at Saint's bowed head. As he

covered from Michael's attack, he espied his track shoes on the floor. They instantly reminded him of seeing Boodie at track practice.

"Hold up, Michael." Saint stopped suddenly. The clock on the dresser showed it was 6:20. He grabbed his hat and walked towards the door. Michael was dumbfounded. "Saint. Where you going?"

"Teresa, if DMB calls, tell her I'll call her back in five minutes." Saint exited the front door and saw David entering the yard. He hadn't gone to work with them that day. "I'll be back in a couple minutes," Saint told him. He suddenly remembered that Fairfields' basketball court was across the street from Brenda's house. Skookie or his gang members usually hung around on the sideline.

"Man, I took a nap and overslept," David explained as Saint took off towards North Thirtieth. Michael watched from the platform step as he ran around the corner.

When Saint walked up from Fairfields Avenue, an intense half-court basketball game was in progress. More than thirty youths were gathered on the other end of the court. The basketball game was on the Madison Avenue end. Saint panned the crowd as he approached. Careless people had been killed on basketball courts when someone just walked up behind them unnoticed and popped a small-caliber bullet into their brain. They'd collapsed on the court in a pool of blood as everyone ran away. Invariably, nobody saw anything.

Boodie was playing in the game. Streetlights buzzed as they began to come on. Saint was still studying the crowd when Pee Wee ran up from behind and surprised him. "Pee Wee!" he hissed. "Don't be running up behind me like that."

"Boodie don't have your guns," Pee Wee said, breathing hard while holding a tennis ball above the reach of a crowd of children with whom he was playing.

"What? How you know?" Saint asked.

In the last game, Boodie made the winning shot and ran up to Saint and Pee Wee. He was breathing hard. He alternated between standing with his hands on his hips, bending over, and walking in tight circles with his head high to catch some air.

"Where my fireworks, Boodie?" Saint demanded, panning the dispersing crowd.

"My uncle found your guns. He won't give 'em back."

"Did you tell him they weren't for you?" Saint asked, angered.

Boodie and Pee Wee walked away towards Madison Avenue.

"Where y'all headed, Boodie?" Saint asked.

"I'm going to see if Monster's home," Boodie answered while walking backwards.

Saint trotted out of sight back to Fairfields Avenue to head home.

At approximately 7:20, a light-blue Volkswagen Beetle sat at the traffic light at the intersection of Plank Road, Fairfields Avenue, and Pawnee Street. The white driver heard six gunshots inside Middleton Drug Store. He then saw a dark skinny male jump up nearby and run away, disappearing in the darkness. The Beetle moved slowly when the light turned green for Plank Road traffic. Middleton's front door opened. A husky young black male staggered out, holding a handgun. He made it to the curb but then, inexplicably, he ran back and reached for the store's door handle—just as the door glass shattered. The black male turned, covering his face with his arms to shield it from the glass. A second black man had crashed through the door and landed on the pavement. Like a startled whitetail deer, he darted across the westbound lane. In the eastbound lane, a Buick Electra's brakes screamed, and the car almost certainly would have hit him had he not jumped over the hood of the still-skidding vehicle. As he sailed through the air, his right gloved hand pushed off the Electra's windshield, catapulting him onto the grass and sidewalk. In what appeared to be a continuous fluid motion, he executed a body roll, bounded to his feet, and vanished into the night. The husky male staggered down the Fairfields Avenue sidewalk.

The Volkswagen driver had already passed the store, but he doubled back after calling the police from a nearby service station. He entered the store and found Billy Middleton lying in a pool of blood by the front door, dead from gunshot wounds. The entire Baton Rouge police force, it seemed, responded to the crime scene, along with the fire department and police canines. As the ambulance left, Detectives Bob and Jimmy arrived. Bob walked up to the front door and listened as, just inside, the Volkswagen driver and the female Buick driver gave statements to a uniformed police officer.

"I mean, he just came through the door glass like a bat out of hell and ran straight that way," the Volkswagen driver explained.

"He wore this colorful-looking knit hat with two little puff balls dangling on strings," the woman said. "If he hadn't jumped, I would have hit him. He touched my windshield with his hand."

A uniformed officer opened the empty doorframe for Bob.

"Has anybody been in here yet besides the EMS techs?" the detective asked him. The officer shook his head no. Bob saw the blood on the floor of the right-front aisle and a pair of eyeglasses on the floor near the front window. Light passing through the lenses cast a rainbow prism on the floor. Bob walked behind the customer-service counter, saw two money trays and an opened register and safe. He squatted and shone his small flashlight inside the safe. Bob tilted his hat upwards and looked up front to see if anyone else had entered.

At eleven o'clock the following morning, Rabenhorst Funeral Home was packed with white business leaders and the victim's political friends. Billy Middleton was well known and liked by many. Retired U.S. Army Lt. Gen. Troy H. Middleton, president emeritus of Louisiana State University and the dead pharmacist's uncle, received condolences and promises from every law-enforcement officer who came through the door.

"I pledge to the bereaved family, and to those of you who knew Billy, that those who committed this heinous, brutal, and senseless criminal act upon our brother, a good husband, and dear friend, will be captured and brought to justice," Ossie Brown, the district attorney, vowed. "I personally will prosecute them to the fullest extent that the law allows. We will have a fast and speedy trial. Justice will be swift and harsh for these hardened criminals, I promise you."

A tearful Pee Wee sat quietly with Middleton's other employees. After the services, he expressed his sympathy to Eloise Middleton and promised police detectives he would try to do what he could to find out who had killed his boss.

Manhunt

An aerial map showing subdivisions within two square miles of the Middleton Drug Store building was posted on the wall of the conference room in the police station. The most experienced detectives and uniformed city policemen were put on the case. Detectives Bob and Jimmy, several assistant district attorneys, district attorney investigators such as Joe Donald Woods, and Louisiana State Police crime-lab specialists were all part of one of the biggest manhunts in Baton Rouge history. They had no leads.

"I'll sign any warrants that make it to my desk," Judge Elmo E. Lear guaranteed.

Brown gave the orders, *"Sweep the streets."*

Within twenty-four hours, police raided known gambling houses, whorehouses, liquor stores, pool halls, and basketball courts at area schools. They stopped suspected drug dealers driving down the streets and even arrested a clerk working in the red-light-district motel. Turtle, a black nineteen-year-old expelled Capitol student turned thug, was arrested as he exited a liquor store wearing a hat that looked like the one seen by one of the witnesses. Turtle came out to find two detectives pointing guns at him. He raised his hands and dropped his brown bag with the bottle of wine. He grimaced.

In several interrogation rooms, detectives questioned suspect after suspect. They checked alibis. Most panned out. The ones whose stories could not be corroborated were placed in lineups or held in jail. The Volkswagen driver studied multiple lineups. Detectives Bob and Jimmy watched, hoping for a positive ID by the witness. There was none.

After a succession of disappointing lineups, they returned to the conference room to eat—fried chicken for Bob and a hamburger for Jimmy. "It's been thirty-two hours and we don't have any substantial leads to make an arrest," Bob said, flipping through his crime-scene report. "No hospital reports of gunshots or injuries from glass cuts, no informants know anything. Something isn't right."

"M-hm," Jimmy replied while munching.

"Is that normal?" Bob asked. He stopped reading the file as if something had just occurred to him. "Remember the night we arrested Skookie when they were shooting at the runner that jumped our hood?"

"Yeah?"

"Every time you see a cockroach, is it clocking a hundred? Is that normal?"

"Oh. No, that's an instinctive survival skill turned on when it's threatened with danger," Jimmy explained.

"And of all the places it crawls after it leaves its cover, the first place it's headed for in times of danger is—straight home, baby!" Bob almost shouted as he jumped from his chair and ran to the map of the crime-scene area. Pointing with his chicken bone he said, "The witnesses said Hat-Man came through the glass like a bat out of hell and jumped her hood. Sound familiar?" Jimmy perked up, stopped chewing, and listened. "Here's the drugstore. Big Husky is at the door. Skinny is on the corner by the flower shop. Hat-Man goes to the door, opens it, waits, then goes in. Something goes wrong. Gunshots! Husky runs out with a gun in his hand, forgets Hat-Man inside, comes back for him, but before he can open the door, Hat-Man crashes through—the adrenaline's pumping. He left two cash drawers on the counter untouched. The safe was wide open. Forget about the money. Self-preservation is the first law of nature, so, he exits with what? The only thing that matters to him."

"His life," Jimmy said, nodding.

"So, he's desperate. No time to open the door—too time consuming. 'I'm going through this glass because I'm dressed for the occasion. I got gloves and my head's covered. I can't cut myself.' So he runs through the glass. Does he turn and go right or left? No! Why? That's not the way home. All the witnesses said he ran straight, even jumped over the hood of a skidding car, to get—where?"

"Back to cover and safety," Jimmy answered.

"Home! You damned right. If he had to get killed, he was going to make it back home. In our stakeout, the runner who leaped our hood wore a hat," Bob said.

"Yeah, but that was a different hat," Jimmy noted. "Almost everybody at the party that night was wearing hats."

Look, the party's here," Bob said, pointing at the map. "Hat-Man passes us here, turns here, goes back, and engages the gang here at Twenty-Eighth Street. He ran three blocks in the time it took Skookie and his gang to walk one. That's a fast son of a b----, huh? Okay, he dances here in the intersection, taunting Skookie as if to lure him and his gang back to him. Then takes off, risking his own life. I haven't figured that one out yet," Bob said.

"I got it!" Jimmy exclaimed. "He wasn't running from the gang. He's running *at* them! Why? Because he's not a part of them, and he knew they were going someplace he didn't want them to go, let's say, to his house. I've seen mockingbirds on the ground dragging their wings, to lure cats away from their nests. It's an instinctive way of protecting their offspring. They'll risk their own lives to keep the cat from going to their nest. That's what he was doing. But where he was luring them from?"

Bob walked away from the map. "I bet Skookie knows who, what, when, where, and why, including his name."

"Yeah, but will he give it to you?" Jimmy asked, skeptical.

The two detectives sat in the interrogation room across the table from Skookie. A pack of Kools and a lighter were the only items on the table. After Skookie sat down, lit a cigarette, and took a few draws, Bob began the questioning.

"Skookie, I was wondering if it were possible that you could tell me something. I'm not asking you to rat. I don't want a statement from you or anything. See, there's no tape recorder. I don't want you to write out a confession or nothing," Bob said.

The only things Bob and Skookie had in common were their cold, black, venomous-snake eyes. They squinted when they talked. Skookie listened and watched Bob's every gesture, reading his body language. Only sixteen years old, Skookie was nevertheless adept at interpreting human behavior, a skill honed during his residency in juvenile institutions. He ignored Jimmy. Bob was the man to watch and listen to.

"Who, ah, where—where were you all going that night when you got arrested?"

Jimmy indistinctly shook his head. Both detectives knew the first word was an error. They hoped Skookie didn't catch it. Bob knew if he got anything from Skookie after this, it would be by absolute grace alone and not attributed to his police training. Bob understood that he should have just asked, "Where were you going?" "Who" implied he was asking Skookie to rat by giving up a name.

"I don't remember his name and I don't recall where we were going that night. I think it was to church," Skookie answered.

Bob expected Skookie's response. Earlier in his career, he would never have made that blunder. It was a sign that he was getting close to retirement. "Skookie, before it's over with, you got ten years looking you in the eye for possession of an illegal firearm. So your little black a-- better remember the Alamo, you hear me? When you see Davy Crockett, call me."

Jimmy grabbed the cigarette out of Skookie's hand, balled it up, and threw it in his face. Skookie jumped up, brushing the ash from his face and clothes.

It was three o'clock in the morning at the Plank Road Krispy Kreme, where detectives often stopped before ending their shifts, a flashing sign told motorists that the doughnuts were fresh and hot. Bob was reading the sports section to take his mind off the still-unsolved crime. He had lots of useless information, and none of the eleven thugs they hauled in with Skookie would even talk to police. They answered no questions and gave no names, suffering a collective memory loss about where they were going that night and whom Skookie and B.C. were shooting at. They knew that if they said anything, they would be as good as dead when word hit the street.

The sports sections of various newspapers featured track and field stars in the upcoming district track meet at LSU's Bernie Moore Track Stadium. Bob found himself poring over the photos as he would a mug-shot book.

"You know," he said to Jimmy while reading the stats on each athlete and the schools they were running for, "as fast as everybody says Hat-Man was running, if I were a track coach, I'd be a damn fool for not having him on my team. Does that make sense?"

Jimmy thought about it as he ate a doughnut. "M-hm," he answered.

"Let's go. It's track season. Get on the radio and have a uniform get all the sports sections of every newspaper for the last two months in the map room."

As both detectives were working in the map room, Ossie Brown rushed in.

"What are you doing here this time of morning?" Bob asked.

"I couldn't sleep. I called a manager at Middleton's about a delivery boy working there who was caught stealing. I sent a unit to bring him in."

"I believe we have our roadrunner here," Bob answered, pinning a copy of a sports article on a bulletin board. "We believe he's on the track team at Capitol High. I think he lives on Washington or Jefferson Avenue, or somewhere in Easytown. He has no criminal record. We've been looking in all the wrong places."

The article's headline read, "CAPITOL WINS!" There was a photo of Saint leaning into the tape. A second photo showed him participating in a broad-jump event.

Brown was soon staring through the double-sided mirror window at Clover Lee "Pee Wee" Hayes sitting at the table in the interrogation room. Bob sat at the opposite end of the table from Pee Wee. Jimmy stood leaning against the wall with his arms crossed. A tape recorder was on the table in front of Pee Wee. Like Skookie, Pee Wee was more concerned with Bob than Jimmy.

"Now, Pee Wee, your big husky friend told us where you lived," Jimmy said. "He's already given us a statement in the interrogation room next door. That's how we knew where to find you."

"You were caught stealing drugs from the storage pen across the street, right?" Bob asked.

"Yes sir," Pee Wee answered, feeling and looking subdued.

"Your friend said robbing Middleton's was your idea. He even said you gave the order to shoot your boss if he caused any trouble, because you didn't like how he talked to you when he caught you stealing."

"Boodie said I said to shoot Mr. Billy?" Pee Wee asked Bob, shocked. "I would never say a thing like that. That's a lie! Boodie lied to you. I told him *not* to do it. Forest Hammond went in the store to get Boodie out before somebody got hurt."

At 6:00 A.M. on April 12, 1973, Saint awoke to a gritty sound coming from the back steps right outside his window. He recognized the sound of sand biting into shoe soles.

The next thing he heard was nine sharp raps at the front door: *knock, knock, knock, knock, knock, knock, knock, knock, knock!* Saint knew it wasn't Skookie. He spun out of bed and started to pull the curtain back, but *something said not to.* He blew gently on the curtains, making them move as if naturally responding to air blowing through the ceiling vents. The brief opening exposed the left blue pants leg of a white man wearing black cowboy boots. Above his thigh, his white hand held the wooden stock of a pump shotgun, aimed at the backdoor. Beyond him, two uniformed police officers were in Mary Blount's backyard next door, aiming handguns at the backdoor.

"Who in the world is knocking at my door this time of morning?" Martin yelled.

"Daddy, they got a whole lot of police in the front yard," Daisy said.

Martin got up and went to the front door.

"Does Forest Hammond live here?" Detective Bob asked. Police officers surrounded him.

"Yes he does," Martin answered. "That's my son."

Detective Bob moved to enter, but Martin blocked the doorway. "Wait a minute. What is this about?" he asked.

"May I come in and talk to him for a moment?"

Martin was hesitant at first but relented. "Yes, come on in."

When Bob entered, three uniformed officers entered with him, a shotgun and revolvers in their hands. "Who are all the trophies for?" Bob asked.

"That's for Forest. He has a scholarship to Southern Illinois. He works for me at night in my business. I own Martin's Personal Janitorial. Wait a minute. Forest, come see!" Martin yelled. "I only have to call him once. He does what I say. I never have a problem with him."

Saint opened the door of his room and stepped to the doorway wearing his red and gold gym shorts. He looked at the assembled detectives and officers.

"Put your clothes on. These officers want to talk to you."

Saint turned back into his room to get dressed.

"Is he a good football player?" Bob asked.

"He's the best player Capitol got. Best in the country if you ask me. They can't stop him on the field," Martin bragged. The officers were unimpressed.

Saint entered the room fully dressed and wearing his bush hat.

"I like your hat," Bob said, then placed handcuffs on his wrists.

'What's all of this?" Saint asked, shocked.

"What you doing?" Martin yelled. "Why you putting handcuffs on my boy? Is he under arrest? Where is the arrest warrant?"

"Oh, no, no, no, Mr. Martin," Bob said. "We need him to look at some pictures downtown. Cuffs are for insurance reasons. My supervisor said the new insurance laws require us to handcuff them if they're riding in back. You know how the law's always changing. That's for protection. Come get him in about an hour."

Martin didn't know enough about the law to protect his son. If Martin had said no and demanded an arrest warrant, he would have had time to secure an attorney before just allowing police to scoop his son up.

Saint was led past two K-9 dogs in his front yard to a police unit parked in front of his neighbor's house. Motorcycle cops were waiting at the corner on North Thirtieth Street. Armed police officers surrounded the house. There were no black police officers present. Before pushing him onto the backseat of the police unit, the officer tightened the cuffs. Saint looked back as the car drove off. He saw Martin and his siblings all standing on the concrete platform. When the family was out of sight, Saint turned and faced the officers in the front seat. Something about them told him they were mad.

"Officer, could you loosen these handcuffs? They are too tight and hurting my wrists."

"Nigger, if you don't want me to get back there with you, you shut the f--- up, hear?"

Saint was hearing, "*Hello, Forest, welcome to the real world!*"

"Sister, we got 'em," a man was saying into a telephone when Saint was brought into the district attorney's office. "We got all three of them nigger sons of b----es. They can't get the death penalty, but we'll take care of them, you have my word on that. I promise you."

The ID room had a camera with a large light. A calendar hung on the wall next to measurement marks. In a temporary holding cell with a sink, toilet, and metal bunkbed frame with no mattress, Saint sat facing—outside the cell—Detectives Bob and Jimmy, Assistant District Attorney Fred Blanche, an investigator from the district attorney's office, three other detectives, and the two white uniformed officers who had driven Saint to the station. Bob squatted at the cell looking Saint in the eyes, searching for a weakness. Neither person blinked.

The detectives tried to convince Saint that Boodie and Pee Wee had been arrested and Boodie said Saint killed Middleton. They demanded Saint give them the gun. Saint insisted he had no reason to be involved in an attempted armed robbery of anyone, not to mention murder.

"You don't have to worry about not going to college," Detective Jimmy said. "The judge won't take you out of school. All we need is the gun. You need to tell us where the gun is." They called on their best training to get Saint to talk. When nothing worked, their real personalities surfaced, and threats were leveled at Saint.

"I don't have a gun," Saint said. "I don't own any guns. I don't know why they would tell you something like that. Where are the pictures, the photographs you told my daddy you wanted me to look at? Why am I here?"

"Look, Forest, we know you're not the triggerman," Jimmy said.

"We know Alton Ramsey—Boodie—shot and killed Billy Middleton," Bob added. "Clover Hayes already told us that you went in the store to stop Ramsey from robbing his boss."

"I don't have no gun," Saint repeated.

The two detectives left, angered. "'I don't have no gun' is all he keeps saying," Bob recounted to Ossie Brown in Judge Lear's chambers.

"Look, you go back down and tell his little black nigger a--, if he doesn't give us . . . "

"What are you going to do? What?" Bob asked. "We've tried all angles with this kid! He has no record, but he's street smart. He knows that to admit having a gun will place him in the same room with Ramsey and Hayes. It'll implicate him in a murder! We can't get him to open the door, let alone go in the room. He's not stupid."

"Tell his father what he's involved in. Let him ask for the gun," Judge Lear suggested.

The Truth Shall Set You Free

Bob and Jimmy entered the ID room and parted like ROTC honor guards, stepping to opposite sides eight feet from the cell. They saw Saint still sitting on the bunk, with his head hung down. He was thinking.

A slow but familiar sound of something shuffling across the floor caused Saint to lift his head. He first saw an old, worn pair of Stacey Adams dress shoes. Moving his eyes upwards, he saw dirty khaki pants legs, then an unevenly buttoned shirt covered with a dark-green sweater, then finally the wrinkled face of an old black man who wore grease-smeared glasses and who hadn't combed his hair. Tear tracks ran down the front of the old man's face. Martin slowly entered the room but stopped suddenly and leaned to the left-inside doorframe. His arms were folded across his chest and he appeared weak.

Saint's defiant demeanor crumbled. "Daddy, are you all right?" he blurted as he rushed to the bars of the cell door.

Martin's head was bowed, sorrow etched in every wrinkle of his face. In an instant, Saint saw all the times Martin had been reaching out to him. He cared for nothing in the world at that moment but his father's health. Martin dragged himself to the cell, his head still hung down. After a deep sigh, he held his head up. When he did, he stood face to face with his son, only the tan iron bars separating them.

"Forest," Martin said, "these officers asked me to ask you something. Detective Jimmy and Bob promised me that you're not in any trouble and for you not to worry about not going to college on your scholarship. They say the judge won't take you away from school. I believe them. Just tell the truth, son. The truth shall set you free. Right is right, son, and wrong is wrong. When you're right, you're right, and when you're wrong, you're wrong. I am right, and you are wrong." Martin's dry lips quivered.

Saint gazed into the sadness of his old father's face. They had never been this close since Saint was a child. Images came rushing back of the times he stood on the seat of Martin's dumptruck, holding on to his father as they rode through town. He remembered Martin's scraggly whiskers scratching his tender toddler's facial skin. Salty tears were now pouring from his eyes. A half-nod by Saint told

Martin his son was ready to tell the truth. "You right, Daddy. You right," he whispered. Saint lost his composure as he reached through the bars, grabbed his father's bad arm, and held on to it.

"Do you have the gun and where is it?" Martin knew that by trusting the white police detectives, he was putting his son's life in their hands, but they'd made him a promise.

Saint stared into Martin's eyes. "Daddy, I just want you to know that I do love you and I will never lie to you again. I know you try to teach us right, Daddy. I hate myself. I'm going to make you happy again, Daddy. I'm'a make you happy like we use to be. I'm sorry I let you down, but I will make you happy again, Daddy."

Saint was confused. *The truth shall set you free.* He'd heard that all his life. Maybe he should try it and see if it worked. He knew he couldn't trust the detectives, but he didn't want to say that he loved his father and then lie to him. He rested both his hands on his knees as if in a football huddle as he cried.

Boodie and Pee Wee left Fairfields basketball court and walked down Madison Avenue towards Plank Road. "I can still do it," Boodie said. "I don't need a gun. I'll tackle him and knock him out."

"No, Boodie, I'm telling you," Pee Wee insisted. "Somebody's gonna get hurt real bad, man, I'm telling you. I don't think we ought to do this. He ain't gonna open the door for you. He only opens that backdoor for his customers he gives a special knock code to. Mr. Billy got three guns in there—a .25 in his right pants pocket, a .38 special under a white towel on his drug counter, and a shotgun in the aisle behind him."

"I just got to find a way to get inside. Monster got a gun I can use," Boodie said.

Boodie and Pee Wee turned on Tecumseh from Madison Avenue just before seven o'clock and approached Monster's house on the corner of Pawnee and Tecumseh. They walked in the middle of the street towards Pawnee. Boodie ran up to Monster's house and tapped on the door. Monster answered, partially opening the door. Pee Wee saw Monster shake his head and close the door in Boodie's face. "Damn," Boodie said as he rejoined Pee Wee. "He said he didn't have anything. But I could still do it, though."

"No, Boodie, I'm telling you. Somebody gonna get hurt, I'm telling you."

They argued in the middle of Tecumseh, thirty feet from Pawnee. It was dark. They were barely visible. Huge trees behind the flower shop created a dark, shadowy area. Plank Road traffic was noisy.

"I figured you let Monster use my fireworks, Boodie," Saint said, surprising the two as he walked out of the dark from behind a tree. "Boodie, I want my fireworks right now!"

A vehicle turned on to Tecumseh. Pee Wee and Boodie ran into the shadows to avoid the headlights. The lights hit Saint's face as he moved to the side of the street.

"Pee Wee! Where you at?" Saint called after the car passed.

Boodie appeared on Pawnee, walking towards the backdoor of Middleton's Drug Store. Pee Wee ran out of the shadows, across Pawnee, and into a dark alley behind the drugstore, a few feet from the backdoor. Saint followed Pee Wee.

Boodie jogged into the alley. "What's the name of that ointment for baby rashes?"

"Desitin or Desenex, something like that," Saint answered.

Boodie rushed to the backdoor and knocked. At the same time, Pee Wee ran from the alley to Pocahontas Street. Saint again asked Pee Wee about his guns, but he denied knowing anything about them. They peered into the darkness towards Plank Road upon hearing footsteps on gravel. It was Boodie.

"What happened, Boodie?" Pee Wee asked.

"I told him I needed the ointment for a baby rash. He told me how much it was. I told him I had to get some more money. I was getting a little scared, but I still believe I can do it."

"No, Boodie, noooo. I'm telling you somebody gonna get hurt," Pee Wee cried.

"All right, man. I'm'a leave it alone," Boodie said.

"Man, what's going on, Pee Wee?" Saint asked. He really didn't know Boodie and certainly didn't trust asking him. He'd already lied about the proposition. Saint had known Pee Wee since 1968, from Valley Park Junior High.

"Boodie was gonna try to rob Mr. Billy," Pee Wee answered.

"I'm going home," Saint said. "I ain't robbing *nobody*. You need to get my fireworks, Boodie. I ain't playing." Saint started walking southwest on Pocahontas away from Pawnee.

"No, Boodie, I'm telling you," Pee Wee said.

"I said all right, man. I'm'a go shoot some pool. Say Saint, wanna shoot a quick game?"

"If you paying for it."

"That's the long way. Let's go back this way," Boodie said.

Traffic noise increased as the trio walked in the middle of Pawnee towards the Plank Road-Fairfield Avenue intersection. As they approached the side door of Middleton's Drug Store, Saint thought about his food waiting at home and changed his mind about shooting pool. He and Pee Wee merged to the left. Boodie veered to the right and edged towards the pavement in front of Middleton's. The signal light glowed a bright crimson for Pawnee's traffic as Saint and Pee Wee walked down the incline to the curb. The light was green for Plank Road traffic. As Saint stood on the curb, he saw Boodie cut across the drugstore's front parking lot on an angle, going towards the pool hall on the corner of Jackson and Plank, half a block away.

"I thought you was gonna shoot some pool," Boodie yelled.

"David's waiting for me at my house," Saint yelled back. When the light changed, he walked across the westbound lane of Plank Road.

"Forest! Forest!" Pee Wee yelled.

Thinking Pee Wee was following him, Saint stopped in the middle of Plank and turned. Pee Wee was still on the corner but pointing at Boodie walking up to the front door of the drugstore. He knocked and waited.

"Come on, Pee Wee!" Saint said.

Pee Wee pointed at Middleton letting Boodie enter. Saint turned to stare down Fairfields Avenue at lights on the other end that led to his house.

Don't go back. Don't go back, his inner voice told him.

An old car with a loud muffler passed through the intersection, leaving a thick hazy cloud of exhaust fumes. He saw Pee Wee, panic stricken. Ignoring the voice, Saint jogged back to the curb. "Damn," he muttered as he went.

"Forest, you gotta go stop him," Pee Wee stammered. "He's gonna try to rob him. I'm telling you. I done seen him like this before. Somebody's gonna get hurt!"

Boodie stood before Middleton and appeared to be counting coins in his hand.

"Why don't you go get him?" Saint asked, turning back to Pee Wee.

"Mr. Billy caught me stealing drugs from his storage pen. He had his detectives friends pick me up. If he sees me around here after I clock out, he's gonna have me locked in jail."

"Wait here. I'll be right back," Saint said.

Boodie stared in Billy Middleton's face. He was a huge, fifty-five-year-old white man, over six feet tall. Just as he said he would, Boodie, using the element of surprise, tackled him and was sitting on Middleton's chest. The initial attack caused Middleton's thick eyeglasses to be knocked to the floor by the front window. On his back, he held his hands in front of his face as Boodie struck him on his head with a heavy bottle.

Saint jogged into the front parking lot. He looked through the windows as he approached the front door, searching for Middleton and Boodie. They were nowhere in sight. Saint looked back at Pee Wee, who had moved away from the corner and was now on the side of Carolyn's Florist Shop, pacing nervously. Saint pulled his multicolored knit hat with the two puff balls down over his face and stuck his sunglasses in place. He opened the door. "Hey, Boo!" His call was cut short. Boodie was striking Middleton's head with a thick bottle.

"Whatcha doing? Whatcha *doing?* Leave that man alone! Come on out of here! Let's go, let's *go!*" Saint shouted, straddling the threshold with the door half-open.

"I can't, man. I can't move. He'll get up," Boodie said.

"Oh, please don't hurt me. I'm sick. I'm dizzy. Take whatever you want. Just let me up so I can clear my head," Middleton begged. Boodie struck him again with the bottle.

"Hold up, man! Wait. Hold up! Don't hit him no more," Saint shouted. He entered the store. The door closed behind him. Remembering what Pee Wee said about the guns, Saint ran to the drug counter in the rear, stepped up on the platform, and saw all types of bottles, clear empty capsules, small piles of powdered drugs, pharmacist equipment, and a white towel. He lifted the towel and saw a blue-steel .38 revolver. He grabbed it, ran back, and handed it to Boodie. "Come on, let's go. Let's get out of here!" he said, backing up and feeling for the door handle.

Boodie hesitated. Then, while holding the gun in Middleton's face, he struck him hard with the bottle on the top of his head.

"What you doin'? Why you still hitting him?" Saint shouted. "Stop hitting him! Hold up. Just keep him down. Keep him down on the floor."

Saint muttered to himself as he walked towards the customer-service counter. "What in the world am I doing in this man's store with this niggah?" At the counter, he saw the cash-register drawer was open but empty. Saint looked around and saw two cash-register trays in the prescription window of the wall that divided the pharmacist's drug counter from the front customer-service counter. He went around the counter, grabbed the two drawers, and set them on the customer-service counter.

Up front, Middleton was involved in a deadly struggle with Boodie. "I'm dizzy. I won't try nothing, I promise," Middleton said in a weak voice. "Just let me stand and clear my head. I'm sick." Middleton knew that if he could get to his feet, he had a chance to pull his pistol, kill Boodie, then get his .38 and kill the mystery assailant in his store. He would be justified in killing both because they were attempting to rob him.

"You promise you won't try nothin', huh?" Boodie asked.

"Oh, no. I won't. I promise I won't. I'm dizzy. My head is spinning. I'm sick. I just need to stand up and clear my head," Middleton said. He appeared weak and frail.

Boodie set the bottle on the floor, stood, and stepped aside. Middleton got to his knees and paused for a moment as Boodie eyed him warily. Middleton pulled his left foot up flat on the floor and rested on his knee. Boodie reached down with his right hand and grabbed Middleton under his left armpit. He pulled the big man up to his feet. Middleton's right hand had already slipped into his right pants pocket. The .38 was in Boodie's left hand, pointed down and away from Middleton as he came to his feet. Middleton slapped Boodie and pushed him against the center merchandise shelving, knocking bottles together.

Saint noticed a floor safe below the cash register, its door slightly ajar.

Middleton pulled the small handgun out of his right pants pocket.

Boodie grabbed at Middleton as he was pushed on the shelving.

Saint heard bottles clanging together towards the front of the store as he bent down, reaching for the safe's handle.

Middleton cocked and fired the gun near Boodie's face.

Pow!

Saint crouched, startled, thinking Boodie fired a shot to frighten Middleton.

Middleton realized he was in trouble as the small .25 handgun jammed.

Trying to keep his balance, Boodie raised his left hand, pointed the gun at Middleton, and began pulling the trigger out of panic.

Boom! Boom! Boom! Boom! Boom! Boom! Click! Click! Click!

Medicine bottles, baby powder, and mirror glass exploded around Saint as he dove forward. He hit a shelf and moved behind a glass counter on the right side, facing the front door.

Outside, Pee Wee jumped up and ran into the darkness behind the florist shop. A white man in a Volkswagen Beetle waiting at the red traffic light heard the gunshots and saw Pee Wee run away.

Click, click, click! Saint, lying low on his stomach behind the counter, listened, trying to comprehend what happened. He heard a continuous clicking noise and Middleton groaning.

"Oh, Lord, somebody help me. I'm shot. Oh, Lord, please somebody help me. Rebel, Rebel," Middleton moaned. A dog was barking from the storage room to Saint's right.

Saint slowly rose to a squat. He moved his head in an attempt to look through the glass counter. He could see nothing for the massive cloud of smoke in the air. Cars turning at the intersection outside illuminated the interior of the store with their headlights, flashing rainbow colors in the haze. The clicking of the gun and the groans from Middleton continued. As the smoke began to dissipate, Saint saw Middleton standing in a light-blue short-sleeve shirt and holding a shiny object in his right hand. Three red vertical lines of blood were streaking down the front of his body. The clicking noise continued. Peering through the counter glass, Saint saw the gun in Boodie's hand. He was still aiming it at Middleton, pulling the trigger. Boodie's eyes were bulging, his mouth was wide open, and he appeared to be in shock.

Middleton was executing a throwing motion as if to get the shiny pistol in his right hand to manually discharge. Finally understanding what he was seeing, Saint stood up.

"Boodie!" he yelled.

The clicking stopped. Boodie, seeing Middleton in front of him with the gun, threw his arms up to cover his face, turned in a circle, and, after regaining his bearings, ran out the front door.

The Volkswagen driver slowly moved his car forward and stopped before passing the store. He saw Boodie stagger out the front door with a gun in his hand.

Saint could think of only one thing: *get out!* Taking a chance of being shot, he screamed and bolted for the door.

"Yaaaah!" Bam! He ran into the customer-service counter, hurting his left hip. He continued towards the door and lost his footing. He found himself lying flat on his back, a lens from his sunglasses

missing. His head hit the terrazzo floor hard, momentarily stunning him. Middleton's first shot had hit a bottle of oil that fell in the aisle. It caused Saint to slip and fall. He crawled back, reaching for the lens on the floor, but couldn't stay any longer. He regained his feet and resumed running. He saw Boodie coming back to the front door but didn't wait for him to open it. Running at top speed, he crashed through the closed door as Boodie turned away. Saint landed on the pavement in front of the drugstore and, in full stride, careened across the street. The driver of an eastbound Buick Electra hit her brakes and would have struck Saint had he not jumped over the hood, pushing off the windshield with his glove-covered right hand. He landed on the grass and sidewalk, executed a football roll, came up running, and disappeared into the darkness.

Saint ran two blocks before realizing he'd left Boodie. He raced back and met him at Twenty-Sixth Street and Fairfields Avenue. "Are you shot? Are you shot?" he asked, gasping.

"No, I don't think so," Boodie answered.

"We told you—I told you to come out! Why you didn't listen? Why you wouldn't listen?! Godd--- it! Why this got to happen to me? *Why?!*" Saint screamed, looking up into the clear star-lit April sky as if now directing his questions to the God of the universe.

Mary Blount was standing in her driveway when Saint and Boodie made it to Saint's house. Teresa, Daisy, Michael, Paul, and David were all in the living and dining room watching television or on the phone when they entered. He and Boodie went straight to his bedroom.

"Forest, I put your plate and milk in the refrigerator," Teresa said as he rushed by. They all sensed something was wrong.

Saint closed the door to his room and began pacing. Boodie collapsed on the bed, leaning back on his elbows. He took the gun out of his waist and looked at it.

"Boy, this sho' is a pretty gun," he said.

"What?!" Saint stopped pacing, grabbed the gun, and, in a single motion, punched Boodie in the face, knocking him back on the bed.

"Come on, you jive-a-- niggah!" Saint wanted Boodie to stand up and fight for potentially messing his life up. Boodie rubbed his jaw and wiped blood from his lips as if he knew he deserved the punch. "This ain't no soap opera! This isn't no game. This ain't no TV! This real-live action. Why you didn't listen and come back? Why? That's a real-live whole air-breathing white man you done shot, you understand that?"

Someone knocked on the door of Saint's room. It opened to a panic-stricken Pee Wee.

"Forest, what happened inside the store?"

Saint pulled Pee Wee in and closed the door. "What happened inside the store?" Saint repeated. He turned towards Boodie. "This stupid-a-- niggah here done shot your boss! *That's* what happened. I told him to keep the man on the floor. How can you mess up keeping somebody down on a godd---- floor? Get off my bed! What happened? You should have come out before I gave you the gun. You shouldn't have been hitting the man on his head with the bottle in the first place!"

"I was trying to knock him out."

"Knock him out? You act like you was tryin' to kill the man. You said you couldn't get up. That's why I went got the gun and gave it to you, so you could get up and back out. No, you should have never went in the store in the first godd--- place. Now look what you done done. You don't know me from now on. We were never together on this day in history. If they catch you, don't call my name! You take your own rap. You shot him. Me, I'm going to college." At that, Saint told the two to get in the fire wagon so he could take them home.

"Forest, come here," Mary Blount called as Saint walked to the fire wagon. "There was a special news bulletin on TV just now saying somebody done shot and killed that man up there at Middleton Drug Store on Plank Road. Now, Forest, please tell me you ain't have nothing to do with that."

"What? Are you serious, Mary? No, we were just coming from down the street."

"Well, all right. I just wanted to make sure. Whoever they are, they in some big trouble. Them white people is going to get them for killing that man. They mad," Mary said.

Saint was driving back on Fairfields Avenue. Police lights illuminated a five-block area from Plank Road to North Thirty-Eighth Street. A car signaled for him to dim his bright lights. When he did so, he had only one headlight. A motorcycle cop pulled him over into the Fairfields Baptist Church parking lot. He studied the officer closely as he unsnapped his holster before getting off his bike and approached with his ticket pad.

"Have you seen three black youth running? One was wearing a colorful knit hat."

"No, Officer, I can't say I have. Why?"

"They just killed a man up there on Plank Road. You got a headlight out. That's why I pulled you over. Let me see your driver's license." As the officer was writing the ticket, he knew that Saint's bush hat didn't fit the witness description of the hat one of the assailants was wearing.

Chapter 4

The Baton Rouge Criminal Justice System

Martin turned to exit the room.

"Daddy," Saint called. He stood up straight and wiped tears from his face. Martin stopped and turned to face his son. "The gun is in the attic in a pillowcase, in the corner by the driveway." Saint felt the least he could do was allow his father the satisfaction of getting the truth out of his son. He was tired of having to lie to his father.

Martin raised his hands towards the detectives. "There," he said. "You got what you used me for. Now, keep your word." The old man then turned and walked out, heartbroken.

Inside an interrogation room, an old tape recorder rested on the table as Detectives Bob and Jimmy prepared to take a statement from Saint. "Forest, like your father told you, you really don't have nothing to worry about, because you were not the triggerman. The judge knows this and he won't take you away from your scholarship," Jimmy explained.

"Now, before you give your statement, I need to read this caption on the tape. It doesn't mean anything," Bob said. "It's just that my supervisor wants it on the front end of every taped statement we record, okay? When I ask you if any promises were made, you just say no so we can hurry and get this thing over."

Saint studied the white men's mannerisms and facial expressions as they all interacted. He nodded, but something kept telling him he couldn't trust them.

"You have the right to remain silent," Bob began reading. "And no promises have been made in exchange for your statement, right? Speak into the tape recorder."

Saint thought carefully before speaking. An inner voice told him he couldn't just give an unconditional no answer. He needed to mention what the detectives had told him.

"Well, since you say it's going to help me and I'll still go to college, no," Saint replied.

Anxiety washed over both detectives' faces. They left and came back minutes later with the tape recorder. Bob cursed, saying the machine didn't record. Jimmy quickly retrieved a second recorder and took another statement from Saint. As Detective Bob reread the Miranda rights, something told Saint to repeat what he'd said the first time: *"Ah, like I said before, since you say it's going to help me and I'll still go to college, no."*

Martin accompanied police and investigators from the district attorney's office to recover the evidence. He pulled the knit hat with the dangling puff balls out of the trash dumpster of one of the offices Saint cleaned. "Yes, this is my son's hat," he said. They also found sunglasses missing a lens and the gloves, pants, and multicolored sports coat Saint had worn.

"This is the easiest investigation I have ever seen in my life," the district attorney investigator said to Jimmy.

"That's because you got a good Christian man working with you," Martin said.

"We need more Christians like you, Mr. Martin," the investigator replied, patting Martin on his shoulder. Martin felt like a true law-abiding, patriotic citizen.

At 2929 Washington, Martin pulled out Saint's breadbox, thinking he might discover something there, but all he found was a half a fifth of white port wine. A police detective climbed into the attic and retrieved the pillowcase that the blue-steel .38 special was wrapped in.

When Jimmy returned, Detective Bob opened the door of the interrogation room and looked down the hall to the right. His barely discernable nod to someone out of Saint's view meant something. *He's communicating,* something told Saint. Saint almost ignored it until Bob, who was exiting the room, stopped suddenly. Saint was following him out, and to his right, he noticed a uniformed officer quickly walk out of sight past a room down the hall. That meant something. *What?* he wondered. Then he recognized the officer as the one who entered his house with pistol in hand and who later called Saint "nigger" when he was in the backseat asking them to loosen the handcuffs. Pee Wee emerged from another room with a uniformed officer. The three men escorted Saint and Pee Wee to the room just shy of where the first uniformed officer had walked out of sight, passing a wall.

"Look," Bob said to Jimmy. "Place them here in dispatch until I run this tape upstairs."

"Well, I can't wait with them. I have to go finish my reports. The captain is waiting for me," Jimmy said.

"You two have a seat on that bench in there until we come back," Bob ordered, pointing to a long brown wooden bench inside the dispatch room.

Saint entered first, followed by Pee Wee. They sat on the end of the bench, three feet from the open door. Across the hall and within twelve feet of the dispatch room's open door was an entrance/exit door that led outside.

A white officer sat facing electronic equipment in the corner across the room from the door. His back was to Saint and Pee Wee. He never bothered to turn around to see them as they entered, but he appeared to be listening.

When the detectives left, Saint was beset by fear.

Look, you have been arrested for murder and gave a statement of your involvement. You are in the police station, his inner voice said. Saint observed several people entering and exiting through the outside door. He could see that it led to freedom. The voice continued. *Isn't it strange that you don't have any handcuffs on after giving a statement? They handcuffed you at home before knowing anything definite about your involvement. What they are trying to do now is kill you. If you stick your head out of the door of this room, they are waiting in this room and outside the room in the hall to shoot and kill you for trying to escape. They have all the evidence they need to justify killing both of you. Slowly move away from this door. Don't stand up. Move further down the bench quietly.*

"We better scoot away from this door. Don't make any noise," Saint whispered to Pee Wee. "They trying to kill us."

Saint quietly scooted away from the door. Pee Wee followed. The uniformed officer never turned around. His gun was on his right side.

After nearly an hour passed, Bob and Jimmy came to the door. They appeared frustrated and disappointed. They placed handcuffs on both youths and took them in opposite directions. The detectives escorted Saint across the parking lot to the old downtown city jail. A light rain began to fall. The detectives took their suit coats off and held them over their heads to keep from getting wet.

In Judge Lear's chambers, the recording of Saint's statement was played for the judge, Ossie Brown, several assistant district attorneys, and investigator Joe Donald Woods, who was Saint's fifth-grade schoolteacher. He was the only black in the room.

On the recorder, Bob's voice could be heard saying, "And no promises have been made in exchange for your statement, right? Speak into the tape recorder."

"Ah, like I said before, since you say it's going to help me and I'll still go to college, no," came Saint's response.

"A promise," Joe Woods said immediately. "Miranda's been violated, Mr. Brown. The statement is no good." He turned to Detective Bob. "You made him a promise he'd still go to college if he gave a statement, didn't you? What would make him think giving a statement of his involvement in a murder would help him go to college if you hadn't given him a promise?" Judge Lear sat back quietly, listening.

"Godd--- it, Bob!" Brown exploded. "It's no good. I can't use it."

Joe Woods walked out of chambers, angry.

The Baton Rouge Jail

Sergeant Daigle, a young, tobacco-chewing, white deputy wearing metal-tip cowboy boots, stuck his brass key into what Saint thought was just a hole in the wall. Instead, it was a door to the old Baton Rouge city jail cells. Daigle waited at the open door while two old, white sheriff's deputies fingerprinted Saint. "We use to hang you nigger sons of b-----s up on those gallows right up there," the taller one said, pointing at the gallows.

"If this was the sixties, we'd hang your nigger a--, too, you son of a b----," the second deputy added.

You're calling my mama a b----, huh? Saint thought. He acted as though they had not said a word, but he saw the gallows the deputy pointed to. As Saint entered the door, Sergeant Daigle kicked him in his backside with the metal tip of his boot. The kick sent Saint sprawling to the floor, holding his buttocks in excruciating pain. His anus began to bleed. Sergeant Daigle then spat chewing tobacco in his face. Saint lay writhing on the floor as all three deputies then sprayed mace in his eyes and face, soaking him with the chemicals while laughing at him.

Saint crawled into the cell and Sergeant Daigle closed the door, sealing the room in near darkness. The cell had five double bunks perpendicular to the wall. Two windows were on each end. A window was straight ahead in the aisle into which Saint had crawled. The mace had temporarily blinded him and had him itching and scratching all over. The cell reeked of urine. He felt a lower bunk, but it was urine soaked. The top bunk felt dry and cleaner. He stood in the open window to allow the fresh air to clear his eyes. A thick wire screen blocked any escape.

Minutes later, Sergeant Daigle accompanied a huge black prisoner into the cell and closed the door behind him. The big man looked at Saint. He then walked towards the other end, but a man placed his foot on the bunk, blocking the new prisoner's passage. Saint had not seen the man, who had been standing in the dark corner at the other end. A tan suit hung on a hanger from the bars beside him. The man wore only his boxer shorts, pinstripe nylon socks, and black dress boots. He had a full beard and about a seven-inch Afro, and a thick coat of hair covered his chest.

"Oh, I didn't see you over here," the huge prisoner said. "Say, man, can I have a smoke?" he asked, looking at a pack of Kools cigarettes and a Zippo lighter on the top bunk. For the first time, Saint turned to look in that direction.

"Yeah, sure," the man said. His voice was masculine and gritty. The big man grabbed the Kools, took one out, got the Zippo, and lit his cigarette. The flame from the Zippo exposed the other man's face, allowing Saint to see him standing in the corner despite his blurred vision. *Boxhead Max*, Saint thought. The big man tossed the Zippo on the bunk by the Kools, drew on his cigarette, and spoke while blowing smoke. "This sho' gonna be a sweet night tonight."

Saint flinched at hearing the big man fall on his back to the concrete floor. Max walked over and stomped the fallen man in his face three times with his dress boot. He then straddled him, grabbed both sides of his head by his hair, and bashed his head against the floor. Blood poured from the man's face and head.

"Niggah, you asked me for a smoke. You didn't ask to use my lighter. I'll kill your b---- a--. Who you think I am?"

Saint was shocked that so much blood could come from a person so fast. He noticed how Max used the floor as a weapon. The big man started yelling. The sound of the keys came first, then a single dim door light came on, and then the outside door opened. Sergeant Daigle and the two old deputies rushed in with flashlights. They saw the man lying in a pool of blood, barely conscious.

"What happened to you?" Daigle shouted. "What happened to him?" he repeated, shining his flashlight on Saint, who turned his back to him and flipped him the bird. Saint's fingers were bloody from pressing his anus through his jeans. Daigle shined his light on Max in the corner but asked him nothing. Max stood motionless as if nothing had happened.

"What happened to you?" Sergeant Daigle asked the big man again.

"Take me out! Take me out! I, I, I fell out my bunk. I can't live in here anymore."

Two trustee inmates were called and carried the man out on a stretcher. The door closed, the light went off, and the cell was again dark.

"Say, Boxhead Max, is that you?

"Depends on who wants to know."

"Max, get dressed. You made bail!" Daigle yelled through the open hatch.

"I live down from your mama on Washington Avenue," Saint said.

"You one of them little young niggahs they busted on that drugstore murder?"

"Uh huh," Saint said.

"I'm sorry it was you, Youngblood."

"Yeah," Saint answered. "Me too."

"Damn, Youngblood. Why y'all go mess with them good white folks' money and drugs? Y'all sho' got them white folks mad at y'all. That was no regular Joe Blow you little niggahs kilt. That man comes from a well-known family all over Louisiana."

"Really, man?"

"Y'all get any money?"

"No."

"No money? Y'all get any drugs?"

"No."

"Damn, Youngblood. You mean to tell me all y'all got out of there was a murder charge? 'Cause that's what them white folks gonna charge y'all with, probably murder and attempted armed robbery since you didn't get any money."

Saint turned away and looked back out the window at the activity across the street. He saw the Greyhound Bus Station and wished he was on one of the buses. The rain was coming down heavily and was blowing through the window in his face. It felt good as it washed his eyes.

"Well, as long as you ain't made no statement to the police, you might can beat the charge. You ain't made no statement, huh?"

"Yeah," Saint said softly.

"Damn!" Max exclaimed, thinking as he tried to analyze Saint's case. "Well, as long as they ain't got the gun, 'cause they need the murder weapon. They ain't got the gun, huh? Tell me they ain't got the gun, Youngblood."

"Yeah, they got it. I have a football scholarship from Southern Illinois University. They said I wasn't in no trouble. Since I didn't shoot the man, the judge won't take me out of college."

"Aw s---, Youngblood. I hate to tell you this, but you can forget about going to college. You might play football but not at no college. You li'l niggahs ain't gonna never see the streets again. Them white folks gonna send all y'all to Angola for life." Max waited by the door as he gave Saint a crash course in reality. "I know you feeling bad, but I don't know what else to tell you. Oh yeah!" Max said, as if remembering something essential. "Y'all stick together, dig? The first move them lowdown mothaf---as gonna do is try to make y'all turn against one another, okay? Divide and conquer. Y'all stick together."

"Say, Max, why you beat that dude like that?" Saint asked.

"They sent him in here to rape you. Watch your back. You'll need this. I'm out of here," Max said as he handed Saint his pack of Kools, his Zippo lighter, and all the money he had on him. The cell door cracked open and Max exited.

Saint flicked the Zippo for illumination and looked at all the blood on the floor. He glanced around to make sure no one else was in the cell. The darkness quickly closed in on him. There was no one cheering for him now. The fact that Middleton was dead began to sink in. Death was something Saint wished upon no one, knowing how much he loved his mother, who had died violently. A strong breeze blew through the fourth-story open window and extinguished the Zippo's flame. Alone and confused in the filthy cell, Saint sat with his arms resting on his knees. Tears formed, but not wanting the deputies to hear him cry, he took off his leather jacket, climbed on the top bunk, balled his jacket up, and buried his face in it to muffle the wailing. It hurt beyond anything he had ever felt. He thought about praying, but God was a great mystery to him and he did not know how to approach prayer. Facing a future even darker than the cell he was in, he wished he could go back and make different decisions. He cried himself to sleep his first night in jail.

On May 18, 1973, a motion to suppress hearing was held before

Judge Elmo E. Lear. Martin was infuriated by Detective Bob's testimony. "We arrested him in his home and read him his Miranda rights in front of his father, Mr. Martin," the detective said. "I didn't know he had a scholarship to play football in college until this morning. Neither I nor anyone present during our interrogation of Forest Hammond ever promised him anything, because we can't make promises."

"You never made any promises to help?" asked defense attorney Warren Hebert. He was a white lawyer for the public defender's office who had just graduated from law school. He was assigned to this murder case to just draft and file motions.

"No sir. That's correct."

"Okay, now, during the taped statement—during the taking of the taped statement, you asked the defendant and this was transcribed by the district attorney's office. I listened to the tape and I think it's substantially correct. You asked the defendant, and I quote, 'We asked you to give us a statement and it was free and you did it because you wanted to, is that right?' Unquote. The answer, quote, '*Ah, like I said before, since you say it's going to help me and I'll still go to college, no.*' Unquote. Now, why would Forest Hammond get the idea or even think that giving a confession would help him go to college when it fact it would not?" Hebert asked.

"Objection, Your Honor," prosecutor Fred Blanche yelled.

"I beg your pardon?" Judge Lear asked, opening his eyes. He had been asleep and hadn't heard a word that was said.

"During the taking of the taped statement . . . " Hebert repeated.

"I don't think this officer could answer that," Judge Lear said, cutting Hebert off. It seemed obvious to Saint that Lear already knew about the taped statement.

"He could if he promised to help the defendant go to college," Hebert argued.

"Well, you can ask him if they promised him any help. He may have been trying to relieve his conscience," the judge said, sustaining the objection. He had been prepared to deal with that issue from the time he sat listening to Joe Woods in his chambers when he first heard the taped statement.

Martin, the next-to-last witness, testified that Detective Jimmy made a promise to him and his son that Saint would still be able to go to college. He testified that there was no arrest warrant and that nobody read his son his Miranda rights at home because he wasn't being arrested. Martin then realized that placing handcuffs on his son was the insurance Bob was talking about, since the handcuffs actually placed his son into custody. He now understood that Bob and Jimmy would lie, as evidenced by their saying they read Saint his Miranda rights.

At the end of the hearing, Judge Lear ruled: "The Court finds the statement and evidence admissible at trial. Let the record show that the defendant's motion to suppress is denied."

"Your Honor, I reserve a bill of exception to seek supervisory writs to the State Supreme Court on this ruling," Hebert stated for the record.

Martin, Coach Bates, and DMB appeared in Ossie Brown's office that afternoon. "I wants to know why your detectives lied in court on the witness stand under oath," Martin thundered. "Nobody told my boy his Miranda rights at my house! That's a lie. Detective Bob told me my son was not under arrest! I asked him myself. He said they had to handcuff him for insurance reasons! I told Bob myself about my son's scholarship to SIU. Bob knew that, ya dig?" Martin was practically breathing fire from his anger.

"It's a matter of proof, Mr. Martin. It was on the tape. The detectives testified to their version. You and your son gave your version. The judge believed their version," Brown replied.

"Look, let me tell you something. I'm a law-abiding citizen. I pay my taxes. My vote put you in office. I give donations to the law-enforcement funds. I expect some consideration around here!" Martin roared at Brown. Two white investigators rushed in but Brown waved them off.

"What kind of consideration, Mr. Martin, are you expecting?" Brown asked.

"Throw the whole statement out! Bob and Jimmy both promised he'll still go to college since he didn't shoot the man. They didn't tell my boy his Miranda rights at my house!" Martin began reciting the Miranda warning to make his point. "Your detectives lied under oath when they said they told my boy his Miranda rights, lying bastards! I was standing right there in my living room when they put the handcuffs on my boy. What more do I need to say?" Martin's lips were quivering as he leaned across Brown's desk, dripping sweat on the desk and documents.

"That is absolutely out of my hands. The judge has ruled. His attorney can appeal," Brown replied. With that, he turned away and looked out his window.

"You can help my boy if you want to," Martin said. "You do it for all the rich white kids you find with tons of dope on their boats or in their vans, trucks, and cars." Martin stalked out of the office with Coach Bates and DMB. In the parking lot, Joe Woods drove up in an unmarked unit as Martin was about to get in his car.

"Mr. Martin, how you doing?"

"I'm mad as hell, Mr. Woods."

"Now, listen to me good, Mr. Martin," Woods said. "I work for the DA's office now. I'm an investigator. I hear things and I know things. You need to get everybody you know, every black and white person you know, to call and ask Ossie Brown to help Forest. He still won't do it because Middleton was a personal friend of Ossie and Judge Lear, but what you will be doing is creating enough pressure to keep your son alive while they got him in jail. Mr. Martin, they'll kill or have Forest killed and make it look like he hung himself. He's smart, but he needs your help now." Looking around, he added, "We never had this conversation." At that, Woods drove away.

In a predominantly white courtroom, Boodie's parents sat with Martin, Coach Bates, DMB, and a few black supporters. At 9:30 A.M., Harris D. Copenhagen, Jr., Boodie's lawyer, petitioned the Court for a continuance. Judge Lear was presiding. "Your Honor, it has barely been two months since the crime and I feel I'm being forced into a speedy trial for murder. I need more time to prepare a defense for my client."

Forest Martin leaves home to seek help for Saint, May 1973.

"Counselor, you've had sufficient time to file motions and prepare for this trial. Motion is denied. We will proceed to select a jury," Judge Lear said.

Fred Blanche and Anthony Graphia made the prosecution's opening remarks: "You will further hear the State's star witness, Forest Hammond, who will testify he saw the defendant fire several gunshots into the victim's back during the failed robbery attempt that Alton Ramsey planned with his other codefendant, Clover Hayes, who worked at the drugstore at that time as a delivery boy."

A twelve-member, all-white jury listened in rapt attention, even though the report of the victim being shot in the back was false. They heard the voice of Alton "Boodie" Ramsey resonate from the amplifier connected to the tape recorder that played his confession. Eloise Middleton tearfully sat on the front row being comforted by family and courtroom officials. She sobbed when she heard Boodie describe the events leading up to his killing her husband.

More than twenty witnesses testified against Ramsey, including eleven police detectives; three state crime-lab specialists; two assistant district attorneys; coroner Hypolite Landry; William Patriquin, the driver of the Volkswagen; and several other employees of Middleton's drugstore. Graphia showed the gun, spent shell casings, and photos of Middleton's dead body on the floor near the front door. At seven o'clock, Judge Lear called a short recess upon being informed that the last witness was being brought to the courtroom.

Saint stepped from the elevator. Directly in front of him was a door. He opened it, and the deputy bailiff pushed him inside a long carpeted hall. Saint passed an office on his right that had all white furniture in it. Ossie Brown sat at his desk talking on a white telephone. The deputy pushed Saint from behind. "Stop looking and keep walking," the deputy growled.

"Now, Warren, this conference never happened," Saint heard Judge Lear say to Hebert. A middle-aged white woman at a typewriter saw Saint behind Judge Lear and tapped the judge on his shoulder, causing him to stop talking. Hebert beckoned for Saint to come to him. Saint felt that Hebert would have alerted the judge himself but was unable to do so because of his proximity to Saint; if he said or did anything, Saint was close enough to see and hear him. The lawyer extended his hand to shake.

"Warren Hebert. I represented you at the motion to suppress hearing, remember?"

"That's right," Saint said, eyeing Judge Lear, who stood eight feet away with his hands clasped behind his back, flexing on his toes. "What's going on? What's all this?" Saint asked. He had thought he was going to see a dentist for a toothache he had been complaining about.

Saint heard the footsteps of a heavy person approaching from behind. It was the white man in the white office. He was tall and heavyset and had slick black hair. He was sweating and holding a manila file folder in his right hand. Ossie Brown, despite having stopped just to his right, ignored Saint.

"Is he ready, is he ready?" Brown asked Hebert. Saint wondered what he was talking about. Hebert said nothing. Saint looked at Judge Lear, who continued flexing on his toes with his hands behind his back.

Saint turned to Hebert. "Ready? Ready for what? Ready for what?" he asked a second time. All typing ceased. No one in the office said a word. "Where's the dentist?" Saint asked, breaking the silence.

Brown began raging, "The deal's off! The deal's off. Take him back. Take him back! I don't need him. The deal's off!" Brown then stomped back into his office and slammed the door.

As the deputy pulled Saint around by his shoulder to escort him back down the hall, the middle-aged white woman patted a figurine of three monkeys sitting on her desk: *See no evil; speak no evil; hear no evil.* She wore white-framed cat-eye glasses, which had been stylish in the fifties.

When Saint opened the door, Aunt Daisy stood between the door and elevator like a defensive linebacker waiting for the ball carrier. A big purse hung on her right arm.

"Aunt Daisy!" Saint exclaimed. "What are you doing here?"

"Deputy, may I speak to my nephew for a moment, please?"

"Make it snappy, lady," the bailiff said reluctantly, pressing the elevator button.

"Forest, boy, you listen to me and you listen to me good. You pray to Yahweh, God of the Hebrews, and whatever you ask him for, at the end of your prayer, you say, 'Yahweh, I ask you this in the name of your son, Yahshua.' Now, you trust what you hear in your heart and he'll walk you right out this mess you done got yourself into, boy. He is the good Lord and he loves hard cases." Aunt Daisy turned to the deputy. "Thank you, sir." She then walked down the empty hallway of the courthouse, saying nothing more to Saint.

Aunt Daisy, resting at home.

When Boodie's trial resumed, the jury was told that Forest Hammond, who was expected to testify as the State's star witness, refused to do so. The State rested its case and the defense began its case. Boodie's father testified for him.

"The fault is yours because you enact legislation that prohibits us parents from whipping our bad-a-- children and makes it a crime if we did so. Then, they grow up unchastised. You force us to spare the rod. So we spare the rod and as a result, we spoil the child, and that's against the teachings of the Bible. They grow up and turn rotten. Then, when we parents have no other alternative but to put something on their a--, put a few marks on our children from whipping them, they tell the social workers and other authorities and you send the police out to arrest the parents and then the parents wind up in jail. I am asking you all for sympathy for me on this one for me and my family. I have other children at home to raise. I am begging and pleading to you for my son Alton's life. This is somehow a terrible mistake. Everybody in here under the roof of this courtroom has made mistakes. I help put you all in office and provide the money for you to be able to cash your paycheck. Please give us all another chance. My family has been good citizens in this

Baton Rouge community so please give us another chance."

"My son! My son!" Susie Ramsey cried. Judge Lear motioned with his head to the bailiff. The bailiff approached Susie and attempted to put his hands on her and remove her from the courtroom.

"You better not touch my mama!" Boodie yelled as he stood up at the counsel table. He then moved towards the bailiff, who had stopped and turned. Graphia ran out of the courtroom and returned with more deputies. The jury was removed. Deputies surrounded Boodie at the counsel table. When emotions were calmed down, the jury was returned. The State called no rebuttal witnesses.

In closing arguments, Boodie's lawyer quoted from the Bible the story of Mary Magdalene, who was caught in adultery: "He that is without sin, let him cast the first stone. He then kneeled down and wrote in the sand. When he stood up, all of the accusers that had accused the woman were gone. Our savior asked the woman, 'Where are they that accuse you?' She answered, 'They are gone.' So, since there were none to accuse the woman, the savior said, 'Neither do I accuse you. Go, and sin no more.'"

Echoing Mathew Ramsey's testimony, Copenhagen said, "If you are honest with your conscience, we've all made mistakes. Be truthful with yourself. In the event that you convict Alton Ramsey, there is still another young man, a seventeen-year-old kid with a college scholarship who has good potential and good grades. He has his life still ahead of him. You have a chance not to end two lives."

Copenhagen endeavored to get the jury to believe that his client fired the .38 revolver not with the intent to kill Middleton but in an unpremeditated act of self-preservation, a powerful involuntary force of nature. His argument supported Ramsey's testimony that he panicked when he saw that Middleton had a gun. The gun discharged repeatedly without Ramsey realizing it. Had not the Hammond kid yelled and called Ramsey, he would still be pulling that trigger until this day. Ramsey was in a state of shock. Billy Middleton got himself killed when he attempted to kill Ramsey.

"Thou shalt not kill," Graphia argued in his closing statement in rebuttal, as he, too, quoted from his Bible. He stood silent before the courtroom and jury, allowing the words to sink in.

Joe Woods entered the downtown jail cell to talk with his former student. He waited until he was certain Sergeant Daigle had walked away and was not eavesdropping on their conversation before he spoke. "Forest, I think you made a bad mistake."

"Yeah, I know, Mr. Woods. I should have never been with those guys," Saint said.

"Forest, that's not what I'm talking about. Warren didn't tell you why you were brought to the courthouse?" he asked.

"No. I been having a toothache and I thought I was finally going to see the dentist."

"No, son. Ossie was calling you as a State witness against Ramsey. He didn't tell you?"

"No. This the first time I've seen Hebert since the motion to suppress hearing."

"Watch your back, boy. I don't like these crackers. Something isn't right here. Be careful and watch your back. I'll see what I can find out and let you know."

Saint was awakened later that night by Boodie. "Hey, Saint! Throw me a cigarette. You know I got found guilty, huh?"

"No, I didn't," Saint answered, as he lit and tossed him the Kool.

"Why you didn't testify for the State?" Boodie asked. "My lawyer wanted you to testify. He said your testimony would have helped my case."

"I don't know where they got that idea from," Saint said. "Why your lawyer didn't call me as his witness?"

Boodie didn't know. He spent the night talking about how it would feel to be walking free in the streets. Saint talked about getting out and still going to college. They stood in the window watching vehicles cross the Mississippi River Bridge as the day sealed them in the seamier pages of Baton Rouge's history.

The morning after Boodie's trial, he and Saint were both in hand and leg shackles, in line to board the paddy wagon for the eight-mile ride across town on Interstate 110 to the parish prison. As the transport deputy checked names on a clipboard, Sergeant Daigle came running down the ramp and told him to only take Ramsey.

"I got room for Hammond. Two seats left," the deputy explained.

"No, the DA's office called, said hold him. They are not through with him yet," Daigle said. "I'll take him back up."

Sunlight shone on a chessboard on a bunk. A hand moved a bishop. The same hand moved a black knight, which took the bishop. Daniel Roger Pugh, a black sixteen-year-old, was playing chess by himself. His baby face had only peach fuzz, but he looked as if he had been in a fight. At five nine and 165 pounds, he did not resemble a thug or criminal. Except for his recently bruised face, his body was free of tattoos and cuts. He had a light skin tone. He stood in stark contrast to the typical prisoner. He looked like a chocolate version of the Pillsbury dough boy.

After the cell door closed, Saint walked straight to the window to meditate.

"Hey, Saint!"

Saint turned but was barely able to see Daniel's face because of the height of the bunk between them. Saint walked around the bunks, eager to see who had spoken. "Man, you sound like my little brother. How do you know me?"

"I've see you in the sports section of the newspaper. I talked to Daisy yesterday at school. I live around the block from her. She told me you were in jail. I'm Daniel Pugh."

"So, you know Daisy Marie Bessix?"

"Yeah, we use to go together last year," Daniel said.

Saint could not suppress a frown. "What are you in here for?" he asked.

"Four counts of aggravated rape, but I didn't do it. I was coming from choir rehearsal at our church and these white men came out the bushes and jumped on me and beat me up on the ground, and handcuffed me, talking about I raped some white girls. I told them I ain't did nobody nothing. They beat me and made me sign a confession."

Saint watched as Daniel reset the chessboard. "Let's play," he said.

Saint smiled. "Michael used to say the same thing. I don't know how to play chess."

Daniel explained how the chess pieces moved across the board. Saint watched and nodded. During the game, the two talked and laughed. Daniel braided his own hair and then offered to braid Saint's. They played chess and talked until the next morning.

"Checkmate," Daniel said.

"I can't see how you keep doing that," Saint protested.

"Youth found guilty in drugstore owner's death," screamed a local newspaper headline. The newspaper story indicated that Hammond and his attorney had made a deal with the district attorney's office for Saint to be the State's star witness against Alton Ramsey. To every criminal, whether incarcerated or free, Forest Hammond would henceforth be labeled a rat, the lowest dishonor a prisoner could have. The penalty for an informant, snitch, or rat was death. The universal prison law on rats states: *the only good rat is a dead rat.*

State Rep. Louis "Woody" Jenkins' office was one of Martin's janitorial contracts. It was late morning when Martin sat rubbing his whiskers before Jenkins.

"This is a hot case, Mr. Martin. It's just too hot for me to handle at the moment. I just can't do anything at this time to help your son. I'll give Ossie a call, but he's not going to do anything, I guarantee you that. Middleton was a well-known man here in Baton Rouge."

Martin went from one of his janitorial accounts to another seeking help. He talked to city councilmen and police jury members, asking them to call Ossie Brown. They all promised to give Brown a call.

Hawkins' Café on North Thirty-Third was the only place in Baton Rouge to get good, hot, crispy, fried chicken, catfish, hamburgers, and French fries at two o'clock in the morning. Martin and owner Hawkins were old friends. Anyone who called Martin "Iron Claw" was from the days before any of Martin's kids were born. Martin hung out at various cafés on North Street during the week and on weekends made Hawkins his routine last stop. Now old white-headed Hawkins had a newspaper headline about the drugstore murder pinned on his menu board.

Martin sipped coffee, as Geneva, his friend, served him a sandwich. "My boy would graduate tomorrow," he said.

Every place Martin visited, whether on business or pleasure, everyone knew that all he would talk about was getting his boy out of jail. Even his sisters in Baton Rouge and New Roads pitied him after he left after stopping to eat. "Poor Martin, he thinks Forest is coming home," Aunt Vivian said. "That was a big white man they killed. That boy ain't never going to walk the streets again. They are going to send him to prison for life and Forest will die up there."

Graduation Day

Capitol High's class of 1973 was seated in the first fifteen rows of the auditorium. Mr. Keel opened graduation ceremonies with a prayer. "Students, families, and faculty members, let's bow our heads for a moment of silent prayer for our graduates," he said, pausing, "and for fallen Lions living in a cruel domain." A seat on the third row was empty but covered with a red and gold football jersey with the number 82 on it, Saint's number.

At the East Baton Rouge Parish Prison, Saint and Daniel were now in a holding cell awaiting transfer. The parish prison was much cleaner than the city jail, which had the appearance of a medieval dungeon. Daniel had done a good job of plaiting Saint's hair. Most young black prisoners in the parish prison had their hair braided.

"Hammond, Pugh, hurry and eat and get ready to go on the line," Capt. M. L. Hugh ordered. "When they get through eating, take and place them on AB-Block," he said to Larry Washington, a tall black deputy.

"I got butterflies," Saint remarked, holding his stomach. He opened his milk and tipped it up, leaving a white mustache around the peach fuzz on his top lip. He began stretching as athletes do in preparation for an upcoming sports event. Daniel watched and drank his milk.

On AB-Block in maximum security, Walkie-Talkie paced in the dayroom gym area, about 130 square feet between the dayroom door, the shower wall, and where the tables begin. He was holding a folded towel under his right armpit.

"Say, Boodie! Your rattin'-a-- fall podnah's on his way over here with another piece of a--," Walkie-Talkie stammered. The twelve members of his clique responded with nods and smiles. Most of them had lived together in and out of juvenile institutions and jail for most of their lives. They even went to school together. Most of them knew Forest Hammond. "We-e-e-e givin' that r-r-rat a-a *trial*," Walkie-Talkie stammered.

Boodie was the first to get up and dump his tray. He lit a Kool. The jailhouse clique got up, dumped their trays, and fired up cigarettes. They all did stretches and shadowboxed as if they were getting ready for a fight.

"Say, ah, Boo-Boodie, ca-can that niggah fight?" Walkie-Talkie asked.

"I don't know, but he plays defensive end on the football team and runs like a deer."

"Say, Walkie-Talkie, me and B.C. missed that niggah with a .38 and 9mm with sixteen shots in the clip," Skookie said.

"Well, I know one thing!" Walkie-Talkie shouted. "Ain't no place to run in here. And he can't fight all us at one time. I'll put this iron on his a-- if I have to. Set up!" He took a nine-inch, stainless-steel knife out of the towel he held.

Deadeye spilled a box of dominoes on table number two and shouted, "Who got the score?" Lloyd Wilson and B.C. sat at table one with their respective partners for a game of spades. Robert Lee and his brother Lazarus joined Walkie-Talkie to play tonk. Others listened to their radios, paced the catwalk, or sat on the floor in front of their cells smoking. Non-clique members watched TV at table two.

Deputy Washington gave a bundle of mail to Saint and Daniel in the foyer of AB-Block. Saint's bundle was stuffed inside a brown paper bag that also contained Edna's red Bible, which Paul had brought to the jail for him to read. The sound of dominoes slamming on the table could be heard. Washington looked through the five-by-seven-inch window in the center of the main door and saw Deadeye banging a domino down on the stainless-steel picnic table. "Give me fifteen, Stick!"

Once criminals know the daily routine, they know what conduct to put on display for newcomers to observe and let their guards down. The jangling of keys out in the corridor told them the deputy was coming. "Everybody! Hit the dayroom!" Washington yelled. All the inmates sitting or walking on the catwalk migrated to the dayroom. Washington closed the dayroom door from a control in the foyer, then opened the food-service aisle door and checked to see if an inmate was hidden from his view. It was clear.

"Both of you are in AB-Block, cell number five," Washington said. "That's your parish prison address. Always put that on your letters you mail out. Y'all be careful and don't trust no one." Washington looked again in the window before opening the door. "It's a good time for you two to go in," he said. "They're playing games."

Saint entered first, followed by Daniel. Each carried sheets, pillowcases, a towel, face towel, soap, toothpaste, and toothbrush.

"Forest Hammond!" Robert Lee yelled when Saint first stepped onto the catwalk. "Them good white folks finally caught you, huh?"

Walkie-Talkie studied Saint, even down to the way he walked.

"Say, Saint! Bring your ol' pussy a-- on up in here," Skookie yelled.

Damn. How worse could it get? Saint thought, hearing Skookie's voice. He was locked in a box with enemies he had made over the years. Saint squinted, seeking to match faces with voices he recognized. Everyone stopped what they were doing and crowded up against the dayroom bars. Saint tried to not look as scared as he was. The way he felt, to utter anything would reveal the fear in his voice. Daniel was so scared he followed close behind Saint with his head bowed like a praying monk. He never looked up. He couldn't wait to get inside the safety of his cell. Once the dayroom door opened, the clique gathered around cell five as Saint and Daniel made up their bunks. Deputy Washington went back to the control center.

Boodie, B.C., Skookie, Walkie-Talkie, and the clique stood on the catwalk, watching them like nosy neighbors. "Them white folks finally caught you?" Robert Lee asked again.

Saint turned around, standing in the middle of the cell. Walkie-Talkie studied him at a closer range. He ogled Daniel, who couldn't hold a stare. He knew that Daniel was an easy target. "What's happening?" Saint finally responded.

Boodie walked up to the door and faced Saint. "You tell me. You know I got sentenced to life in Angola, huh?"

"Damn. No, I didn't know," Saint said, shaking his head.

Nap, an inmate sentry standing by the main door, heard the jailer. "*Keys!*" he yelled.

Seconds later, a deputy entered the service aisle and yelled, "Mail call!" All the prisoners migrated to the front of the block in front of cell number one, the orderly cell. The mop wringer, mop bucket, broom, and toilet brush were stored here. It stayed open twenty-four hours a day.

Saint and Daniel sat on their bunks reading their mail. A prisoner angrily stomped by their cell on his way to the dayroom. "Man, nobody writes me. Something told me not to go with them niggahs that night. Now look at me," he lamented.

When Saint opened a dirty envelope with a 2929 Washington Avenue return address and tried to read it, he fought back tears. He knew he was not in a place he could openly cry. He sucked in air deeply and placed the letter in his bag. He then opened a thick letter with a school picture. "DMB wrote me. She sent me fifty bucks," he told Daniel. Money was attached to each of his letters from his typing class. Mrs. Stelly sent him twenty dollars. Saint stacked the money next to his pillow. He opened letters from lots of former girlfriends. Linda Martin sent twenty dollars. She was not related to Saint but was his girlfriend in the tenth and eleventh grades. Saint always went to Linda's house, where her mother, Ms. Duke, would braid his hair in cornrows. Other girls sent five- and ten-dollar bills stapled to their letters.

Walkie-Talkie, Skookie, B.C., Deadeye, and Boodie walked past on the catwalk unnoticed and saw the money. After reading all his letters, Saint pushed the money under his pillow, leaned on his left arm, and held DMB's photo in front of his face. The large eight-by-ten color picture blocked his view of activity in front of cell five on the catwalk. He studied DMB's eyes, nose, lips, eyebrows, and long black silky hair, realizing he had never held her and kissed her.

Daniel was lying on the upper rear bunk, facing the wall and quietly crying.

Heads up, heads up!

"Huh?" Saint asked. It sounded like someone from the locker room at Capitol. *Heads up? Look out for what?* Saint wondered. Although someone turned up the music on a radio by cell one, a sudden eerie silence fell over all of AB-Block, having the effect of an explosion. Saint slowly lowered DMB's picture.

To drop down low and press his upper body and head flat against the mattress was all he had time to do. The galvanized mop wringer slammed against the thin wall, making a loud crashing noise and just missing his face. Saint kicked the man who held it and rolled out of the bunk to the floor. He scuttled on all fours to the rear of the cell and turned around. The six-by-eight-foot cell didn't have much room to maneuver. As if operating on an innate emergency defense system, Saint backed up to the wall, then took one and a half steps forward—having touched the wall with the heel of his right foot, measuring the distance. Boodie charged.

Walkie-Talkie and the clique gathered as spectators on the catwalk around the cell door. Boodie held the galvanized wringer overhead. Raising his arms above his head, Saint feigned being a still target. Boodie went for the fake, committing all his strength to the downward swing of the wringer. Saint recoiled flush to the wall as if trying to blend into it. The wringer skimmed the left side of his face and crashed into the terrazzo floor. Saint's left and right fists smashed into Boodie's face so hard he was knocked back against the bunk, causing him to release the wringer. Saint was so intent on defending himself that he never saw Eager Beaver grab his money from beneath the pillow and run out of the cell. Daniel saw him, however.

Saint grabbed Boodie's hair and began ramming his head into the edge of the top bunk. They slipped to the floor. Saint held on to Boodie's hair and continued to ram his head on the metal edge of the bottom bunk, speaking with each blow as he tried to crack his skull. "Boodie, . . . what's . . . *wrong* . . . with . . . you?"

Walkie-Talkie entered with Deadeye, who jerked Boodie out of Saint's hands. Boodie's eyes had begun to roll back in his head.

"Not now, not now. Wait, wait," Walkie-Talkie told Boodie.

"No, don't wait," Saint said. "*Now*, niggah! Let's get it on since we can't get along." Saint moved about anxiously in the rear of his cell, his back to the wall.

"It's on now. Who you think you is?" Boodie asked, breathing hard.

"A Lion," Saint shot back. "Who you think you is?"

Boodie struggled against Deadeye, who pushed him out of the cell. He pointed and cursed. "Niggah, you ain't s---!" he shouted. "Walkie-Talkie, I can take him. Let me take this niggah," Boodie pleaded.

"S---, Boodie, look like that niggah was about to take your a-- out on that bunk," Walkie-Talkie answered with a sinister grin.

"Your mama ain't s--- for birthing your big a--!" Saint shouted. He couldn't understand why Boodie was acting like that against him. He saw clearly that he was under the influence of Walkie-Talkie but was puzzled by the suddenness of it all.

"Ooh, Boodie. Damn! That niggah talking about your mama," Robert Lee said.

"I'm-a kill you!" Boodie yelled from the dayroom.

"Boodie, let me ask you something, and listen to me good," Walkie-Talkie said. "How did you miss that niggah with a whole mop wringer, not one, but t-two times?"

"I told you that niggah was fast."

"And while he was laying down," Walkie-Talkie said, as the twelve-man clique went into the dayroom to plot against Saint.

Daniel had moved to the rear corner of his bunk. Saint tied his shirt around his waist and picked up his mail and a red bandana someone had dropped. "Forest Hammond, I think they took all your money," Daniel said, as though they were not friends any longer. They obviously wanted Saint and not him, he reasoned.

Saint raised his pillow. All his cash was gone. "Them rotten bastards. Daniel, I hope you can fight, 'cause they coming after us, you and me. Can you fight? You know how to fight?"

"Coming after me? For what? Can I fight? No. I mean, I don't know."

"What?" Saint asked. "You don't know? What you mean you don't know?"

"I told you I played the trombone in our band, and I sang in our church choir. Mama didn't allow us to watch all that violence on TV."

Saint placed his foot on the toilet, tying his Converse All-Star sneaker tight. Walkie-Talkie passed the cell counting money. Saint knew it was his money but couldn't prove it. Anger began to churn until Saint could almost taste his own bile.

"Daniel, you know what a fight looks like? Say yes," Saint almost begged.

"Yes, Forest Hammond, I know what a fight looks like," Daniel said. "I'm not stupid."

"Look, get down here. Show me how you hold your guards," Saint said.

Daniel got down from the top bunk and stood before Saint in the middle of the cell. He assumed the stance of a polite Marquis of Queensberry-era boxer. "I don't have no certain en garde stance, because it depends on who it is I would be fighting, but I fancy the tuck and extend style." Daniel looked like a French painting.

"Fancy. En garde. Tuck and extend," Saint repeated. He could not believe what he was hearing. "Daniel, that's not going to work in this place. I swear. I ain't lying. Ah, show me how you say you played that, ah, trombone horn again."

When Daniel did, Saint positioned his hands as a fighter. "That's your guards. Just stand like this," he said. "When they come at you, play the trombone on their a--. You can do it! Hit 'em hard, you hear?"

"Forest, I don't want to be no sissy," Daniel said.

"Then you better learn how to fight in three ways—quick, fast, and in a hurry, you hear me?" Saint was in Daniel's face, emphasizing the gravity of their situation. "Daniel, whatever you do, don't give up."

Walkie-Talkie walked up to the cell door, pointing at Daniel. "Say, Danny, looky here. Come see in the dayroom." He left quickly.

"Who? Me?" Daniel asked Saint. "Was he talking to me? I don't know him."

"Look, Danny is another form of Daniel. It ain't my name," Saint explained, "Yeah, he was talking to you! Go see what he wants. Play the trombone on 'em. Bite 'em if you have to."

Nap moved into position to monitor sounds up by the main door.

In the dayroom, the twelve-member clique surrounded Daniel. "Look, you gonna hafta let me trim you," Walkie-Talkie told him. "Now, it ain't gonna hurt. If you don't, then we gonna take that a-- and you gonna hafta fight and prove you're a man. If you give it up, you a whore."

In his cell, Saint was pacing as he heard Daniel groaning from fists smashing against his face and body. He walked to the dayroom door and watched. Daniel had become a human punching bag for the clique. His face was swollen. Nap left his post and blindsided Daniel. The blow sent Daniel stumbling into the wall. Mucus and blood splattered on the wall by the shower in the near corner of the dayroom. Boodie hit Daniel in the face with such power that it knocked him to his knees.

Saint backed up and returned to his cell. He saw the pack of Kools under his bunk, retrieved them, and nervously tried to get one out. He tore the pack open as sounds of the beating reverberated in the cellblock. He got a cigarette and flicked the Zippo. His hands shook. He dropped the Zippo and ran out on the catwalk towards the big green main door. Nap, who had returned to his post, moved as Saint sprinted by with his right hand balled and raised.

June Bug covered Daniel's head with the plastic shower curtain to muffle his voice. Lloyd, Reginald, Foots, and B.C. held Daniel's arms and legs. Boodie stood behind Daniel, choking him with a broom handle. B.C. pulled Daniel's pants and underwear to his ankles.

"Mama, *Forest—help me!*" Daniel screamed. Saint half-turned his head upon hearing it. He searched for a place to knock where someone would hear. There was none. "I can't run," Saint whispered. "I ain't scared. It don't matter."

Face Challenges with Confidence

At the graduation ceremony at Capitol, Coaches Bates and Lyles, both wearing red and gold Lions jackets, gave affirmative nods to Mr. Keel's words. "Depending on the depth of your education, it will enable you to face challenges with confidence."

"Turn this b---- over!" Walkie-Talkie commanded. "Keep him turned over and hold him." Deadeye walked up and punched Daniel's covered head, causing his body to go limp. "Spread his legs," Walkie-Talkie ordered as he greased his penis and stepped in between Daniel's legs.

"*Walkie-Talkie!*" As if talking to everyone, Saint slowly moved through the dayroom door, staring at the floor and wrapping the red bandana around his right fist. Another scream followed. "*Leave my little brother alone, you bunch of mammy-f---in' animals! Try me, you mothaf---as. You wanna try to f--- somebody, come try to f--- me, niggahs!*"

The surprised clique suspended the attack immediately. They released Daniel. Walkie-Talkie took a step towards Saint.

"To get some a--, niggah, you got to bring some a--," Saint said, looking up into Walkie-Talkie's eyes.

"The keys coming! The keys. Kill it!" Nap yelled from up at the main door.

"Everybody out!" Walkie-Talkie ordered. "Clean this mess up. Hurry, hurry! Act normal."

The medic deputy peeked through the window. He couldn't see Daniel for the crowd of prisoners on the catwalk. The medic opened the service-aisle door and pulled his cart to the bars. A trustee inmate also brought a laundry cart, to collect all prison-stripe clothing.

Daniel dropped like a tree onto the lower bunk in cell five.

"Sick call! Laundry!" the medic deputy shouted. The clique stood in their cell doors, watching the deputy dispense medication to ill prisoners. Other prisoners handed their dirty prison clothes through the bars to the trustee, who placed them in the cart. Saint gave up his stripes, then went back and squatted by Daniel, tending to his injuries with a wet towel. He put on Daniel's long-sleeve, olive-green pajama shirt.

When the medic left, Walkie-Talkie posted each clique member in position in the dayroom. They were fully dressed, with extra clothing. Saint only had on the bandana around his neck, Daniel's pajama shirt, his red and gold gym shorts over white nylon undershorts, and his Converse All-Stars. He knew that the clique was preparing for him, but there was nothing he could do. Boodie walked up to the cell door, pointing his finger. Saint stood up quickly, thinking Boodie was coming into the cell again.

"Hey, you. Catch the gym," Boodie said.

"Don't you want to come in?" Saint asked. "You're welcome in here," he said, taunting him. Boodie jogged away. "Gym! You ain't said nothing but a word. I thought you'd never ask!" Saint yelled. Everyone heard him.

In the dayroom, Boodie got into position near a giant Igloo water cooler that sat on the end of the table that ran along the central wall dividing AB-Block from AC-Block. Walkie-Talkie poured table salt in both of Boodie's hands.

Saint took the bandana from his neck and wrapped his fist. "Say, Daniel, you know what? I'm supposed to be graduating this morning."

Saint walked up to the cell door. He looked right at the main door, then turned left. Before entering the dayroom, he saw the shining floors. "Aah, I see y'all been mopping this terrazzo. My daddy would say, 'Y'all put too much damn water on the flo'. I asked y'all to damp-mop the flo', not soak it! What you trying to do, flood the damn building? What's wrong with y'all? All you bastards is fired,'" Saint said, mocking Martin.

Boodie stood by the Igloo table with his arms and legs crossed as if waiting for a bus.

"F--- your daddy," Robert Lee, B.C., and others uttered simultaneously.

Saint edged towards Boodie. He turned his head to the others, but the clique ignored him. They had begun watching television and playing cards and dominoes. Encouraged, Saint lowered his guards from in front of his face. Just as Saint's head was turning back, Boodie flung the salt from six feet away.

Clique chatter erupted. *"Get him, Boodie! Get that niggah. Hit that niggah, Boodie!"*

Catching salt in both eyes, Saint started to rub them but stopped suddenly when a voice inside him said, *Drop to your knees.* Saint heard the voice clearly, despite the noise made by the shouting clique. *Drop to your knees* came from somewhere within. It was stern but friendly. Saint dropped and Boodie caught only air when he swung with both fists. Saint felt his face against the soft tissue of Boodie's stomach beneath the white football jersey he wore. Saint was in perfect position.

It worked, Saint thought, feeling exuberant for a split second. He knew he was in an intense fight. He buried his face in Boodie's stomach, hugging and lifting Boodie's 230 pounds off the floor just as he learned in tackle practice at Capitol. He carried and jammed Boodie on the bench seat between the wall and Igloo table. Boodie was trapped. From on top, Saint blindly punched him in the face. Boodie's shoulders were pinned, preventing him from using his arms.

"Deadeye! Pull him off," Walkie-Talkie ordered. "Y'all fight standing up."

As Deadeye helped Boodie up, Saint quickly washed the salt out of his eyes at the dayroom sink. Saint then stood with his back to the wall again, to keep the clique in front of him. The two former teammates, now codefendants and bitter enemies, squared off once more. They clashed like mountain rams fighting for breeding rights. When Deadeye separated them, Boodie swung, trying to sucker punch Saint, but Saint caught both his wrists. Boodie violently jerked to free himself, but Saint wouldn't let go. They wrestled and tugged, turning over the trashcan during their struggle and slipping in the cigarette ashes and wasted food on the wet floor. Deadeye emptied the remaining trash on top of them both, burying them. Boodie was breathing hard. Saint fought against releasing Boodie's wrists even though his head was caught between Boodie's powerful legs in a scissor-hold.

Walkie-Talkie got down on his hands and knees like a professional wrestling referee and began slapping the floor with his hand, counting, *"One! Two . . . "*

"Break that rattin' b----'s neck, Boodie!" Robert Lee yelled.

"You can body bag that niggah now, Boodie," Skookie said.

Straining to pull his head free and feeling as if his ears were being pulled off, Saint was still holding Boodie's wrists as he climbed on top of Boodie between the shower and dayroom door. Saint sat on his chest and punched him in the face with both fists, busting his lip. At Walkie-Talkie's gesture, Deadeye pulled Saint off again.

"Y'all need to stand up and fight," Walkie-Talkie said. The clique agreed.

Disoriented, Saint now fought with his back to the clique instead of against the wall. Lloyd sat on the table edge, signaling Boodie to charge Saint. B.C. got down on his knees behind Saint. Boodie charged with his head down and eyes closed, swinging. Lloyd jerked Saint's shirt collar, causing him to tumble back over B.C. Boodie landed on Saint's head. The dayroom got quiet.

"Say, Walkie-Talkie," Saint said. "Get him off me. You said we should stand up and fight, remember? We're wrestling."

"I said that? I don't remember saying that. Do you have a witness that can testify that I said that?" Walkie-Talkie asked, amusing his comrades. "Well, that law don't apply no mo'. See, that was the old law. We now under a new law, see. It's all right to wrestle now. Y'all know how white folks always keep changing laws on a niggah to give us more time."

"Oh, I see now," Saint said, trying another angle. "So, it takes all y'all to gang up on one, huh? I see. All of y'all against the one me."

"Damn! You a smart mothaf---a I don't see how you figured that s--- out." The clique roared with laughter. Boodie punched at Saint with his left fist because Saint held his right arm.

"And I messed my life up for a niggah like you," Saint declared.

"Shut up, you rattin' b----!" Boodie shouted angrily. He was unable to hit Saint for his blocking him with his forearm. "B.C., go get the s---ter brush, so I can close this rat's mouth."

Through the maze of tables and human legs, B.C. ran to the catwalk.

Saint grabbed the bottom of the bench seat and, straining, pulled himself from under Boodie and escaped under the table. Saint stood up on the opposite side, against the rear wall. The clique laughed as he staggered from his dizziness. Saint got on top of table three. The clique congregated amidst clothes hanging across the dayroom on four shoestring lines. The lines were tied at the bars high above the television and connected to a heat vent at the top of the rear wall. Saint pulled on one, bouncing laundry onto the floor.

"Niggah!" "Don't!" "You better not!" "Dirty my s---, and I'm-a kill you!" "I'm-a put something on your a-- now," they growled, chasing Saint as he jumped from table to table. He kicked and forearmed them, knocking them into each other and sending them crashing into the bars and falling onto the floor.

"Get him. Get him. Get that niggah!" Walkie-Talkie screamed.

Boodie climbed onto the table behind Saint and bear hugged him. Saint strained as he reached down to grab Boodie's pants cuffs. He struggled to stand upright as he pulled Boodie's feet up off the tabletop. Once Boodie was lifted, Saint fell backwards and head-butted Boodie with the back of his head, busting his nose. Boodie groaned as he released Saint and grabbed his nose and stomach. With a vengeance, Saint stood and stomped on Boodie's face, slamming his head against the stainless-steel tabletop, then jumped to table one.

Walkie-Talkie had directed the attack from under the TV, out of harm's way. Saint worked his way to the Igloo, fighting off attempts to grab him. He tried pushing the Igloo over. The fifty-five-gallon insulated drum was full of water and ice and was heavy.

"That's our cold water. You better not turn our water over!" Robert Lee shouted. He acted as cheerleader for the clique.

Saint backed up and rammed the Igloo as though he was hitting a football sledge, pumping his legs and pushing it off the table. The top came off when it crashed, spilling water and ice on the floor. That terrazzo instantly became dangerously slippery. When the water mixed with the trash, the floor took on the appearance of a muddy football field, and everyone began slipping down.

Saint ran off the bench seat and body blocked three clique

members, knocking them onto their backs. He kicked, punched, and slung debris in their eyes. Saint chattered while crouching and running in place. Deadeye charged him, but Saint stepped onto and pushed off Boodie's chest with his feet, driving his right forearm into Deadeye's face. The impact sent the big man stumbling backwards onto the sink, breaking it. Water shot up and it appeared to be raining in the dayroom. Saint fell to the floor and crawled to the open dayroom door.

Keep Your Balance

Halfway through the graduation ceremonies, Mr. Keel continued. "You will stagger before you fall. That's life, filled with ups and downs. But fight, I say, to keep your balance in life that your educational experience here at Capitol High has given you these last four years."

Saint stumbled through the dayroom door onto the catwalk, exhausted. He grabbed the bars to hold himself up. He looked at the main door, then back at the pursuing clique. He pushed off the bars and staggered down the catwalk, wiping his face as he went. He stopped and turned around next to cell three. Standing in the middle of the catwalk, Saint squared off, waiting for them to come. He was tired, weak, and thirsty. He kept his arms lowered to his sides because they were heavy. He was drained of strength and energy.

All that water, he thought. *I wish I had gotten a drop on my dry tongue.*

The clique lined each side of the catwalk. Walkie-Talkie came through the middle from the rear. "What's this I hear?" he asked Saint. "Breathing hard? Are you tired? You know your arms are down? That means they're heavy. You know you can't get tired in here."

Saint hoped he would keep talking a few more minutes. He was too tired to filibuster.

"Don't let him rest. Charge him!" Walkie-Talkie ordered.

They all threw punches at the same time, hitting Saint and knocking him against the bars. Unable to run and too tired to fight, he never knew he could feel so helpless. His punches were merely slow, harmless waves of his fist that allowed the clique to hit him at will.

"That's for putting your hand in my face and dancing with my ol' lady," Skookie said.

B.C. rushed out of cell one and struck Saint on the back of his head with the wooden toilet brush, making him stumble forward into a barrage of fists that knocked him back again. B.C. jumped onto his back, hitting him twice on his head and choking him with his left arm. Saint waved his fist at the clique to keep them off while he pulled on B.C.'s left arm. Like a madman, B.C. repeatedly struck Saint's head. Saint violently jerked back towards the bars, trying to knock him. B.C. dropped the brush and held on with both hands, riding Saint like a bucking horse. Saint caught an arm in front of him and bit it. Boodie reached for the brush, but Saint kicked it away. Boodie caught Saint's leg and bent down to grab the brush. The clique swarmed Saint, seizing his legs. Boodie hit him repeatedly in the face with the brush. Walkie-Talkie stood back as he looked on. "Take his eyes, knock him out, and bring him in this cell," he said.

Fist blows landed in a torrent that made Saint's eyes swell and shut immediately. Unable to see, he raised his right arm and clawed B.C. in the face with his sharp fingernails.

B.C. screamed and fell to the floor, holding his bleeding face. "Ahhhh! *My eyes, my eyes. I can't see. I can't see!*" he cried, squirming.

"You was gonna testify for them good white folks, huh? You ain't no star athlete. You a State's star witness, you rat!" Boodie shouted.

"Boodie! What you talking about?" Saint screamed. He suddenly remembered. Though he was temporarily blinded, the vision was crystal clear.

The man extended his hand. "Warren Hebert. I represented you at the motion to suppress hearing, remember?"

"What's going on? What's all this?"

"Is he ready, is he ready?"

"Ready? Ready for what? Ready for what? Where's the dentist?"

"The deal's off! The deal's off. Take him back. Take him back! I don't need him. The deal's off!"

"Forest, I think you made a bad mistake. Warren didn't tell you why you were brought to the courthouse? Watch your back, boy. I don't like this. Something isn't right here."

When Saint's right arm was secured, Boodie alternated between striking his face with a fist and hitting him with the wooden brush in his other hand. Saint twisted and turned, grabbing the bars and hiding his face against them. Boodie hammered his head repeatedly.

He then beat Saint's right hand to numbness while June Bug bit his left hand to make him release the bars.

After pulling him loose, the clique carried Saint to cell four, but he broke free and fell back against the bars. He covered his face the way boxers do when trapped on the ropes. The clique pounded and pounded at his head, each one trying to find a clear opening. Walkie-Talkie slammed him in the stomach, taking his breath away and sending him to the floor. Deadeye dragged him into the cell as they kicked and stomped on his head and body. The clique filled the cell. They appeared to have been in a war and were showing signs of fatigue. Saint sat on the floor, gasping in pain. He tried to see them but couldn't for his swollen eyes.

Walkie-Talkie entered the cell with a *Morning Advocate* article. He began reading: "'In the opening statement, Special Counsel told a twelve-man jury that Hammond had agreed to be the state's star witness against Ramsey. The court was informed that Hammond later for unknown reasons refused to take the stand and testify. Ossie Brown, District Attorney, had agreed to take a plea of guilty without capital punishment if Hammond would have testified against Ramsey according to the plea bargain that had earlier been worked out.' "Without capital punishment" meant eligibility for parole, probation, commutation, or suspension of sentence.

Trying to cut a deal with the DA, huh? Yeah, this b---- is a rat. S--- on my d--- or blood on my knife."

B.C. staggered into the cell. He took a metal garbage-can lid from Robert Lee and smashed Saint's face, pushing his head over in the toilet and flushing it. Deadeye pulled B.C. off.

"Saint, you got to give that a-- up so this beating can stop," Walkie-Talkie said.

"I ain't doing nothing with all y'all in here," Saint retorted.

"All right then! Everybody get out. Let me trim this rat," Walkie-Talkie said.

Through a slit of his swollen right eye, Saint saw the clique grinning as they exited the cell. He climbed onto the top rear bunk. Walkie-Talkie climbed on the top front bunk with the knife and handed Saint a can of Royal Crown hairdressing. Saint began exaggerating his gasping. He reached for the grease but caught Walkie-Talkie squarely in the mouth with a violent blow, knocking him back against the wall, snorting and farting from the surprise.

Walkie-Talkie retaliated by swinging, cutting, and stabbing Saint, hitting him in his arm, chest, and multiple times in his hand—slicing all his fingers. He thrust the knife at Saint's stomach. With both his hands, Saint caught the knife and Walkie-Talkie's hands. The knife pierced Saint's left hand; blood poured onto the mattress. Walkie-Talkie withdrew the knife and jumped back to the bars. Saint pulled the mattress from the top bunk and held it against his body with his left arm. He balled his hand to slow the bleeding, but the numbness wouldn't allow him to make a fist. The most he could do was form a cup where the blood from his lacerated fingers collected. He threw the blood in Walkie-Talkie's face. He stabbed Saint's exposed left arm that held the mattress against his body. Saint could feel the steely knife puncturing his flesh. He knew he had to get the knife.

"Take me by yourself, you mothaf---a," Saint whispered. "I'm-a take that knife, kill you, then f--- you, you dead pussy-a-- mothaf---a."

Boodie heard the bunk and wall buckling and thought Saint was having the meat put to him. He didn't understand the sprinkles of blood coming out of the cell, splattering on the catwalk. He peeked inside.

"What? That niggah ain't f---in'. He still fighting! Y'all come on!" Boodie yelled.

The clique returned. Daniel heard Saint's groans and moans from the torturous beating as fist after fist made repeated contact with his swollen face.

"*Aaaah-ha-ha-ha.* Stop. Stop it. I'm-a do it. I'll f---. I'll f---," Saint cried.

"Then all this beating will stop and be over with," Walkie-Talkie assured him. "We don't wanna rape you. We want you to give that a-- up knowingly, voluntarily, and willingly, like the judge was gonna ask you in that deal you tried to make, you rattin' b----. Now, y'all get out."

As they exited, Saint yelled, *"I'm-a f--- all you niggahs!"* Then, inexplicably, he began laughing. Walkie-Talkie stared at Saint's bloody teeth as he sat on the rear bunk, laughing derisively. "I'm gon' f--- all you niggahs," Saint repeated.

Daniel saw the clique stop in front of cell five and return to cell four. They attacked Saint with renewed ferocity, cursing and beating him as if trying to kill his spirit. The pack mentality was in full control. "You laughing? Laugh at this!" They kicked Saint under the rear bunk. Daniel heard him groaning. His gym shorts were pulled off. His once-white but now bloody-red nylon undershorts were ripped away and thrown on the catwalk. The pajama shirt was soaked with blood. He was gasping like a dying bird, balled up on the floor under the bunk. He felt with his tongue where a tooth had been knocked out. His eyes rolled back as he blacked out momentarily. He felt cold, unaware that he was experiencing the initial stages of traumatic shock.

"Come out from under there," Boodie said, taking the knife from Walkie-Talkie and stabbing at Saint beneath the bunk.

"I come out. Don't stab no more. I come out," Saint said. "Give me grease. Give me grease," he pleaded. His words and sentences were now broken as he became disoriented. He was nearly immobile. Walkie-Talkie took the knife as Saint crawled out. Saint positioned himself on his knees on the floor with his head hanging so that he could make out images through the tiny slit of his right eye.

"If I don't tame this Lion this time, I'm killing his a--. Knocked my damn gold crown loose," Walkie-Talkie said, feeling his own front tooth.

The clique returned to the dayroom. Saint crawled to the front lower bunk next to the door. Walkie-Talkie, standing on the catwalk outside the cell, guarded the door and watched Saint slowly get into position on the bunk. Walkie-Talkie handed him the grease, placing it in Saint's extended, trembling left hand. Saint was lying on his left side with his buttocks to the wall. He stuck his right-hand fingers in the can and came out with a huge wad of grease. He gasped and swallowed. His throat felt as though he had swallowed sand.

I'll give you some a-- if you just give me a drink of water, he thought about saying. He wanted to laugh but now couldn't. His body was going into shock. He had no energy to talk. His lips were swollen. His jawbones ached.

Walkie-Talkie became aroused as he watched Saint place his hand behind him and rub. He grabbed his groin as he cautiously moved into the cell, still holding the knife and watching Saint. Blinded, but tracking with his ears, Saint could hear him as he entered the cell. Saint got another wad of grease out of the can, placed his hand behind him, and rubbed again. Walkie-Talkie slowly moved past him towards the rear of the cell. He was unbuttoning his pants and taking his penis out. He stood at the foot of the bunk, still hesitant about mounting Saint.

"Turn over, ho'," Walkie-Talkie ordered.

Saint rolled over on his stomach and he rested on his forearms. In that single motion, he bent his right leg at the knee and dangled it tight against the bunk, barely touching the floor. He began an indistinct swinging movement. His left leg extended on the bunk. The blood-soaked Converse All-Star sneaker subtly moved back and forth, trying to grip a dry spot on the bloody floor, but it kept slipping. Walkie-Talkie didn't budge. He needed to be stimulated again. Saint propped himself up on his left knee, which raised his buttocks away from where the metal bunk attached to the wall. In doing so, he hung his huge, heavy head down between his shoulders and arms. From this upside-down position, he opened his eyelids enough to see Walkie-Talkie watching him. The knife was in his right hand; his penis was out of his pants but not erect.

Walkie-Talkie reached for his penis and took a half-step towards the bunk to mount Saint but stopped suddenly. He stared at the area where the bunk attached to the wall. Saint's turning over on his stomach exposed the spot on the blanket where the two huge wads of grease had been wiped. Walkie-Talkie then saw Saint staring at him out of the crevices of his eyelids. He noticed the unguarded door and jumped back near the toilet in alarm.

"What do you want?" Coach Bates shouted at winter practice. "A hole wide enough for a train to go through! The hole is only gonna be open for a split second. You got to do the rest! Dive through it. Get the first down!"

"You slick motherf---er," Walkie-Talkie whispered.

The right sneaker stopped. The ball of his foot gripped the terrazzo. Saint had only one chance and no strength to move. His lungs hurt. It was painful to breathe. He needed energy to push himself off with his arms. He sighed deeply, exhaling and unable to move. As he inhaled, he watched Walkie-Talkie put his penis back in his pants. Oxygen filled his lungs. His arms became filled with power. He felt strengthened. Pushing off the bunk with his arms while thrusting himself forward, Saint went through the narrow cell door, turning his body from being hit with the knife as Walkie-Talkie lunged. The wide swing missed Saint's neck and hit the bunk, cutting Walkie-Talkie's hand as it ricocheted into the service aisle. Saint crashed headfirst into the bars on the catwalk. His arms were too heavy to hold up and block the collision. He fell to the floor and immediately covered up, expecting another attack from the clique. The clique, bewildered, remained in the dayroom.

"Oh. No mo' beating? No mo' beating, huh? Don't stop now,"

Saint muttered, his words unintelligible. He turned and saw the clique sitting in the dayroom. He pulled himself up by the bars, staggered into the dayroom like his crippled neighbor Papa, and slowly placed his feet on the bench seat of table two, directly in front of the television. He was gasping, disoriented. Like a person paralyzed from the waist down, Saint used his arms to aid himself in standing upright. When he stood, he spread his arms out wide so the clique would see him.

"Look at me. Look what y'all did me," he muttered. "I no rat, no rat. I make no deal. Set up. They set up." Saint could barely speak. He stood there, naked and covered with blood for them to see. His eyes rolled back again. He felt as if he was going to black out. His outstretched arms hung like wet eagle's wings. Everyone in the clique frowned and turned their faces away from Saint's grotesque and marred appearance. They were too ashamed to look.

"Look at me," he said again. They refused. Saint tried to lift his leg to step down to the floor but did not possess the strength. He tried to raise his arms to a fighting guard position but couldn't. "Come, come on. I fight all you moth'f---. I'm Cap, Cap, Lion, niggah."

The clique turned to look but quickly turned away again. Saint felt himself getting colder. His legs felt cold. He could not bend his knees to get down. He inched his feet to the edge and leaned forward, slipping off the bench. The jar from landing on the floor sent excruciating pain throughout his body. He felt every bone. Blood oozed out of his sneakers, spattering everywhere. His huge head was too heavy to balance upon his neck. His eyes rolled again. Once on the catwalk, Saint saw Walkie-Talkie shaking his head as he staggered by him.

Edna's words entered Saint's mind. "He that fights or runs away shall live to fight another day." This fight was not over.

No one could understand anything Saint said. His lips and face were misshapen and too huge to form words. He was only blowing air through his swollen lips and making sounds. When he reached the green main door, he stumbled and crashed into it. The swelling of his body and head with fluids insulated his nerves, and the impact of falling against the iron door caused no pain.

In the AB-AC Lobby just outside the cellblock, Columbus the hall man turned left but looked to his right upon hearing a faint thud. "Oh my God!" he exclaimed after peeking through the tiny window and ran off down the corridor.

Saint got up slowly. Pulling up on the bars, he saw a pack of Kools. "Live, live to fight."

Felix Hatch remained in cell one, away from the carnage his friends had committed. He had attended Capitol and was in jail on an armed-robbery charge. Hatch was a baseball player. Saint assumed the Kools were for Hatch.

"Say, Hatch, cigarette?"

"Help yourself, Saint," Hatch said, shaking his head. He didn't believe that Saint was a rat, but the leaders of the clique were his friends, and he could have helped but didn't. The newspaper article was hard evidence that Saint had tried to cut a deal with the same district attorney who would be prosecuting all of them.

When Saint reached down, blood poured into the pack off his arm.

"That's all right, Saint," Hatch said. Seeing that Saint couldn't manage the pack, he stepped out onto the catwalk, tore the pack open, got a cigarette, lit it, stuck it in Saint's swollen lips, and went back into the cell. Saint took one draw and it had an immediate soothing effect.

"Come here, you rattin' b----."

Saint turned around. Boodie was six feet away with both arms reaching for his neck. Saint tried to raise his guards, but Boodie grabbed him by the throat and began to choke him. Pressed up against the green door, Saint finger-stepped his hand up Boodie's body until it reached his throat. He couldn't squeeze. Boodie pressed Saint back against the door as Saint yielded to the pressure of the chokehold.

The big green door swung open. Deputy Washington struck Boodie with a riot stick, making him release Saint, who fell backwards against Washington's leg before landing on the cold floor.

"Get back, you animals. Hit your cells!" Deputy Washington screamed. "Everybody, right now. Look what they did to this boy! Columbus, get a mattress out of cell one so we can drag this boy out of here up front and get him to the hospital."

Saint's body jerked as he lay on his stomach on the cold floor.

"But when you fall, oh, but you will fall, children, you will fall," Mr. Keel said in a quiet, low voice. Then: *"Get up!"* The class of 1973 stood up, cheering, tossing their caps, and hugging each other. *"Get up, with your Lion Pride! Execute the gifts and educational tools you've received here these four years. Remember your red and gold alma mater, for you will forever be a Capitol High red and gold*

mighty Lion. Thank you and congratulations, young women, and congratulations, young men. May God bless you and be with you in this life."

"Another, 'nother day, another day," the nude Saint uttered. His blood-soaked sneakers hung over the edge of the mattress. As they dragged him away, his shoes divided the corridor in half, with the middle line being a long red trail of blood.

Chapter 5

The Plea

Deputy Washington and Columbus held Saint up in a shower as a white female deputy washed his blood-covered body and searched for stab wounds. Saint regained consciousness momentarily and tried to talk, but neither deputy understood him. They thought he was trying to fight them.

Then Columbus said, "He's trying to get some water. Lean him back so the water can get in his mouth."

Saint drank some water but then blacked out again as they held him up.

A tall, blond Louisiana state trooper stood on the loading dock of Earl K. Long Hospital. In front of him was a small, mostly black crowd waiting for rides or a taxi. Soon an ambulance drove up to the door of the emergency room. A sheriff's patrol unit parked just shy of the ramp. A deputy exited and ran up the ramp as EMTs rolled Saint into the emergency room. The state trooper shook his head. The presence of the sheriff's deputy told him it was a jailhouse victim.

A white nurse moved swiftly with the stretcher. She was holding Saint's head near her breast. "Oh my God, look what they done to him!" she exclaimed.

Saint felt his body relax just before he blacked out again. As they washed his body he regained consciousness, still thinking he was in a fight. The nurse and aides struggled to hold him down.

An orderly who worked in the emergency room heard the deputy utter the name Forest Hammond. He got on the phone and put the word out to find Martin. Martin was in a café on North Street when the news reached him. He raced down Airline Highway, running every red light between North Street and Earl K. Long along the way.

"Mr. Martin, your son took a real good head bashing," the doctor told him. "His condition is stable but critical. It's a miracle he's alive from the amount of blood lost. He was in shock when we got him. I don't know how he survived. He's an athlete?"

Martin nodded.

"I thought so. In the future, he has to avoid any rough sports. His memory might be affected slightly or his ability to concentrate. He has several mild concussions. He will need rehabilitation therapy. I don't think he will experience the loss of any bodily functions. No internal organs were punctured. He'll have to be kept quiet."

"When can I see my boy?" Martin asked.

"I don't think that is a good idea at this time, Mr. Martin. He looks pretty bad."

"I don't care how he looks. I want see my boy," Martin insisted.

"I don't think the deputies will allow you to see your son. I'd suggest that if you know a lawyer, he can get you in. Good luck, sir."

Martin drove to Rep. Woody Jenkins' office. After several hours, Saint was transferred back to the parish prison. Jenkins called the prison and got Martin, his children, and DMB a special pass to see Forest.

The female deputy who had stood in the shower to aid his son led Martin, DMB, and the siblings to the parish prison infirmary. The deputy opened the door but stopped the siblings from entering.

DMB slowly followed Martin, who pulled the curtain open. The grotesque scene before him took his breath away. Nothing resembled his boy, the son he had raised. He walked in, looked at the nametag on a rail at the foot of the bed, and turned away, shaking his head. Refusing to accept the obvious, he proceeded to the next curtain and pulled it back, only to find an empty bed.

"That's it, Mr. Martin. That's him!" the deputy said.

Martin shook his head. He looked again at the first bed as he removed his hat and wiped tears from his eyes.

DMB walked up only to glance at Saint before cringing and turning away.

"IIII want to see thaaaat boy you bastards came to-to-to *myyyy house* and took away." Martin bent over, resting his hand on a cart. He was biting his good arm. He walked back to Saint's bed, took his glasses off, and wiped his eyes. He cleaned his glasses and replaced them, studying the tubes in his son's nose, the IVs in his arms, and his monstrous appearance. Martin turned to the deputy. "Where's my boy? That's not my boy. I wanna see my boy, my son! Lord have mercy. Who the hell did I help slaughter my boy like this?" Martin lamented. "I want him just like he was when you lying bastards came and took him from my house! What kind of program you operating here, a slaughter camp?"

Martin turned back to Saint. He reached out to touch him but didn't, for fear of hurting him. "Forest," Martin called. He studied his son's wounds, the stitches in his hand, fingers, and arm, his gigantic swollen head, and his closed eyes and huge lips. He tried to envision what kind of fight he had been in. "Them mothaf---as," Martin muttered. "Oh, God, please forgive me," he said, making the sign of the cross. "These rotten bastards will make Christ cuss." Martin walked out past the deputy and left.

Somewhere in the midst of 168 pounds of swollen human flesh and blood, Saint managed to blink his right eye. He tried to call out to his father. "Haddy, Haddy," he uttered, unable to move his lips. He twitched a swollen, stitched finger in an effort to beckon Martin to come back. He wanted Martin to know that he had heard him.

Three days later, Daniel sat at Saint's bedside and spoon-fed him. The swelling of his eyes had gone down to small puffs, and one could see that the whites of his eyes had changed to completely red. Still in trauma, he drooled as he stared into space. His lips remained large. He sat tilted up in the hospital bed. His arms and head were still bandaged. Daniel moved around, talking to Saint but getting no response. He spoke as if he were talking to a plant.

After feeding his friend, Daniel got a red Bible out of Saint's bag and read.

"Hey, Saint, I know what we can do. We can pray for help. Can you hear me? All right? Just sit back, okay? I'll pray for both of us. I don't know why I didn't think about this earlier. Lord, we come to you as sinners and two people who have repented their sins. We need your help now, oh Lord. We don't know how much longer we can take this treatment. These white peoples got us locked up behind iron bars and we's innocent, Lord. Me and Saint both renounce Satan and all his demons. We desire to worship and serve you only, oh God of David."

As Daniel prayed, Saint was conscious but continued to stare straight ahead. He slowly raised his arms, covering his head and face as flashbacks of the attack overwhelmed him. He moaned.

"And oh lord, I ask this prayer in the name of your only son, Jesus Christ. Amen.

Saint lowered his arms, whispering softly as he drooled, "Yah-Yahshua."

On October 15, the courtroom chatter was loud. Blacks occupied the entire right side and half of the left seating area. Billy Middleton's widow, retired Army Lt. General Troy H. Middleton, who was also president emeritus of Louisiana State University, and relatives and friends were present on the front row, all wearing black sunglasses.

Saint, wearing a brown suit, was brought into the courtroom in handcuffs. He recognized Judge Lear. Saint stood on the opposite side of the rail. Four huge sheriff's bailiffs were present, with one standing immediately to Saint's right. Assistant District Attorney Anthony Graphia talked with Saint's new lawyer, near the judge's bench. Joe Woods was also present. Several assistant prosecutors and investigators at the counsel table were turned around, talking to the Middleton family.

"Good Lord, Ossie, hurry and send more deputies in here," Lear was overheard to say. "My courtroom looks like it did during the Black Muslims trial."

DMB gently touched the scars in Saint's face, but his attention was on his new attorney, Woodson T. Callihan, who was talking to Graphia near Judge Lear. "I feel butterflies," Saint said when he saw his lawyer and Graphia covering their mouths with manila folders as they spoke.

DMB dug into her purse and retrieved a stick of gum that she gave to Saint. "Big Mama said chew gum when you got butterflies," she told him. "They'll go away."

"What are they saying that requires them to put folders over their mouths to talk?"

"I don't know, Saint, but it can't be anything good. They white people," DMB replied.

Martin was watching when Callihan beckoned for him to follow him into the jury deliberation room.

"Forest, how you like my new dress? My godmother bought it so I could wear it to court today," Daisy said to her brother, smiling. She thought his bloodshot eyes caused him to look like an alien. She instinctively backed away from Saint when he only stared back at her.

"Forest, after all this time I finally learned how to curl my own hair," Teresa said. "What do you think? Do you like it? I cooked your favorite meal last night, red beans and rice and cornbread," she added, smiling. Teresa tried to ignore the scars and red eyes. Saint responded with a blank expression, as if trying to comprehend what she was talking about.

"Hey, Forest," Paul called. "Don't get mad at me, but I've been wearing your jacket and some of your other clothes too. I took good care of them. I keep the room clean." He quickly lost his enthusiasm when Saint just looked at him, expressionless. "Something's wrong with Forest," he whispered.

Michael was elated to see his big brother and couldn't wait for old times to resume. He bobbed and weaved like Smokin' Joe Frazier. "Hey, Saint! Come on. Let's play! Paul won't play with me," Michael said, too loud.

His zeal caught the attention of the bailiff standing by. "Hey, be quiet! Absolutely no playing in this courtroom," he commanded.

Michael dropped his hands and hid behind Paul. Judge Lear and the attorneys turned to see. Saint looked down at his cuffed hands. He turned, gazed at the bailiff, and shook his head. He then turned and looked at Daisy's pretty dress and cracked a slight smile. Tears formed in his eyes. Daisy's weak smile began to widen. Saint tilted his head and smiled at Teresa as he studied her curls. Teresa smiled until she noticed his right lateral incisor was missing and assumed correctly that it had been lost in the fight. He nodded his approval to Paul. Michael continued to hide behind Paul, his eyes squeezed shut.

Just as fighters do when caught on the ropes, Saint painfully bowed his head and raised his cuffed hands to protect his face. Salty tears rolled down his cheeks into his mouth and dripped to the floor. "Come, come on, S-S-Smokin' Joe. Ali is on the ropes."

On hearing that, Michael opened his eyes but didn't move. His siblings, all in tears, edged back, watching and thinking that Saint was crazy.

"Take his eyes, knock him out, and bring him in this cell." Voices screamed in recall, igniting flashback trauma. "Smokin' Joe pounds and pounds at his head, hook after hook, trying to find . . . opening," Saint said." Tears streamed down Aunt Daisy's face as she looked on. Saint waited.

Michael peeked around Paul at his brother's marred face and dark-red eyes. Saint was hunched over. He had his healing, half-balled-fist up to his face. He was in a fighter's stance. Everything was normal except for the handcuffs. That was still his big brother! Michael dashed out from behind Paul, ran to Saint, and hugged him around the waist. Saint embraced all of his siblings and DMB, telling them he loved them.

In the Jury Room

The jury-room door opened and Callihan motioned for Saint, who limped past the victim's seating area and jury box and entered the room. Martin was sitting at a table alone, his bad hand resting on a document on the table and his good hand wiping his eyes.

"Daddy, why you crying? What's wrong?" Saint asked, alarmed.

"Son, this new lawyer says you must plead guilty or they gonna slap an armed-robbery charge on you and give you ninety-nine years or you might get the death sentence for murder if you go to trial," Martin explained.

"Yes, Forest," Callihan said. "There is just too much overwhelming evidence against you to be acquitted at trial. By pleading guilty, you avoid the death penalty. If we don't accept the State's offer through the district attorney's office, you are facing, well, that's really forty-nine and a half years for attempted armed robbery and capital punishment."

Although Louisiana's death penalty had already been ruled unconstitutional, the legislature had created a system of guilty verdicts "with" or "without" capital punishment. "Without" provided eligibility for parole, probation, commutation, or suspension of sentence after serving a certain minimum; "with" did not provide these. Neither amounted to the death penalty, but they could give the illusion of such to an ignorant defendant.

"But I'm not guilty of no murder. I ain't murdered nobody. I was trying to stop Boodie."

"I understand, but the jury won't believe that. I talked to the judge. He said if you plead guilty he will give you a pardon after two years. He won't oppose any request for clemency you make," Callihan explained.

After nearly two hours of trying to persuade Saint to accept a guilty plea to murder, Callihan attempted to show him the criminal code, but Saint walked away to a window and stared at the initials *I.N.R.I.* on the smokestack of a ship docked in the Mississippi River. Saint didn't want to hear all of that guilty-plea talk.

A bailiff peeked in. "The judge said to hurry up," he told them. "He don't want to be late for his lunch appointment."

Callihan insisted that if Saint pled guilty to murder instead of going to trial, he would not get the death penalty. He told Martin that Saint would not serve his sentence in Angola but instead would go to an industrial school for first-offender youths at DeQuincy, where he would be able to maximize his rehabilitative efforts and come home on weekend passes. Callihan made it sound like a trade school that also had a sports program.

Saint held his head as a migraine started. He still heard a ringing in his ears from the beating and everything was confusing. He refused to accept a plea bargain.

"Where is Mr. Bell?" Martin asked. Murphy Bell headed up the public defender's office. "He said he personally would represent my boy at trial and could clear him of this charge."

"I don't know, Mr. Martin. We met at the office this morning like we always do before trial. He knows the trial starts this morning. I can't account for his whereabouts," Callihan said.

"Well, can't you tell the judge you aren't prepared to go to trial?"

"He won't believe me, Mr. Martin. I think your son should take the plea bargain."

Two public-defender investigators entered and began asking Saint for names of character witnesses. He gave them names of his teachers at Capitol High and of managers and presidents in offices he had cleaned. They all seemed to be cramming to prepare for trial at the last moment. Callihan sent for Coach Bates, who was seated in the courtroom. Bates, after speaking briefly with Callihan, walked over to where Saint stood staring out the window towards the Mississippi River.

"Champ, they want me to talk to you and tell you to plead guilty. I'm not going to tell you what to do. They figured you would listen to me," Coach Bates said. "You be your own man and make that decision. Whatever you do, son, stand up like a man and be a good example for your whole family out there. Quitters never win and winners never quit. We're gonna get this victory, son." In tears, Coach Bates extended his hand but Saint grabbed and hugged him.

Martin sat alone at the table, crying. Saint walked over to Martin and patted him on his shoulder and rubbed his back.

"Daddy, don't cry, Daddy."

"I don't understand this. Oh, I wish Edna was here. She was smart. She would understand all this legal talk," Martin said, wiping his tears. He was hurt.

Saint picked up the papers off the table and looked at them. He didn't understand any of the legal terminology or Callihan's legalese, and he didn't trust Callihan.

Martin turned to Callihan and Coach Bates. "Let me talk to my boy," he said finally. Callihan, Coach Bates, and the two investigators stood by the door. Callihan had said Saint wouldn't go to Angola, but Martin wasn't so sure. Saint was only seventeen years old and had never been in any trouble, nor had he lived in any institution in his life. Martin didn't think Saint would survive in Angola, and he wanted to tell him something in case they never saw each other again. He asked Saint to sit.

"Before me and your mama got married, before you were born, she got pregnant, but not by me. I raised so much hell about it when she brought Vincent back with her from up north that she sent him to California to live."

The bailiff opened the door again. "The judge said to hurry up. It's been almost four hours since y'all been back here," he said. "He's running late for his lunch date."

"Vincent's your half-brother," Martin continued when the bailiff left. "After he grew up, he was so bad, your aunt Fern sent him to me, hoping I could straighten him out. Even after we got married, I never forgave your mama. I kept punishing her for that. I guess I wanted her to, ah, I don't know. I never thought about how what I did would affect my other kids. I was selfish, but I loved Edna and I do love you, Forest. I always have. I got this for you before you left to go to USI. I guess I forgot to give it to you." Martin set a tiny black velvet box on the table. Saint ignored it.

"It's, it's SIU, Daddy, SIU. Southern Illinois University." Saint knew his dad always got things mixed up like that.

"I made plenty money. Women got bold and started calling the house, cussing Edna out, ah, and woman stuff, you know. I wish I'd never touched any of them. I never thought my payback would lead to her, ah—"

"Killing herself, but it did," Saint said, angered. He stood up abruptly.

"Sit down, son. Let me tell you. Sit down, please."

Saint refused to sit. "I guess we all make mistakes, huh, Daddy?"

"Your mama didn't kill herself, Forest," Martin said flatly.

Saint sat. "What do you mean, Daddy? She killed herself. I saw the rifle laying on her. The barrel was laying at her heart. I saw it."

"Naw," Martin replied. "Y'all were so young. I, I just couldn't tell you then, you see. You would have grown up hating that boy like you hated me. Edna wouldn't want that. Edna was too smart, too strong for that. She was an Indian-Jew woman, strong. You were asleep. Daisy Lee said she was shot while talking to her on the phone. I knew then. That boy, Vincent, he shot and killed my wife, your mama." Martin held his hands together, rocking back and forth and shaking his head, feeling released of the burden that had been on him for years. "Your mama loved him so much she would never forgive me if I turned him over to the authorities. I just wanted to get him as far away from me as possible before I did him something. I couldn't live with him being there. I know you grew up hating me, but that's all right. I figured someday you'd find out the truth."

"Gahlee, Daddy. I grew up all these years hating you and thinking she killed herself."

"I wanted to tell you, but you grew up on me so fast. I gave her lots of money, Forest. She would send that money to California to keep that boy out of trouble. I wish I could let her know I forgive her. But it's too late."

"It ain't too late, Daddy. She knows. I know. At least I know now. It ain't too late. It's not too late," Saint tearfully whispered.

Coach Bates walked over, gestured to Saint, and pointed to his watch. Martin wiped his tears. Saint helped Martin up and embraced him. Saint picked up the black velvet box off the table.

"Let's go, Daddy. I'll be all right. I'll take care of myself. Don't cry. Don't worry about me. I'm-a make you happy again, Daddy. I'll take care of myself."

Back in the courtroom, as they stood before Judge Lear, Callihan whispered, "When the judge asks you if any promises have been made to you, just say no. Say no. Answer yes when he asks do you understand your rights. You'll be going to DeQuincy."

"You are charged in a bill of indictment with violating, on the tenth day of April 1973, Louisiana Revised Statutes 14:30, in that you murdered Billy Middleton. Do I understand that you wish to plead guilty to this offense?" asked Judge Lear.

"Yes sir."

"*No! Forest! No! No!*" Teresa and Daisy screamed. Teresa raised her long leg and stepped over the gate, attempting to climb over and go to her brother, but a bailiff grabbed and wrestled with her until another bailiff came and helped him. Judge Lear became nervous. The noise level rose in the public seating area.

Graphia, holding a file folder, waved it, telling Judge Lear to continue. Graphia then followed a bailiff out of the courtroom. When the door opened, Martin saw Ossie Brown standing by the elevator with Murphy Bell. A few seconds later, the bailiff reentered with five more bailiffs behind him. They all carried riot gear and shields and stood in front of the audience.

"Why he's not going to trial!" someone shouted. "We want to see a trial!"

"No, Forest, please, no, no, no! Don't!" Teresa cried again.

Three bailiffs ran to the gate to help hold her while two others restrained Daisy. Another bailiff rested his right hand on his weapon and extended his left arm, pointing his finger in Paul's face, warning him not to cross over the rail. Graphia, with the file folder still in his hand, stood at the exit at the back of the courtroom as more deputies entered. He gestured to Judge Lear to hurry and get to the sentencing.

"Turn around and pay attention to the judge," Callihan instructed Saint, who kept looking to the left at his distraught family as the judge spoke. When Judge Lear asked Saint in a single long question if he wanted to waive his right to a trial by jury and to confront his accusers and to waive the right against self-incrimination, Saint didn't hear or understand what he said. Judge Lear was watching the commotion in the courtroom as well. Callihan nudged Saint with his right elbow. "Turn around and pay attention to the judge and answer him. He's talking to you," Callihan said.

Saint saw the stenographer's hands suspended above her keyboard as Callihan spoke to him. He saw Judge Lear looking at the crowd, then back at him. Judge Lear appeared to be waiting for an answer from Saint. Saint turned to Callihan. "What did he say?" The stenographer's fingers were punching keys on her keyboard.

"Do I understand you wish to give up and waive the right against self-incrimination?" Lear asked again. He omitted asking again if Saint understood and waived his right to trial by jury and to have his attorney cross examine his accusers.

"Yes," Saint answered. His body faced Judge Lear, but his head was still turned towards his family. He saw Michael standing in front of Paul, looking at him.

"Do you understand those rights and wish to waive them and enter a plea of guilty?" Judge Lear asked. He looked at the crowd, looked at Saint, and waited for an answer.

Callihan tapped Saint and leaned towards him. "Say yes. Say yes!"

The stenographer's hands again were suspended motionless above her keyboard.

Judge Lear turned to Graphia. "Has there been a plea bargain in this matter?"

"Your Honor, in view of the plea of guilty as charged to the murder indictment, the State will not prosecute Bill Number 5-73-478," Graphia stated, reading from his file.

"That's the attempted armed robbery?" Judge Lear asked.

"Yes sir," Graphia answered.

"Yes, Your Honor, I would like to state for the record that the State has agreed to accept the plea of guilty without capital punishment," Callihan explained.

"That's correct, Your Honor," Graphia said. "And also not prosecute the charge of attempted armed robbery," he added.

"All right, this Court will accept the plea. Is the defendant ready for sentencing?" Judge Lear asked in one breath. "The sentence is automatic," he said.

When Saint heard the word "automatic," he wondered if they had lied to him again and it were still possible for him to get the death penalty.

"Yes, Your Honor, we waive any delay for sentencing," Callihan answered.

Judge Lear was speeding through the process so quickly that he didn't wait for Callihan to finish speaking. "By the authority vested in me by the State of Louisiana, it is the sentence of the Court that you be confined to the custody of the Department of Corrections at the Louisiana State Penitentiary at Angola for the rest of your natural life."

Saint stood looking at the little black box and raised his hand, appreciating his beautiful graduation ring that Martin had given him only moments earlier. He tried to speak.

"Yes? You want to make a statement?" Judge Lear asked.

Saint nodded, raised his hands, and took the gum out his mouth. "If, if you think I'm gonna spend the rest of my life in Angola," Saint began as he turned to the Middleton crowd, the DA, and his family and friends, then back to the judge, "you got another thought coming."

Judge Lear was infuriated. He grabbed his gavel and slammed it down on the wood base on his bench. "This Court is adjourned! Bailiff, get him out of here!"

A bailiff placed his hands on Saint's shoulder and escorted him past his family.

"He didn't do anything!" Teresa cried. "Y'all are just prejudiced white people!"

The commotion built as the black members of the audience protested. Deputies stood in front of the Middleton family and white audience to protect them. More deputies filed into the courtroom with riot shields and formed a barrier around Judge Lear.

A Ford cargo van traveled up U.S. 61 from Baton Rouge and turned left on LA 66. A handmade sign said: ROAD OF NO RETURN. The van crossed a flat bridge and another sign advised: DON'T DESPAIR. On the reverse it read: YOU WILL SOON BE THERE! Each of the five convicts from East Baton Rouge Parish saw both sides of the second sign. Chris McAllister was the only white convict among the five. The other four were Larry Mullens, Gilbert Franklin, Lonnie "Turtle" Woods, and Forest Hammond.

"The great athlete, going to the Louisiana State Penitentiary," Turtle said and chuckled. He studied the scars on Saint's face as if he were a doctor determining their rate of healing. "Now, me, I can see me going to penitentiary, because I'm a dropout, I smoke dope, I gamble, I commit burglaries, and might rob a store every now and then," he said. "But not you. You go to school. You made good grades, played sports, became a great athlete, and you got life. S---! I got fifteen years and it's killing me."

Saint sat in shackles connected to Turtle and the three others. He said nothing as he stared out the window. Sunlight coming through the thick foliage of the Tunica Hills hit his face.

"Say, Saint, you gonna do that life sentence?" The other convicts didn't know Saint and just looked at him when Turtle asked the question. They knew about the drugstore murder. They heard about Saint saving "another niggah's a--." That news had spread all over the parish prison and had even reached Angola before his arrival. Any seventeen-year-old, first-offender kid who went up against a madman like Walkie-Talkie and his clique deserved respect. Not to mention he got stabbed and beaten for nearly three hours and never gave up. Most young convicts had only to see a knife before dropping their drawers and asking for the grease. They dreaded being stabbed. The three who didn't know Saint felt privileged to meet him.

"Turtle, I'm going to Angola to get out of Angola," Saint answered.

Mullens, a career criminal like Walkie-Talkie but not as cynical, laughed. "I'll be out by," Saint paused, reflecting as if listening, "by the new decade."

Turtle's hands were shackled to his waist, so he spread his fingers and counted. "Let's see, next year is '74, '75, '76, '77, '78, '79, '80. That's seven years. You think you gonna live that long, Saint?" Each of the five convicts would have to answer that question individually.

"I don't know, Turtle. I don't know," Saint whispered.

Chapter 6

Louisiana State Peniversity at Angola

Louisiana State Peniversity, Angola 101. Beginning date: November 8, 1973.

Saint saw people differently since the parish-prison war. The painful experience and suffering left him with a new but all-too-real view of fear.

From this day forth, you better work on getting out of here, a still, small voice said.

"Hey, baby! You gonna be for me," were the first human words Saint heard when he arrived at Angola. Prison whores were shouting to agitate fears they knew were simmering within the hearts of the five new "fresh fish" arrivals disembarking from the white prison cargo van below them.

"*Boy, at the rate you going, you gonna be in penitentiary before you twenty years old. Mark my words.*" Martin's words echoed in Saint's mind like someone yelling in a tunnel. Deputies placed brown paper bags of personal items in each convict's hands—hands that were still fastened with handcuffs and chained to their waists. A storm-fence gate opened to a paved walkway that extended for over a hundred feet to a burgundy entrance door of a large, two-story, pale-green building that was called the Reception Center/Admitting Unit (RC/AU) of the Louisiana State Penitentiary at Angola. RC was downstairs and AU was upstairs.

The five shackled men baby-stepped as they entered their new home. AU convicts stuck their heads out of upstairs windows, ogling the new arrivals as if they were photos of a prime rib entrée on a restaurant menu. The red bandana was tied as a sweatband around Saint's combed-out hair. The camouflage Vietnam bush hat hung on the back of his neck. Wearing his black leather jacket, blue fishnet T-shirt, bleach-stained flared jeans, and Converse sneakers, Saint led the line. As if entering a rival team's field, he wore his confident, football-game face.

Beneath the main front-gate canopy were two old black men. One stood near an armed Angola guard, who squinted from the sunlight as he looked at Saint. The other one sat on a bench in the shade. An armed guard tower stood to the right of the front gate.

If they are prisoners, they look too old to run or escape, Saint thought.

Saint's transfer to Angola was almost immediate, just as Boodie's trial for capital murder occurred less than two months after his arrest. Boodie's case had been processed through the Baton Rouge criminal justice system as if it were a parking ticket. Like all district attorneys, Ossie Brown knew that the sooner a defendant was in penitentiary, the harder it would be for him to return to society. Once a convict entered the front gates of Angola, it was tantamount to stepping back into time—two centuries ago. Angola was a present-day microcosm of the Southern slave-trade era. Angola is a foreign country within the state of Louisiana that the free public knows little about and cares about even less.

"It is my duty and pleasure to inform all of you that you are now the official property of our great and wonderful State of Louisiana. Now, y'all sit y'all's a--es down on that bench right there, ole t'ang," an old Angola guard said to the new arrivals.

Saint sat on the bench in the lobby as Turtle and the others entered the office, where they were strip searched. Saint saw that the office furniture was outdated. On the other side of a wall of iron bars, old convicts moved about their daily business and stopped to see if they knew any of the newcomers from the streets of their old neighborhoods. Saint studied them, from the skullcaps on their heads to the shower slippers on their feet. He noticed their accents during dialog with others and noted how they walked and how they laughed. Some were so black they looked as if they had been roasted in a furnace or had worked in the hot sun all of their lives.

What did the legislators have in mind when they created a life sentence as a form of punishment? Saint desired to ask the prisoners how long they had been in Angola and how much time each still had to serve. He felt that their answers might help him gauge whether he had a chance of leaving this place. He reasoned that each convict had stood before a judge—another man like himself with sins, faults, and shortcomings and who read from a law book, pronouncing certain words that stripped them of their freedom and confined them to the custody of the state of Louisiana for a certain number of years.

He pondered whether they had police officers who testified under oath to tell the truth but lied to cover up their unethical conduct and illegal practices. *What are these prisoners' stories?* He tried to envision the heartwrenching agonies, the physical and mental beatings, they suffered over the years that had left them incarcerated in Angola. The prisoners acted and looked as though they had been beaten down by some force—a force called the Louisiana criminal justice system.

After Saint was stripped and searched, he made plans to send his street clothes and hat home to Paul. A tall redneck guard named Goff, supervisor of the Identification Department, insinuated to the veteran Angola convicts that the five men he was leading naked to the Identification Department were prison whores-to-be. They were given prison photo-ID cards and numbers they would never forget. Each was also issued new prison clothes, towels, sheets, a blanket, and a Department of Corrections rulebook. As Saint received these items, he vowed to reject everything the State gave him. He felt that free room and board, medical treatment, or anything else he got was costing him his life. This would be his daily promise to himself.

Saint created an imaginary, sinister creature he called the Death Angel. Being processed in AU was like having the long sharp talons of a giant bird of prey penetrate and sink deep within his psyche. Saint understood that he was in Angola, but he refused to let it change him to be like others he found here. They seemed institutionalized. The only thing meaningful he could identify with was that he was still a Lion of Capitol High, where winners never quit and quitters never win.

It was nightfall when a guard walked Saint down the C dorm corridor. The other four had been taken to D dorm, on the other side. Convicts in rooms along the corridor were yelling, "*Freeman! Freeman!* I need to talk to you." The guard, called the "freeman" by inmates, was a prison VIP.

In AU/C dorm, all newly arrived prisoners sat or lay on pale-green, plastic mattresses that covered the entire floor area. All of the double bunk beds were against the walls around the room and were already occupied by prisoners who arrived weeks earlier from judicial districts throughout Louisiana's sixty-four parishes. Convicts crowded around a huge, illiterate, black guard with a mail sack on his shoulder. A New Orleans convict took mail from the guard and began calling out names.

"Say, *Vietnam,* you got mail!" He waved a letter towards the right corner of the room. Six-foot-three, twenty-one-year-old John L. "Vietnam" Hardy, a black army veteran, emerged from the corner. He noticed as the freeman told Saint to get a mattress off the stack and find a place to put it. Saint got a mattress but found no place to put it other than to stand it on end.

"Say, li'l brother, you can put it right over here," a black convict said, pointing to the left rear side of the dormitory that New Orleans convicts had claimed. "Ain't nobody gonna mess with your bags. They'll be safe. They don't steal over here."

Vietnam got his mail as Saint passed him. He noticed Saint's scarred face and bloodshot eyes. Everybody deduced from his appearance that Saint had been in a fight. Vietnam saw the New Orleans convicts eyeing Saint as he carried his mattress. "Say, *Saint!*" Vietnam called. Saint turned around, surprised. "That's Baton Rouge side back in the corner over here. All that's New Orleans." Saint detoured, never saying a word to the first prisoner. "Say, BigOne," Vietnam muttered to a convict lying on a bunk next to his. "That bunk you laying in is for Saint, right there. Now, get out this corner." Saint watched the big convict as he politely gathered his belongings and left without saying a word or even putting up an argument. "Say, Gentilly, look at this niggah Saint we been waiting for," Vietnam remarked to his friend on the bunk above his. Saint and Gentilly touched fists and exchanged greetings. Gentilly then returned to writing his letter.

"That niggah gonna be a ho' for sho'. That's your bunk, Saint. Take it."

Saint wondered why a man he had never met before, but who obviously knew him, was looking out for him. After making his bunk, Saint sat and shared the aisle with Vietnam. He offered Saint a camel, but Saint had Kools and smoked one of them. Vietnam gave Saint a camouflage bandana. "Say, little brother, you gonna need this," Vietnam said, extending a folded towel to Saint while watching the convicts from New Orleans.

Saint's hand dipped from the weight of the towel. "Damn! What's in this? A gun?" he asked. He unfolded it to see what looked like a bowie knife.

"Three rules go with having a knife, Saint. Don't let the niggahs catch you without it. Don't let the white folks catch you with it. If anybody f---s with you, kill 'em. Whatever your lawyer told you back in court about keeping a good record and stayin' out of fights, you leave that in

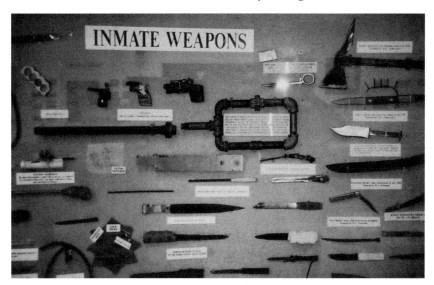

Angola inmate weapons found during shakedowns by guards.

court. You're serving the time, li'l brother. You're in penitentiary. Your lawyer's at home with his wife and family, ya dig?" Vietnam explained. Saint nodded and slid the weapon in his bag, where it would be easily accessible. "Four things will get you killed up here, Saint. Messing with the prison whores, gambling, stealing from convicts, and drugs."

"How you know me?" he asked.

"Linda Martin knows my ol' lady Paulette Miller, who came to see me last month. Linda came with her. That's when she told me about you. I've been waiting for you ever since we saw on the news that they sentenced you to life. Stand and look out that window," Vietnam instructed. "You see all them lights down there that looks like a little city?"

"Yeah, over to the left way down there?"

"Yeah. That's the big-yard walk. That's the best place to be in Angola with a life sentence. They got a law library down there with law books you need to read. The freeman turns the television off at ten thirty each night before the dorm lights are turned off. This is AU. Four or five fresh fish get gang raped every night by them crooked-a-- niggahs from New Orleans. It starts not too long after the lights go out. You'll be up here on the hill about forty-five days before they classify you to your job assignment. They got a wagon-train-looking thing they call the 'hootenanny' that's pulled by a tractor that takes us out in the field to work while in AU."

The AU Classification Board consisted of a warden, security head, and classification officer. By the time they met, Saint had gotten a physical, received pain pills for his toothache, been tested for aptitude, taken a typing test, worked in the farm line in the muddy fields of November and December, and been shot at by a guard.

"You read the rulebook?" Warden Hilton Butler asked at the meeting.

"Yes sir," Saint answered.

"Are the men who attacked you still in parish prison?" Colonel Wall, the security head, asked.

Saint shrugged. "I don't know." He noticed breadboxes in the corner.

"You really type ninety-five words per minute?" Kelly Ward, the classification officer, asked. He was a young white man with freckles, sandy brown hair, and gold-framed eyeglasses.

"Yes sir."

"Those scars on your face—did they come from the injuries it says here in this letter you sustained in the parish prison?" Warden Butler asked. He smoked a pipe and looked over the rim of his glasses as he questioned Saint.

"Yeah."

"You must have fast hands," Colonel Wall commented. "Send him to big yard, Hickory II, farm line. You just recently made eighteen, huh?" he asked.

"Yes sir. My lawyer said I would go to DeQuincy," Saint said.

"You got too much time. DeQuincy is for short timers," Butler replied.

"So, you're saying I could never go to DeQuincy?" Saint asked.

"Exactly," the warden answered.

"I wonder why they told me that? They told me and my daddy. Well, can I have a breadbox?" Saint asked, changing the subject. He realized it was no use arguing with these white people. He couldn't wait to tell Martin that Callihan had lied to them.

"We are backlogged in the Psychological Evaluation Testing Department," Ward said. "I need a good typing clerk to get all the files processed. Give him to me."

"So, ah, are you a gal-boy or what?" Colonel Wall asked. The board members got quiet as they listened to see if Saint would lie or tell the truth. They felt that all convicts lied, especially when asked about this. Saint eyed each board member and exchanged stares with Wall.

"Well?" Warden Butler prompted loudly.

"Or what?"

"You're one of them smart-a-- convicts, huh?" Warden Butler asked.

"I never heard that answer in all my years working this farm," Wall said. "I asked him was he a gal-boy or what and he said, 'Or what?' He's not being smart, Warden. All right, Kelly, you got 'im." The Colonel took a liking to Saint just from the answer he gave. "All right, Or What, make sure you read your rulebook. Watch your back. A lot of convicts will be watching it too."

"Can I have one of those breadboxes?" Saint asked again.

"No," Butler answered abruptly.

"Sure. Take one," the Colonel answered. "Let him have it. We burn them by the dozens."

"All right, you're classified to the Testing Department."

Visitation at the A Building was crowded on Sunday, January 6, 1974. Families rented charter buses out of New Orleans to come to Angola on Sundays to visit incarcerated relatives. Martin, the siblings, and DMB visited Saint shortly after he was classified.

Saint before his first visit from his family.

"Saint, you can have these. I thought they might help your eyes heal faster," Paul said. He couldn't wait to give his brother a pair of Ray-Ban 49'ers, the most popular sunglasses of the seventies. Martin was seated when Saint came to the table and kissed him on his cheek. He then hugged each of his siblings. DMB stood and gave Saint a warm and gentle embrace. She knew they would have their time together.

Saint sat at the table. "Daddy, Callihan lied to us about me serving my sentence at DeQuincy. DeQuincy is for short timers. Callihan knew this and lied to us so I would accept the plea bargain instead of going to trial."

"Well, look. Here's Nolan Edwards' business card. He's Governor Edwards' brother. He said he would take your case, but he wants you to write and tell him everything that happened to you, from the crime to the time," Martin told Saint, handing him a card. "That's all I got to say about that. I'll wait for y'all outside."

"All right, Daddy," Saint said. He stood and hugged Martin. "I love you."

"Hey, Saint, why you lie to me?" Michael asked after Martin left.

"When did I lie to you, Michael?"

"You told me DMB was a 101-year-old granny. You had me thinking she was old and wrinkled and you used to make me sick when you described her to me," Michael said. Paul laughed. Saint smiled. DMB looked confused.

"Daddy found your white port in your breadbox when they was looking for that gun," Daisy said. They listened as their brother told them about life in prison and about the knife he had.

The guard came over to the table and gave Saint his two-minute warning. Saint said goodbye to his siblings and they left. Michael ran back and whispered, "Are you gonna get that first kiss today?" Saint smiled, pushing him to catch up with the others.

Saint and DMB slowly approached each other, then he grabbed her and they kissed. He was overwhelmed by feeling her warm, soft body. Martin had doubled back and stood watching for a moment before leaving. Michael peeked and watched for a few seconds, smiling.

Saint broke off the kiss. "My first and last kiss, huh?" he asked. "You're not coming back here to see me, are you?"

DMB didn't answer. She cried in her handkerchief and rushed away through the gate. Saint stood watching her fine figure as she hurried off. He then turned the card over and looked at it.

After getting settled down in the Testing Department, Saint was amazed at how the convicts had mastered the art of henpeck typing. They actually pecked forty words per minute.

After inquiring among the convicts, Saint learned that working at the Louisiana governor's mansion was the most assured way for a lifer to get his freedom. All lifers sought the gold seal on the governor's act of clemency. Saint typed a letter to Woody Jenkins to ask his help in getting him transferred to the governor's mansion.

Ninety percent of the convicts in his Reception Center dorm had been on death row for over fourteen years each. When the U.S. Supreme Court declared the Louisiana death penalty unconstitutional in 1972, they were all resentenced to life imprisonment. The former death-row convicts got along as if they were true family members. They cared for one another and it showed. They functioned as peacemakers, settling lots of disputes between other convicts who wanted to kill others with knives. They knew how valuable a life was and the consequences for taking one.

The former death-row convicts looked at Saint as their little brother. They provided him with educational material concerning Louisiana law. Eugene "Shiphead" Scott, from Baton Rouge, gave Saint the old, unraveling *Black's Law Dictionary* he'd had all the sixteen years he was on death row. Others gave Saint mint-condition documents to help orient him in the manner of drafting and arguing legal issues on paper in post-conviction pleadings. Everything given to him was geared towards getting him to know the law and how to apply it. Saint placed the materials in neat stacks around his bunk and spent the evenings playing basketball with the older convicts who were once great young athletes. It was fun.

"Say, you, Saint!" a prisoner named Flannigan shouted with a wide grin. "Don't nothing come to a sleeper but a dream." Saint slept late on weekends and was lying in his bunk. He hadn't touched the documents under his bunk for weeks. "You can come here and get caught up in sports and playing poker, spades, and dominoes and think you can sleep that life sentence away. But these good whites folks will plant your a-- back there at Point Look-Out Cemetery. In here, won't nothing happen unless you make it happen. You got to know what you're up against to know what you got to do. You got to know your case and the law that applies to your case better than your lawyer, better than the judge, better than the district attorney opposing you, understand?" Flannigan emphasized.

Woody Jenkins responded to Saint's request, saying his case was too hot and he couldn't help him get transferred to the governor's mansion.

As Saint read the legal documents of various cases, he noticed a pattern. All the pleadings had similar headings and wordings. Saint was glad that Edna had made him read the World Book Encyclopedias she bought the family for Christmas 1963 in Zion City.

"Heads up, heads up!" Saint yelled as he stood before the bullpen. "Look, I'm going to call the first half of you and take you to the testing room, then come back and get the rest of you."

He called seventeen names. and the inmate guard watched seventeen men walk out of the bullpen and stand behind him. Then the guard began to close and lock the gate.

"Say, Slim! When you gonna call me out of this motherf---er, huh? I been in here all morning. I'm tired of being in here!"

The older convict's yelling at a younger, new arrival quieted the bullpen. Convicts recognized war talk instantly. This was it.

"Niggah, you blowing on me like you talking to a ho'," Saint said, looking the man in his eyes. "You got something on your mind? You feel like you wanna charge me? Charge, niggah." By penitentiary law, unless Saint was a known whore, a convict could not yell, curse, or talk to him in just any manner, regardless of how young he may be. If he was a man, he was entitled to full respect. Saint was young, with no hair growing on his face, and the repeat offender thought Saint was a whore or had the potential to be one.

The inmate guard closed the gate before anything happened. While the convicts were being administered the psychological evaluation test, Saint went to his office across the hall, where he would type alone until he was notified to get the rest of the convicts. He reached over and turned on a radio that was on the window ledge by his desk. When he turned back to sit straight in his chair, two men were standing four feet from him. The tall one who disrespected him was leaning against the wall with his hands behind his back. A short, dark-skinned convict was beside him, looking around as if for something to steal.

"Say, Slim, you got something on your mind?" the tall man asked. From his accent, it was easy to discern he was from New Orleans. The dark-skinned one was new but a longtime criminal who had finally gotten caught. Realizing he was literally cornered, Saint leaned back in his chair and clasped his hands behind his head. "Slim, you must have something on your mind. I don't even know you. You blew on me like I'm a ho'. I blew on you like you're ho'. You disrespected me. I disrespected you. You was talking like you had something on your mind."

The man avoided eye contact with Saint while Saint replied, "I was telling you to go ahead and charge."

The man nodded while staring down at the floor. His dark-skinned sidekick was very antsy. "Well, all right. I just wanted to see. Okay," the tall man said and left with his sidekick.

Saint sat for a few seconds, trying to understand what all that meant. He resumed typing. The words seemed to come from the radio: *Go to the dorm. Go to the dorm.* Saint stopped typing, looked at the radio, then adjusted the tuning. *Go to the dorm. Go to the dorm,* the voice said again. Saint placed his fingers on the homerow keys, but his hands seemed paralyzed. *They wanted to see where you worked. They are going to get knives and come back to kill you.*

The two men rushed back downstairs to the Testing Department corridor and ran into the office and into Saint's corner. They both had big knives.

"What's wrong with you? What's wrong with you, Saint?" Sheen asked. He was sweeping the dormitory when Saint walked in, sat on his bunk, and looked at his hands.

"I don't know. I can't type," he answered. "Something told me to go to the dorm."

"Where Saint at?" Schoolboy's voice could be heard out in the corridor as he yelled. The commotion drew a convict crowd instantly. Sheen turned and saw the crowd bursting through the door. Flannigan, Miller, Schoolboy, Big O, Shiphead, Skiza Fats, the Word, and Bird were concerned for Saint.

"Saint, what did you do to Leonard Turner?" Tyrone "Schoolboy" Watts asked. He and Turner were from New Orleans. "Do you know who that is? Jesus Christ. Do you know he was looking for you? Him and Black was gonna kill you if they found you in that office. They opened the door to our office and Turner said, 'Say, Schoolboy, you know where Slim at that call us out the bullpen? I'm getting ready to take him out.' I said, 'Who you talking about, Saint? You can't be talking about Saint. Saint just got here. Saint don't mess with nobody. I know him. He said you blew on him in front of everybody. He came and checked you out about it and you blew on him again.'"

Everyone listened closely as Saint explained, and they all agreed that he did the right thing. They knew that Turner was feeling Saint out. If Saint had tried to talk to the career criminal using civil language and a diplomatic attitude, he was inviting trouble for himself. It would have been a definite sign of weakness.

Schoolboy brought Saint, Turner, and Black into the office and persuaded everyone it was a misunderstanding. Each gave his word that it was over and there were no hard feelings. Turner and Black had their knives in their boots. Saint had Jim Bowie in the back of his legal tablet on his clipboard. If they didn't want to let things go, whatever would be would be.

Go to the dorm, the voice had said. *It saved my life. Damn,* Saint thought, awestruck, as he rested in his bunk and chain smoked. He told no one about the voice. He didn't have to.

Sixteen pages of legal paper finally contained the facts Saint felt Mr. Edwards needed. It was an extremely difficult task. Saint's typing speed didn't help. The day he first began typing about the beating and describing what happened, multiple hands seemed to spring up from the keys and hit him in the face. Saint yelled, grabbing his face as he fell backwards out of the chair. Flannigan and the rest just looked at him. After exiting the testing office, Saint stood in the doorway staring back at the keys of his typewriter. It would be weeks before he resumed typing his statement.

Shiphead watched Saint each morning as he broke out in cold sweats as he slept. He was twisting, turning, and talking in his sleep. Shiphead often woke him. Everyone knew he had nightmares. The flashbacks, meanwhile, had triggered something else.

A green Air Force cap was pulled down on his head, making Saint looked mentally challenged when he entered the AU office. He wore reading glasses. A wad of chewing gum stuffed behind his top lip gave him monkeylike features. Two "coon-a—" freemen were in the AU office talking about deer hunting when Saint walked in with his clipboard, hobbling like the crippled Papa. "Excuse me, chief. I'm from RC. I needs Lloyd Wil—Wil—" he stammered.

"Lloyd Wilson?" one freeman asked impatiently.

"See, he needs to sign right yere befo' he leave to go on walk."

"Sign what? Let me see," the guard ordered.

Saint held on to the clipboard, showing him the testing documents for Lloyd to sign. "See, he got to sign right yere by this shere *X,*" Saint pointed out. He sounded like an uneducated New Orleans convict thug.

"Yeah, C dorm, to the left," the freeman said.

Saint walked out of the office, then turned out of sight and stopped.

"They got a sumb---- like that testing inmates. I wonder if he knows what he's doing?" the other freeman asked. "Well, anyway, it's cold as hell. I'm in my deer stand aiming at a ten point, but I can't pull the trigger. My damn trigger fingers was frozen!"

The Papa imitator hobbled down the corridor towards his former AU dorm. Little One, a short fresh fish from New Orleans who had a notorious uncle on the big yard, greeted Saint. "Slim, what's happening?" Little One yelled, seeing Saint scanning the Baton Rouge corner as he entered C dorm.

"What's happening, Li'l One? Where's Lloyd? I need him to sign some forms."

"Say, Lloyd!" Little One yelled, looking back towards the right corner. "Slim got some papers for you to sign!"

When Lloyd stepped out from between double bunks, the big smile on his face dissolved like candle wax. He saw Saint standing there with the clipboard.

"Sign by the *X* on the first page. Answer the three questions on the second page. You didn't complete your psychological evaluation," Saint said, handing Lloyd the clipboard.

"Slim, I want to thank you for keeping us out of the field all them days, man," Little One said. "I can't stand that field. It was killing me. Slim had us up here watching soap operas every week. Whenever you come down on the walk, I'm-a take care of you, hear, Slim?"

Lloyd dropped the clipboard and leaped back with his fighting guards raised. Everyone in the area jumped, looking around for what caused Lloyd to be acting that way.

"I know you got your blade. Go ahead and use it," Lloyd said, staring at Saint.

"Slim, he's talking to you?" Little One asked. "Lloyd, are you talking to Slim?"

"Did you answer the questions? Did you finish the test, niggah?" Saint asked, frowning at Lloyd, then grinning at Little One. Lloyd was too scared to talk. "Niggah, I don't need a blade for you," Saint said and walked straight to him. Lloyd's first two punches missed Saint, who simply leaned left into Lloyd's right side—his left hand grabbing Lloyd's pants at the waist on the backside. His right hand grabbed a handful of Lloyd's hair. Saint rammed Lloyd's head into the ceramic-tiled wall. Lloyd collapsed to the floor.

"Slim! Why you doing this? What he did you, Slim?" Little One asked frantically.

Saint stood waiting for anyone to come out of the Baton Rouge corner to assist Lloyd. Three men emerged, not to help but watch. They had heard of the incident and understood the confrontation between Lloyd and Saint.

"This niggah was in a clique in the parish, trying to rape me and my friend," Saint said.

Lloyd began moving. Saint grabbed him by his hair, dragged him like a mattress to the threshold of the shower room, and rammed his head into the metal doorframe. He grabbed him again by his hair and pants and ran with him into the ceramic tiles of the shower room, shattering one. Saint tried to kick the cinderblock out of place to make a larger hole so he could throw Lloyd through it from the second floor.

Little One gently tapped Saint's shoulder and whispered, "Slim. Hey, Slim, don't you think that's enough, Slim?"

Saint kicked Lloyd in his ribs, stomped on his head, then got down on his knees and punched him in the face. "B----, get up and fight." Saint stood and rammed Lloyd's head again into a ceramic tile, shattering it before he hit the floor.

Little One jumped on Saint's back to stop him. His homies helped, grabbing Saint's arms. "No, Slim!" Little One shouted hysterically. "Don't do it! You gonna kill him! You gonna kill him, Slim! Don't kill him, Slim!" He didn't want his friend to get a murder charge.

The distraction allowed Lloyd to stand up, but he staggered over a low shower wall and tumbled onto the floor. Saint freed his arms and moved towards Lloyd, pulling Little One's arm off his neck. Saint finally caught Little One by his shirt and threw him into the shower.

Little One backed up with his hands in front of his face. *"No, no, no, Slim! It's me, Slim!"* He backed into the water control. Water shot out of the shower spout, hitting Saint in the face and shocking him out of the flashback and back to the present. He jumped aside and backwards to keep from getting wet. Little One gave Saint his cap and glasses back and Fats gave him his clipboard before he left.

"Niggah! You gonna be somebody's ho', *ta'day!* I'm-a get *all you mothaf---in' animals!* Why you helped them crowd me? You still want to f--- my daddy? Where the clique *now,* you mothaf---a?" Those were the three questions Lloyd had to answer to "pass the test."

Afterwards, Baton Rouge prisoners in AU wrote letters to their parish-prison friends, telling them Saint was waiting for the clique. Every clique member who heard it was stricken with fear. They knew they had a definite enemy with an attitude awaiting them in Angola. Saint did what he had been taught by the Louisiana criminal justice system. He used his job position to get his enemies.

Saint sat on his bunk, watching shackled clique members come in the front gate, as he had done. They didn't know how or when they would be attacked, only that they would be. They looked for Saint to come to the dormitory, as letters described he'd done with Lloyd. Saint was a step ahead. He arranged for the freeman to bring the clique members to him one or two at a time, when he placed them on testing callout. While they took their psychological evaluation tests, Saint came in from behind with a wooden club and battered them. With Jim Bowie in his hand, he made two clique members stand in a corner, daring them to raise their hands to protect their faces. Seeing the big knife petrified them. Saint punched them in the face until they collapsed. Then he kicked and struck them with the club. The other testing-class convicts ran to the back of the room, where they watched and listened. "Don't kill 'em, Slim," one AU inmate called out.

"Y'all wanna try to put that d--- on me now, niggahs?" Saint saw their swollen heads and faces, cuts and bruises, but had no pity for them. This was their punishment for doing what someone else wanted them to do and not being man enough to follow their own minds.

Bird, the white barber for the RC Lobby, walked into the dorm from the weight pile. He saw Saint at a window as he watched ducks swimming in a pond. "What's happening, Saint?"

"Hey, Bird, what's happening?" Saint turned back to staring at the ducks.

"You mind if I have a word with you?" Bird asked. Saint was surprised to see that Bird had stopped directly behind him.

"No, Bird. What's going on?"

"Look, I'm not getting in your business. You're your own man, but you see that piece of s--- you waiting for the freeman to walk to the patrol so you could dirk him down? That would be a terrible mistake."

Bird was referring to one of the inmates who had been in parish prison with him. Saint neither nodded to affirm nor shook his head to deny. He listened to the young white barber, who resembled a hippie with his long hair and full beard.

"I know what you're thinking. So what? The mothaf---as tried to f--- you—everybody gets tried, Saint! I killed three white-boy convicts the same day they tried me. I got three life sentences from St. Francisville. You got family that visits you. That piece of s--- gets no visits. Don't be stupid like I was. You gonna get out of this mothaf---a. You gonna be out there making babies while that piece of s--- is in here waiting to go rot at Point Lookout. You need to bury the hatchet. It's gonna get out of hand. You gonna kill somebody and never get out. Everybody knows what you been doing. With all the rats they got here on the hill, it's a wonder the good white folks ain't locked you up in maximum security. You can bet they already know." Bird read Saint's body language. "Come on, Saint, man. You can do it. You're smart." With that, Bird walked away.

Noise from the gate rolling open caught Saint's attention. The first one through the gate was the freeman. Next came a man with a bloody head and bulging eyes. Saint had earlier reached through the bars of the bullpen and struck him with a rock. Shackled, the man baby-stepped through the gate. He never took his eyes off Saint, who pulled his arms from out of the window bars and faced him. The man tried to walk faster. Saint opened his jean jacket, revealing Jim Bowie and a hatchet stuck in his waistband. Saint frowned and took several giant steps as he ran towards him. The man left a trail of urine behind as he hobbled away as quickly as he could. Saint stopped, shot the man the bird, then returned to the window to watch the ducks. "Aaaah!" he yelled, waving his hands and causing the ducks to fly away. He wondered if the ducks were a metaphor for the sitting duck he was about to kill.

Paul Ceasar, the convict photographer, arrived at Saint's office to take pictures that he charged a dollar for. Saint changed clothes, went outside on the side of his office, and squatted and posed for a picture. He still had the wristband he used to pace himself at track practice on his right arm and the Ray-Ban shades Paul had given him that helped his bloodshot eyes heal.

Camp A was known as the old Angola Slave Quarters and the horse lot. It was also the home of the Angola Light Heavyweight Champion, Bull Cobra. After spending a year on the hill living in RC, 90 percent of the convicts were transferred to Camp A Big Stripe. Saint was one of them. He filed his first writ of habeas corpus in the Nineteenth Judicial District Court in Baton Rouge in April 1975, but Judge Lear denied it the next day. Saint received letters from his teammate Steve Ingram. He was doing well at Southern Illinois University playing defensive end. Though happy for his friend, Saint was tortured by thoughts of what might have been.

He had worked in the field seven days a week in 1975. In hot weather, the farm line tilled the soil for irrigation canals, cut weeds,

Saint in 1974, out in the Reception Center yard.

or hoed endless crop rows. On the winter end of 1975, Saint was in the field harvesting corn and picking cotton with a long bag on his shoulder. Instead of playing football, he was a cotton-pickin' niggah.

Camp A Big Stripe's front yard had a beautiful view of the western horizon during sunset. The scarlet, purple, and blue sky inspired Saint to pray to the heavenly being who spoke to him from time to time. In Edna's red Bible, Saint read Psalm 8 of King David: "O Yahweh, our Elohim"—Edna had handwritten this in place of

"Lord our God"—"how excellent is thy name in all the earth!"

You need to go down on the big-yard walk. There is a law library down there you need to be in, a still small voice said during one particularly beautiful sunset.

Chapter 7

The Fighting Inmate Lawyer

"Verse twenty-three: 'Jesus saith unto her, "Thy brother shall rise again."'" Cheyenne did five pushups per verse as he read his Bible to an illiterate inmate in the cell next door to him on the maniac ward.

"Big Red's on the catwalk," a convict yelled. It was a greeting and a heads-up to the guard and inmates.

At the far end, Cheyenne watched through a half-inch-square piece of broken mirror affixed with chewing gum to the bottom of the bars near the floor. Its angle clearly captured Redford's husky image growing even larger as he approached. "Strong is smell of spotted hyena!" Cheyenne shouted, causing Redford to stop in his tracks. Redford had been walking near the windows ten feet from the cells. To walk closer invited convict maniacs to drench him in body waste and fluids. Cheyenne stopped reading when Redford stood in front of his cell, staring down at his naked, sweaty body. "No man come unto me except he needeth me," Cheyenne said.

"Cheyenne, cut the crap," Redford ordered. "Get dressed. The Colonel wants to know if you'll find and train him another champ. It'll get you off this maniac ward and back to doing what you love doing. The Colonel said you got the run of the farm."

"Tell Chief Hyena Cheyenne said go look in mirror to see what manner of man he is. He is same man from yesterday."

"Look, Cheyenne, you got life for—"

"For raping white flesh this penis never took pleasure penetrating!" Redford leaped back as Cheyenne jumped to his feet and grabbed for him through the bars with his long, black arm. His other hand held his penis.

"See. You're almost there. You're turning into a maniac."

After a month of living on the big yard assigned to Hickory II Unit, bed number 17, and working in the hot fields, Saint reported to the law library every evening. He always checked the roller bar on an old Royal typewriter to make sure it was working properly before typing on his case. At 8:30 one night, Victor Linkletter, a sixty-five-year-old, white, potbellied safecracker, stood up front, sipping coffee from a white Styrofoam cup and looking out the window at guards gathering in the control center.

A freeman opened the door and yelled, "Nobody is to come out of the library!" Deadeye had crawled to the middle of the control center with his pants down to his ankles and severe head and facial wounds, covered with blood. He tried to talk but was incoherent. A freeman came back and yelled, "We need eight of y'all!".

Eight convicts working in the law library carried a stretcher with Deadeye's huge body to the penitentiary hospital. Unconcerned, Saint continued typing on his statement of case for a second writ of habeas corpus. He went to the law library as though it were a required night-class course. He had also enrolled in academic school in order to get his GED.

While Saint lived at Camp A, Boodie and other clique members arrived at Angola from the parish prison. They lived on the big yard. It was so heavily populated that one could live on the walk for months and not be noticed by those who knew him. Boodie and the clique members loved hanging out in the regular library at night, looking through picture books and talking to their associates.

One night, Boodie, Skookie, Foots, and B.C. all exited the main library for the restroom down the hall. Ever cautious, they went in groups, even to the latrine.

"Damn, the light ain't working," Boodie said, having pushed the light switch up.

"You don't need light to wipe," B.C. told him, laughing. "Get on in there."

The four walked in, leaving the door open so light from the hall could illuminate the restroom. They entered separate stalls and closed the doors. All locks on the doors were broken off. "That's lightbulb glass we was stepping on," Foots said.

Each man had his pants down to his ankles, sitting on the toilet.

"They need these stalls in our dorm. No telling who you be s--- tin' next to," Boodie said.

B.C. replied, "You ain't lying—" The door slowly closed, sealing the room in darkness. "Hey! Leave the door open, brother. I need some light."

After a few seconds, B.C.'s stall door was kicked in, striking him in the face. The sound of blows and grunts echoed in the restroom.

Attempts to yell were cut off in the dark. The sound of toilet paper spinning off the roller indicated that someone was trying to hurry to his feet. The heavy weapon struck each man's head, stunning him and knocking him down. The stall walls collapsed, making the men easy targets. A toilet flushed continually, caused by someone lying on the handle, unconscious. The lone assailant kicked and struck them until it was safe. With their pants down, he dragged them by their hair to set their faces on each other's genitals. The tool he used had busted their faces open and left teeth scattered on the floor. The door behind the man opened. He turned to see only a disappearing leg as the person fled. The door closed.

Colonel Wall puffed a cigar as he leaned against the restroom door and observed the bodies that lay on the floor atop each other, their pants down to their ankles. It had all the appearances of a homosexual orgy.

Cheyenne walked up, holding an anatomy and physiology book he had just checked out of the regular library. He stood by Colonel Wall, observing and listening.

"Jesus Christ, what a mess!" Wall said, shaking his head. "This is what you call getting caught with your pants down." He saw teeth, blood, and little pieces of black material he couldn't readily identify on the floor and in a couple of the convicts' mouths. They were swollen from jagged cuts and torn flesh on their heads, necks, arms, hands, fingers, and legs.

"I swear to God, Colonel," Alley Cat reiterated. "It was dark. I couldn't see a thing. He had his back to me. When I opened the door and saw him, I ran before he saw me."

"Is this a war between Baton Rouge and New Orleans?" the Colonel asked Cheyenne. "This is Baton Rouge, here? Red, ask Doc to see what that black stuff is in their mouths." The Colonel pointed at the nearly comatose bodies. A freeman came out of the library with a crowd of convicts, who then carried them all on stretchers to the penitentiary hospital. The control-center porters cleaned up the restroom, and the white convicts from Oak Unit arrived and repaired the stalls.

Colonel Wall walked away with Cheyenne and Alley Cat. "You found my man yet?" he asked Cheyenne. "That will put you back in the boxing room." The Colonel oversaw security and the boxing program. Cheyenne covered all the sport fields, courts, and weight piles, but every young fresh fish he asked to box declined.

The freeman field foreman always selected one or two seasoned convicts to be head lane bosses. Badboy, age twenty-six, was from New Orleans. He had been in Angola since he was sixteen. Today he was head lane boss. The foreman told him what needed to be done and he told the field niggahs who comprised the farm line.

Saint stopped working momentarily to tie his head with the camouflage bandana. He sported the Ray-Ban shades Paul had given him.

"Say, Slim," Badboy called. Saint turned to him, saw the two guards in the background, and knew they had sent him. "Mr. Charlie said he wanna see a--holes and elbows else he's gonna call the patrol and send you to the dungeon."

Saint lit a cigarette, put his gloves back on, and started hoeing his soybean row.

"Say, Cheyenne, you found anybody to train yet?" Badboy asked when he walked up to the head lane and joined Cheyenne at the water cooler.

"These are some of the most sorry-a-- niggahs I ever seen in my life. They don't wanna suffer pain. The only killer instinct they have is shooting round ball in hoops."

"The niggahs who jumped them niggahs from Baton Rouge got a killer instinct," Badboy said, squatting. "I bet if they find them, that's your champ. Wall been talking to every rat on the walk in Angola trying to find out. They gonna get indicted in St. Francisville and get more time." He watched as Saint worked past the others on the line. "See that niggah Saint over there with that army bandana? Talk on the walk says he went out in deep water against a clique in the Baton Rouge parish prison and saved a niggah from getting raped. They beat and stabbed that niggah, but he never gave up. Alley Cat sleeps right next to him in Hickory II. He said he can't sleep at night. He be fightin' in his sleep. That might be that niggah, huh?"

Cheyenne squinted at Saint, then pulled down the front rim of his straw hat to block the sunlight. "Adisaa," Cheyenne whispered. He turned to Badboy with a big smile. "Badboy, you no more Badboy. You good boy."

Cheyenne walked up to Saint and began working next to him for a few moments. He chopped his row like a professional and soon passed Saint. He stopped for a moment, wiped sweat, and waited for Saint to catch up. "*Mababuzangu wali lima shaba hi* [my ancestors worked this field]," Cheyenne said. He stared down the long row. "*Bali shaba laini kulima.*"

Saint stood up and held his aching back while looking down the row. "What you said?"

"This is a long row to hoe. Swahili," Cheyenne explained. "You learn? I teach you."

"I ain't got time. I got to learn how to get out this mothaf---a," Saint replied.

"How much time the good white people send you to hell for?"

"Natural life."

"They send you to hell for eternity?" Cheyenne grimaced. "*Kufyanza mbawa nguruwe.*"

"Where you from? Africa?"

"My ancestors from Africa. During slave trade they escaped to Virgin Isles, West Indies, and Jamaica. I am fourth generation of my people from Angola since coming here in 1856."

Saint found it amazing that he was working next to an almost genuine African slave. "What was that last thing you said in Swahili?"

"I curse the good white people. Why did great king command soldiers to kill monkey in coconut tree?"

"What? You're talking to me?" Saint asked. Cheyenne repeated the question. "Ah, 'cause it was throwing coconuts at 'em? I don't know," Saint said.

"Think serious, Saint," Cheyenne prompted. As Saint worked, Cheyenne observed his long arms that gave him an extended reach. He liked his long legs that would allow him to dance, slip, move around, and evade an opponent. He liked his height and the fact that he was slim and not overweight. He liked his small chin. The only thing he didn't like was the fact that Saint chain-smoked.

"Ah, let's see," Saint said, bending over backwards, stretching and complaining about his back pain. "The king was out hunting for a special, uncommon monkey. The king's son was dying from a disease and only this special monkey ate this remote bug that allowed him to s--- a turd that had special enzymes in it that could save the life of the king's son if he ate that s---. S---, I don't know."

Cheyenne gave a slight chuckle, amused by Saint's vision. He then exploded into laughter, causing the whole farm line to stop working and look up. Cheyenne hadn't laughed in a long time.

"Look, Saint, monkey would not throw coconuts down and king was hungry. King had no use for monkey. Monkey is commodity. No coconut, no commodity, no use for monkey. Understand me?"

"So, way out here in the middle of nowhere, under this blazing sun, you just felt like walking up here telling me about your ancestors, how long this row is, a king, and a coconut-throwing monkey? Hell, no. Why you telling me this African tale?"

"It is happening now, this very moment," Cheyenne whispered. "Look, I am Cheyenne, best fight trainer in Angola. I train only fighter to get out Angola through boxing program. Basketball, football, and baseball players grow old and die here. Mafia reach inside Angola and pull strings to get good young fighter out and back into free world regardless of sentence."

If one can do it, two can do it, the voice told Saint. He looked around for other listeners, but the closest convicts were out of earshot of Cheyenne's whispers.

Watching Saint, Cheyenne knew he had struck a nerve in the youngster. "Look, I can train anyone—even you—so good, when rats tell Colonel, who is over security and over boxing programs, that you ambush enemies from parish prison, he will not lock you in maximum security. You will not be indicted in St. Francisville and get more time. Why? Because champ fills seats on fight nights and gets greedy king much, much coconuts." Cheyenne began laughing.

"Well, what can you teach me?" Saint asked, as he continued to hoe the row.

"I teach you nothing," Cheyenne answered.

"Wait. I thought—didn't you just say you can train me to be the champ?"

"I said no such thing. I said I can train anyone, even you. For me to train anyone they have to ask me to train them. They have to want to be champ."

"Well, now what kind of s--- is this? You brought it up. You started talking about this. Why I got to ask you?"

"Because if I want you to do it and you get mad at me for hard training, you will quit because of me. If you want to do it, you will suffer pain to train and be champ. You have to want me to teach and train you. You must ask me to teach you how to fight and train you to be champ," Cheyenne explained.

"What? I got to ask you just like that?" Saint exclaimed.

Cheyenne knew it would be humbling for Saint, as it was for all good fighters. He knew that ego and vanity got in the way of many young convicts who wanted to fight but wouldn't because of peer pressure.

With Cheyenne and Saint slowing down to talk, several older

black convicts had caught up and were now in earshot. Saint thought about the proposition for forty yards of hoeing. Neither Cheyenne nor Saint spoke. Cheyenne acted as if he had never had a conversation with Saint and began talking to the other convicts.

The farm line and guards on horseback moved down the rows and became barely visible in the distant field. The sun was setting. The more Saint thought about the ambush and his desire to get out of Angola, the more he considered the deal. "You know, Cheyenne," Saint finally said, "maybe I have a little time to spare. I guess you can train me." Cheyenne ignored him. "Say, Cheyenne, look here," Saint called.

"Catch up. *Bali shaba laini kulima,*" Cheyenne replied. As Saint tried to catch up, Cheyenne worked harder and faster to keep his distance from him. They were approaching the end and the call for head lane was near. Cheyenne saw Saint hustling to catch up with him.

"Ah, say, Cheyenne. Ah, will you, ah, you know, go ahead and teach me how, ah, you know, ah, to fight, so ah, you know, so I can, ah, ah, *be the mothaf---in' champ!*" Saint whispered forcefully, letting Cheyenne know he wasn't going to say it again. Cheyenne laughed as Saint bent over backwards, stretched, and then continued working. The 300 convicts were stretched across the soybean field.

"You ever see mongoose dance?" Cheyenne asked.

"Dance of a mongoose? No, what's that?"

"Stick and move, stick and move, stick and move. Mongoose greatest strength is speed. Mongoose is boxer with killer instinct. Boxing is just stick and move. You will have to know, understand, and believe that. Moving target is hard to hit, Saint."

"You got that right," Saint replied.

Ready for a Bullfight

Colonel Wall puffed at his cigar while listening to Cheyenne, then called Deputy Warden Michael Beaubouef to assign Saint to the Legal Aid Office. Saint's new job was that of an inmate lawyer. It was the best job for convicts in Angola. It paid twenty cents per hour. Field dogs (convicts who had been working in the fields for over a year) got incentive pay of two cents per hour. Beaubouef carefully screened anyone assigned to the Legal Aid Office. Angola did not want political activists in the law library who would sue the penitentiary.

April was the Angola rainy season. Cheyenne, featherweight Lee Rocquemore, lightweight Chico Gonzales, welterweight Edward Scott, seconds man Alley Cat, ring stool and waterman Graveyard, and twenty-seven other young convicts gathered behind Hickory II at the weight pile. Saint observed from the footwork of Rocquemore, Chico, and Scott that they had lots of fight experience.

"Cheyenne, that's five miles you're talking about," Saint complained when they were told to run seven laps around the big yard. "I've been smoking like a train. I ain't ran in almost three years. I might have to stop for a break."

"If you stop, you don't get second chance. That's my rule," an unsmiling Cheyenne said. Saint realized he was serious when it came to fight training.

The group ran off, leaving Saint smoking his last Kool.

"Saint, man, you know how to run," Graveyard said. "You ran track. All these niggahs ever did was run from da police."

"Yeah, and all I ever done was run from da niggahs," Saint replied. "Five miles, damn," he muttered. The rain came sooner than expected, extinguishing Saint's cigarette. The entire big-yard lawn was soaked within minutes.

Chico led the pack, 400 yards ahead of Saint, who was dead last. The runners strung out like a long train around the big yard. Saint pushed himself as he passed first one and then another. Runners began dropping out. By the fifth lap, Saint plodded along, 20 yards behind Chico and Scott.

Cheyenne watched as they headed into the final lap. *"Keep moving. Keep moving. Moving target is hard to hit."*

With nine runners remaining, Graveyard and Alley Cat yelled at Saint to keep going and not stop, but his calf muscles were throbbing. He wanted to quit. He began limping at times to keep moving. As he moved into fourth place, he slowed down to a turtle's crawl but ran despite a persistent limp. The bounce in Chico's step was gone and he and Rocquemore battled for first place. Scott was third. As the four approached the finish line, Saint surged forward, leaning into the imaginary tape. Graveyard and Alley Cat gave Saint the victory by his lean. Saint stumbled and fell on the rain-soaked grass, vomiting while crawling on his hands and knees. He rolled over on his back, letting rain fall on his face and in his open mouth. Rocquemore, Chico, and Scott bounced and danced around Saint with their wrapped hands held up as if they had knocked him down.

My champ, Cheyenne thought.

Saint's legs were so sore he couldn't walk. Graveyard carried him from the yard to his bunk inside Hickory II.

After the evening meal, Saint was next in a long line at the Main Prison Control Center window, signing for his certified-stamp mail. Any mail coming from the courts or an attorney had to be signed for by the recipient. The inmate petitioner's date and signature showed when he received mail relating to time-sensitive pleadings and court orders. As soon as the mail log was signed, the clock began to run in time-sensitive legal matters.

A letter from the East Baton Rouge Parish clerk of court had arrived for Saint. It was the transcript of the boykinization (reading of rights to a defendant) of his guilty plea, dated October 15, 1973. Perry M. Johnson, the clerk of court in Baton Rouge at the time of Saint's crime, wouldn't send him a copy of it. Mike Cannon, a new clerk of court, sent the transcript without hesitation, because Saint was entitled to it.

After reading the four-page transcript, Saint went inside the law library and sat at his desk to think. Sioux Dog and Shorty skimmed the transcript, then Victor walked down and took it to his desk, reading it while sipping on a cup of Angola black gold.

"Who you said named you 'Saint'?" Sioux Dog asked. "Somebody must love you up there, because that ain't s---."

"You ought to sue those bastards,," Shorty said. "I wish Judge Parker would have f---ed up like Lear did when he sentenced me to these twenty-five years. I'd have it made like you."

"Saint!" Victor yelled. "You need to file your writ of habeas corpus in district court. You got two main claims: involuntary plea of guilty and ineffective assistance of counsel." Victor used the *United States Supreme Court Reporters* as a license to show others he knew what he was talking about. He had two personal decisions in them. In his younger years, Victor had been arrested and was sitting in a hick-town jail. The jailers wouldn't give him any paper, so he filed a writ of certiorari using a paper bag and hand towels. "*Would you believe it, the sons of b----es granted the motherf---er, Saint?*"

"What happened in court that day?" Shorty asked Saint.

"A lot happened. My sister Teresa was screaming and reaching for me with one leg across the gate and the bailiffs were holding her back. Callihan kept nudging me in the side, telling me to 'turn around and pay attention to the judge.'"

Inmate lawyers and convict clients. Saint is in the back row, center, wearing a knit hat. Daniel is on the left, wearing a knit hat. In front of him is Victor Linkletter, holding a cup. George "Ashanti" Witherspoon is in the front left with Bennie "Idi Amin" Hicks beside him. Henry "Auary" Lewis is in the middle row, far right.

"(REPORTER'S NOTE: *The accused then turned to his attorney and asked,* 'What did he say?')" Victor read aloud. "I don't see nowhere in here where you personally entered a plea of guilty. You never pled guilty, Saint. Do you know what this means?" Victor asked excitedly. "You were never convicted."

"You're going back to court," Sioux Dog said.

When Saint left the law library at two o'clock each morning, he did so with three or four *Southern* and *Federal Reporter* law books. He read cases on his bunk using the light from the catwalk outside the dorm. At the library, pillars of law books surrounded his desk.

The boxing room was in a twelve-by-twenty-foot room on the side of Hickory I Unit. It had two benches on the walls, an old taped-up heavy bag hanging in the center, a speed bag, a big fifteen-pound medicine ball, and ring equipment in the far corner, including the ropes and turnbuckles for the blue and red corners. From a window, Cheyenne could see a section of the fence line out on the big yard that the boxing teams ran on.

Saint ran five miles, seven days a week, for four months. Old convicts became accustomed to seeing him run and noticed that he ran like no other boxer they had ever seen. After the second lap, Saint designated the long straightway as his sprint zone. In that zone, he stretched his legs in such a way that it appeared he was floating. Incorporating his football, track, and now boxing training, Saint was a running machine and seemed to never run out of breath or get tired. He ran as if he had no lungs. He developed a formula to run long and hard, whereby he would take seven sprint steps on a single inhale and seven sprint steps on a single exhale. It placed him in overdrive mode and didn't burn him out. The running and exercises became a way for him to release his personal anxieties. They made him feel good and train longer and harder. Saint did exercises and stretches behind Hickory III. He also trained in the martial arts with black-belt Muslims, learning all the kung fu kicks.

Saint in the big yard, Hickory II Unit, in a martial-arts stance.

After six months in the boxing room under Cheyenne's tutorship, Saint had not even touched the heavy bag. All Cheyenne had him doing was running five miles a day and practicing footwork. Cheyenne showed Saint how to use his footwork in the ring to maintain his balance. He was shown how to stand, walk to the left, walk to the right, skip backwards, skip forward during stalking, move laterally to the left, then to the right, run from an opponent, use the ropes, block punches, slip punches, and pivot—and he had to do all of that on the

Auary, Saint, Ronald "Kung Fu" Vallery, and Ashanti in the big-yard walk between Walnut and Pine units.

balls of his feet, as if suspended in the air. His heels never touched the ground until his training was finished each day. From the time Saint got up until he went to bed, he walked everywhere on the balls of his feet—never flatfooted.

Since there were several inmate lawyers, Saint could train at will. He doubled his training, with a session in the morning and one at night. He was jumping fifteen rounds of rope per session. When Saint entered the boxing room each day, he always found Cheyenne doing something he considered crazy in front of or on the heavy bag. He looked like an African witch doctor the way he stood in front of the bag, leaning from the waist in and out, in and out, as if he were a cobra hypnotizing an enemy. It was what Saint would learn and do every day until he mastered it. That crazy thing was called the dance of a mongoose.

One day while teaching Saint how to parry, Cheyenne talked about how good Jerry Celestine was. Saint and Jerry came to Angola the same day but never met. "Nobody will ever hit Jerry with right hand," he boasted. Jerry had been Cheyenne's fighter, and the New Orleans Criminal Sheriff's Department had retrieved him after Colonel Wall cleared his transfer. Saint, upon hearing that, determined to be greater than Jerry.

Saint was throwing jabs, right hands, left hooks, and uppercuts before Cheyenne would let him touch the heavy bag. Finally,

Cheyenne brought him to the bag to execute the punches. "Saint, always come out jabbing. Throw every punch off your jab. *Moja* is one jab. *Moja, moja, moja, moja, mbili* (right hand), *tatu* (left hook), *nne* (right uppercut). Always make two punches sound like one punch. It's all about speed. Don't worry about power. Power will come. In mongoose dance, always pivot left to slip right hand. Nobody will ever hit you with right hand." Cheyenne repeated the drill over and over.

In eight months, Saint was sparring with other fighters. At 173 pounds, he was a light heavyweight. The fighters he sparred with were in the lightweight class. Saint used complete rounds to practice running from his sparring partners to see if he could avoid making any bodily contact with them. Cheyenne's intent was to have his light heavyweight move around the ring like the little lightweight boxers. It would become natural to Saint.

Cheyenne would not allow Saint to fight before his time and out of his class. Other trainers let Colonel Wall manipulate them, and their fighters would end up with a lost eye, impaired hearing, fractured ribs, broken jaws, loosened teeth, and countless broken noses. All light-heavyweight fighters were being hammered by the merciless Bull Cobra, who trained at the Camp A horse lot. No one could get past the first round with him. It was common for him to beat his opponents to bloody pulps in front of the free people and guards who watched and cheered for him.

Graveyard held an inflated football dummy and rushed at Saint, putting pressure on him to throw punches. Saint threw fast and powerful combination after combination while dancing, pivoting, and hitting the dummy, stopping big Graveyard in his tracks. From inside the Administration Building, Colonel Wall watched Cheyenne, Saint, Alley Cat, and Graveyard through binoculars as they worked out on the sunny big-yard field. On a security desk behind him was a damaged roller bar taken from a typewriter in the law library.

"Cheyenne's new fighter will be a good challenge for the Bull."

"Ah, Chief, you thinks he ready for the Bull?" Redford asked, surprised.

"I think with the right promotion, we can fill the rodeo arena," he replied.

"Chief, you don't think he first needs some fight experience, huh?" Redford asked.

"Oh, I think he's ready! He's had enough fight experience," the

Colonel said. Like working a puzzle, he fit a chunk of black rubber retrieved from the restroom assault exactly into the roller bar.

Cheyenne positioned Saint against the wall in the boxing room to simulate being caught on the ropes. "Let's go. You on the ropes. Go into your protection. Protect your head."

Saint leaned against the wall and raised his gloves to his face. Cheyenne pounded away at his head with sixteen-ounce sparring gloves. Saint suddenly had a flashback.

"Take his eyes, knock him out, and bring him in this cell."

Saint threw a right forearm into Cheyenne's face, putting him on his back. Colonel Wall and Redford entered the boxing room at that moment to see Saint standing over Cheyenne.

"Saint! Why did you strike me?" Cheyenne yelled, holding the left side of his face.

"And you got him outweighed by, what, fifty pounds, Cheyenne?" the Colonel asked.

"That's illegal blow, Saint! You cannot mix kung-fu with boxing ring, Saint," Cheyenne protested as he got to his feet.

"Ah, man, I'm sorry. I don't know, man. I blanked out. I'm sorry, Cheyenne."

"I think it's time Saint show who's the king of the river, him or Bull," Wall said, impressed. He was grinning and puffing on his cigar. "What you think about that, Cheyenne?"

"Colonel, I am not finished. No one ever fought first fight with champion fighter. Bull can kill, ah, hurt my fighter. Give me three months. He will be ready, I promise." Cheyenne stared into Colonel Wall's eyes, then at Saint. He knew what was about to happen. "Saint will not fight without me in his corner."

"Bull's gonna paint the ring with your blood, you slick son of a b----," Redford said, getting in Saint's face. "I'm going to bet my whole paycheck that he takes you out."

"Or What! You ready for a bullfight?" the Colonel asked.

Later that day, four guards escorted Cheyenne down the walk towards the maniac ward. Graveyard, Alley Cat, and Saint exited the boxing room for the evening chow. Without warning, Saint jumped to the ground and began disrobing and throwing his clothes towards the guard tower until he was wearing only his jockstrap and sunglasses. "I'm tired of being locked *up*. I want to be *free!*"

Graveyard followed behind Alley Cat, picking up Saint's fading Capitol High gym shorts and other clothes. "Saint! Put these gym shorts back on before they write you up for indecent exposure."

Saint pulled the shorts up high and took off running hard around the track, trying to burst either his lungs or his heart wide open. Hickory III convicts jumped off the walk and ran to the track to watch Saint run or perhaps get a free look at his rear without the threat of being beaten nearly to death. The convicts cheered as Saint passed them and leaned into the imaginary tape.

Graveyard realized Saint was venting. He jogged up to Saint with his clothes and workboots. "Here," Graveyard said. "Put this on before we have to kill some of these niggahs out here. What you trying to do—bust a gut?"

"Just wanted to make sure I got long, long wind," Saint said, barely panting. He then told them what happened to Cheyenne and about his fight with Bull Cobra.

"What? The Bull?" Alley Cat and Graveyard shouted in unison.

Ross Maggio was named warden of Angola in 1977. He came in cracking his whip. To cut down on the killings, he wanted every able-bodied convict working in the field so they'd be too tired to kill when they came in. He saw there were too many dorm orderlies and reassigned them to the fields. He instituted major shakedowns and confiscated hundreds of knives. He shook down entire dorms at two thirty in the morning, when the convicts least expected it. Freemen strip searched convicts daily at the most inconvenient times and places and often found knives. The shakedowns reduced the stabbings and killings tremendously. "I got too much time for this!" was the convicts' response.

Convicts were being written up for even minor rule violations. Disciplinary court always took twenty-five days of good time away from each convict, extending his stay in Angola. In retaliation, convicts began to slow the entire prison process to a snail's crawl. They slow-walked everywhere they went—to chow, callout, work on the compound, or especially the field. A field foreman called Warden Maggio on his radio and told him that by the time the farm line walks to the jobsite in the field, it will be time to turn around and walk them back. Maggio gave the order: "Walk their a--es to Camp J!" Camp J was still under construction. All 365 convicts on the farm slow-walked to Camp J that evening.

That night, Warden Maggio herded the entire big-yard convict population into a giant outdoor bullpen. A helicopter hovered above, bathing the prisoners with searchlights from above. Several

Jeeps with fifty- and sixty-caliber machineguns were parked facing the convicts. Over a hundred armed guards with machineguns and M-16 rifles stood facing the convicts. Maggio and Colonel Wall approached the prisoners and asked what their grievances and demands were. Maggio instructed the convicts to select their spokesmen. Saint stepped up along with Auary and Ashanti, two convicts from Hickory II, to be spokesmen. Billy Sinclair represented the white convicts in Oak Unit.

After all the spokesmen from each of the sixteen dormitories met and discussed the grievances, Saint became angry and told them they were selling out. Most of them wanted their whores back. "For the public to know what's going on in here and get involved, somebody's got to die. That's the cost!" he said. Saint walked to the rear of the bullpen, where the old and sickly convicts were. There he sat in an Indian squat with his back to all the convicts and silently cried. The only one he wished to hear from now was the still small voice. He had not heard from his invisible friend in a long time.

The next morning, Saint sat at his desk reading *The Godfather*. Only he and Victor were present in the law library. The others were in disciplinary court in D-Block. Victor was at his desk pecking away on the ancient typewriter. A control-center freeman opened the door and stuck his head in.

"They need a lawyer at Camp J Court. Let's hurry! The patrol is waiting for you at the A Building. This is coming from the warden's office."

Saint joined the patrol and crossed the parking lot, carrying his clipboard and Department of Corrections appeals binder. Camp J was the newest camp at Angola. A backhoe, bulldozer, and other machinery sat in the yard. There were no signs of inmate life. Officer Lehman, a red-complexioned black freeman with curly hair, brought Saint to a room set up to hold court. Col. Walter Pence, a short white man in his fifties who had the reputation of being the fairest disciplinary-court chairman in Angola, sat at the table along with Dwayne McFadden and Mason Green.

Lehman brought the first client out of his cell. Saint noticed Lehman telling the young white convict something. It had to be alarming, because the convict looked terrified. He was covered with red scars and blue bruises and walked in obvious pain.

After hearing the report read, the convict stood there mute. Saint instantly moved for a continuance on the grounds that the inmate did not have a copy of the report. The board granted it and gave Saint a copy. Saint and the convict walked twenty feet away to talk. "What happened, man?" Saint asked. The convicted said nothing. "This is an incident report. Tell me what happened. How you got all those bruises on you?"

"Your continuance is up. Come back," Colonel Pence said. "How do you plead?"

"We enter a plea of not guilty," Saint said, beginning to argue.

"No! Guilty. I'm guilty. I'm guilty!" the client yelled.

Well, I'll be damned, Saint thought. He had never seen anything like this.

"The board transfers you to Camp J lockdown indefinitely and orders the loss of twenty-five days good time. Next case."

Saint sighed, feeling it was going to be a long, long day.

It appeared that Colonel Pence was carrying out a fixed agenda handed down by the warden's office. Herbert Hatcher of New Orleans was next on the docket. "The charge is aggravated disobedience. The above named and numbered inmate was given a direct order to go to work in the main prison farm line. He refused and was taken to Camp J lockdown. How do you plead?"

"Counsel moves that the board give us a copy of the report and grant a continuance so I can speak with my client about the nature of the report." Saint saw blue copies within the stack of files on the table. None of the inmates had been given a copy of their reports.

Hatcher was afraid as he and Saint walked from the table. Two white guards came in and stomped their feet near the door as if knocking mud from their boots. Saint saw that as sending a message to Hatcher not to talk. He read the report, then switched places with Hatcher so that Hatcher's back was to the board. "Look, li'l brother, I'm on your side, understand?" Saint whispered. "You need to tell me what happened over here. Why y'all scared to talk? Just talk to me. I got your back. Tell me what happened."

"Slim, they beat us! All of us. They held me down on the floor and beat and kicked me for nothing. I didn't do nothing. I asked them last night, 'Why y'all jumping on me? I didn't do nothing!' The warden told them to kick our a--."

"Wait, hold up, little brother. Slow down. How you know the warden told them that?"

"He was standing right over there when they were doing it. I could see him! I heard him tell them, all the guards, 'Kick that son of a b---- a—. Every one of them f---ing with me,'" Hatcher said.

"You saw Warden Maggio? You heard Warden Maggio?" Saint asked, realizing the gravity of the charge. He didn't want Hatcher to be telling him any hearsay.

"Everybody saw him! He was standing right there telling the guards to kick our a--. Look! You think I'm lying?" Hatcher asked Saint. He pulled down his gray sweatshirt, revealing bandages from the base of his neck to his clavicle. "Look! They broke my collarbone last night when they kicked and stomped me. They took me to the hospital in Baton Rouge. Maggio told me, 'If you say anything or tell anybody what happened we're going to kill you.' We can't get no mail, no visits, no TV, no radios, no cigarettes. We can't even lay in the bunk, and my shoulder's killing me. They won't even give me any medicine for the pain, and I'm hurting right now," Hatcher cried to Saint.

Saint flipped his legal tablet to the middle and began writing. "Give me your mother's phone number. I'm going to call her and have her send you a lawyer here tomorrow to take pictures and get a statement from you. You tell him the same thing you just told me. Don't worry about the good white folks. They just threatening you because they know they done f---ed up."

A Courtroom Fighter

Saint stood before the board with a succession of beaten convicts and demanded copies of their blue incident reports. As fast as he could, he moved for continuances and wrote the names and contact information for first of kin on his legal pad. Every convict at Camp J Court that day had been beaten and had the bruises to prove it.

"I move for a continuance," Saint said yet again.

"Why?" Colonel Pence asked. The board was growing impatient.

"Because DOC Appeal Number 420 says so," Saint replied.

"What does it say?"

"A twenty-four-hour continuance shall be granted to all inmates that appear before the disciplinary board for a hearing to prepare his defense against the report if he hasn't received a copy and notice of the charges against him before appearing before the disciplinary board. I could ask for twenty-four hours, but all I want is ten minutes, Colonel."

"Ten minutes. All the incident reports are the same," Pence said.

"But these are separate reports and not a class action. I have to find out what each inmate's story is. Now, if you want to treat this as a class-action case, the freeman can bring every convict in the big-yard farm line, all 365 of them, and we can handle this as one big case. Otherwise, my client needs his continuance so he can tell me what happened to him personally."

"It makes no difference," Pence argued.

"It makes all the difference in the world if you count the twenty-five days good time you take away that will keep these men who are husbands, fathers, brothers, sons away from their families twenty-five days longer. 'Makes no difference' depends on what side of the fence you're on. That's easy for you to say because you go home every night to your family. They could get killed within that extra twenty-five days they remain incarcerated here when they should have been released. Taking twenty-five days good time alters the original release date as set by the law for when the defendant would finish serving his sentence. That's the difference," Saint argued. The board was not pleased with his legal maneuvering.

Saint continued. "If 360 convicts were walking really slow in a double line, the report has to show that the field foreman asked the first two inmates in front of the lines to walk faster. If they refused to do so, then they should have been taken out of line, placed on the side, and written up for a valid violation. Then, the next two workers should be given the same order. That same process should have occurred 180 times to justify writing up each inmate for the identical rule violation. I don't think everybody out there wanted to take part in the slow-walk. But they couldn't walk no faster than the person in front of them walked. If they walked out of line to go around them, they would be shot by the guards and charged with attempting to escape. Right is right and wrong is wrong. I am right and the report is wrong. Am I right?" Saint asked.

"No, you not right," Colonel Pence answered, angered.

Saint knew he was right. He knew the board knew he was right. The convicts knew he was right, but the board didn't want to be beaten by an inmate lawyer. They were angry at Saint and showed it. Saint likewise was mad and didn't let up.

"Motion denied. It's 10:30 P.M. Court's at recess. Disciplinary court is normally over with by 2:00 P.M. This is unprecedented," Pence said.

"I object and will appeal the board's decision," Saint replied.

Saint entered the law library and leaned back on the door, exhausted. The appeals binder was in his right hand and his clipboard, thick with blue incident reports, was in his left.

"Saint!" everyone at the table yelled at once.

"What? Y'all thought the good white folks had got my a--, huh?" Saint asked, smiling.

Shorty slowly walked over and suddenly punched him in the gut.

"Ohhhh! Shorty, why you did that?"

""Where you been all this damn time?" Shorty yelled.

"In a war back there at Camp J. Let me tell you." Saint gave twenty-five reports with phone numbers to each lawyer as he explained what happened.

"Don't you ever do that again, you hear me?" Shorty shouted. "This Angola! These white folks will kill you and throw you in one of them ravines and claim you escaped."

"Hello. May I speak with Mrs. Dorothy Hatcher, please?" Saint asked. He was using the telephone on the walk at Hickory Unit. Each unit had a phone the convicts could use to call outside Angola. "Mrs. Dorothy, I am a friend of your son, Herbert. I'm calling you to inform you that the guards here in Angola have almost beaten your son to death. He might not make it until tomorrow. They beat him real bad and broke his collarbone and had to take him to a hospital in Baton Rouge last night. He's here in Angola at Camp J and they won't give him no pain medicine. They want him to die so he can't tell what happened and who beat him. Warden Maggio told the guards to beat Herbert and a lot of other prisoners, Mrs. Hatcher."

When Mrs. Dorothy heard that, she dropped the phone and ran screaming through the house, "They killed Herbert! They killed Herbert!" A young man came to the phone. Saint conveyed the same information to him and urged that they send an attorney to take photographs and get a statement from Hatcher.

"I move for a continuance," Saint said on the second court day at Camp J. He was not backing off. "*Whatever you are, be the best,*" he could hear his football and track coaches echoing from the Lions' locker room.

"How much time do you need, Forest Hammond?" Deputy Warden Michael Beaubouef asked on the third day of hearings. He was sitting as chairman, next to Colonel Pence.

"I'd say, ah, about ten minutes, Warden."

"I tell you what, Forest Hammond. Why don't you just go and wait in the lobby for the patrol to take you back to the law library. We'll get Herman or Prentice to be counsel. They're good lawyers. Holding court until nine and ten thirty every night, that's ridiculous, and I'm not going to stand for that this day."

The deputy warden could see in Saint's eyes that he was cursing him in his mind. Saint left his client and walked into the lobby.

"So, you're that smart-a-- niggah, huh? Boy, you must don't know where you're at, do you?" Lehman drew his right fist back. "You don't think I'll bust you in your face, huh?" Two short, white twin brothers flanked Lehman anxiously, ready to pounce. The muscular guards looked like professional wrestlers. Lehman searched Saint's eyes for traces of fear. Instead, he saw confidence. Saint looked in Lehman's eyes and smiled invitingly, with both arms lowered to his sides and his back a foot from the wall. He held the clipboard and appeals binder in separate hands. They had seen fear in the eyes of the convicts they'd beaten. They all saw something else today.

"Wait for the patrol out in the sun," Lehman finally said, backing off. Maybe Saint had resources in the free world that could get him and his entire family killed.

Warden Maggio called a meeting at the Administration Building with all main prison classification officers, heads of security, and deputy wardens. "We got a very volatile situation and I want all of us to be on the same page," he began. "The front gate is packed with lawyers trying to see their clients, who happen to all be at Camp J. Inmate lawyer Forest Hammond is somehow responsible for this onslaught of attorneys at the front gate. He's the only person, excluding employees, who has routinely been in and out of Camp J."

Colonel Wall did not like where this was going. "Well, now, Warden, don't you think you're being a little too hasty here?" he asked. "I'm just cutting to the chase. Now if he's caught with a knife, I will accept that, but I don't want a knife found in his bunk. That kid don't do drugs, so no dope found in his bunk. I say 'found,' because I know you people got rats that can plant dope in his a-- if you want to. If anything comes up, I'm investigating it personally if I have to sleep in his bunk overnight with the convicts to find out what happened."

"Forest Hammond!" Larry Smith called. The only black classification officer in Angola, he was coming from the meeting, where he had listened to the arguments. The lawyers were entering the control center when Saint turned. Smith motioned for him to step to the side on the cellblock walk so they could talk. "Boy, your name ringing in the Administration Building like Catholic church bells for a high Mass. You got these folks mad at you. They want you out of the Legal Aid Office. This is all about politics. You're going up against an institution, son, a state conglomerate. You can't win by yourself."

"What do you mean when you say 'politics'?" Saint asked, listening carefully.

"You could say 'politics' comes from 'poly'—'many'—and 'tics'—'tricks.' You put the two together and it means many tricks. These folks will utilize as many tricks or politics as they can to defeat you. You're confined in their penitentiary," Smith explained.

"Mr. Smith, I'm not on their side. Right is right and wrong is wrong. I'm right, they wrong. Am I right?" Saint asked. Smith hesitated. "Mr. Smith, you're suppose to say, 'You're right,'" Saint prompted, smiling.

"You got a life sentence. You need to think about being able to work and live with these people."

"When I accept this life sentence, then I'll think like that."

"All I'm saying is, when you got your head in a lion's mouth, you got to pull it out slow."

"You better warn 'em," Saint said, grinning. The two men laughed.

"Boy, you're crazy. I done warned you, now," Smith said.

On the next court date for the main prison, a long line of inmates stood by the wall outside disciplinary court.

"Now, Mr. Hammond, I want to give you a clear admonition that the board will not tolerate any more of your redundant arguments," Deputy Warden Frank Blackburn said. "State your defense, make your point, and be finished one time around, you understand? We're not as stupid as you think." Saint nodded, knowing better than to start a conversation with Blackburn. "I need a verbal answer for the record," Blackburn said. "State your name."

"F. Hammond. I hear you loud and clear, Warden Blackburn."

"The above named and numbered inmate was given a direct order to go to work. He refused. He was placed in lockdown. How do you plead, guilty or not guilty?"

"Counsel motions for the board to dismiss the charge because the report is not signed or dated. DOC Rule 7 says that in the absence of the same, the report shall—*s-h-a-l-l;* that makes it mandatory—

must be dismissed," Saint said and watched Blackburn search for the empty signature line. "Bottom right, at the blank line, and top left, where it says *date*," Saint prompted.

"Motion denied," Blackburn said without conferring with the board.

"What? Motion denied?" Saint pulled his client back. "This a setup," he whispered. "They gonna find you guilty and take your good time. I'll get your good time back when I file your appeal with the secretary of corrections. You'll get it back; don't worry."

"No argument," Saint said to the board.

"The board finds you guilty and sentences you to loss of twenty-five days good time and ten days in isolation. Next case!"

The walls were closing in. Saint soon stopped going to disciplinary court and stayed in the law library, working on his own case. He had been helping everybody but himself, it seemed.

Not Down for the Count

The fight banner read: ANGOLA THRILLER! THE MONGOOSE vs. THE COBRA. The convict crowd sat in a caged area next to the civilian crowd. The ring was set up in the middle of the rodeo arena. Torches were burning at the four corners of the ring, making the event look grand and exotic. There were families in the stands. Ticket and concession sales were high.

When it came time for the main event, Saint was in the ring looking at a beautiful woman who resembled DMB. "Damn! She looks good. You know what, Cheyenne?" Saint asked.

"What is it, Saint?" Cheyenne thought it would be a last-minute question about some fighting technique he wasn't sure of.

"I have never been naked in bed with a woman before. She could pee on me," Saint said.

"You speaking for both of us, Saint. All I ever put the meat on is these damned penitentiary whores," Graveyard said. "I got a brother live in New York, New York. That's a city so nice, they had to name it twice. One day, Saint, when we get out this motha', we gonna go to New York, get a hotel suite in one of them five stars, with two king-size beds in it, and get us some weed."

"And some white port wine," Saint added.

"Yeah, bring it on, brother. Talk to me!" Graveyard shouted. He and Saint began fantasizing. "She could s--- on me, Saint," Graveyard said.

"You been locked up too long, Graveyard," Saint said. "That's a little too far for me."

"Saint! Graveyard!" Cheyenne yelled. "You can't be thinking about women now. Cut that out, Graveyard. You make sure Saint gets water."

"All right, Cheyenne. Saint, you do need to concentrate. If we don't stop looking at these white folks women, neither one of us gonna get out."

"You got that right," Cheyenne said. "The good white people will turn boxing match to lynching. Now *concentrate*, Saint. This is real bullfight tonight."

"Saint, go let that niggah know this your ring," Graveyard said.

Saint walked around the ring, feeling for soft spots and dips in the canvas and checking the spring in the ropes.

"Watch that niggah Bull, Saint," Alley Cat said. "He don't fight fair. You can take him.

Between handling the horses for the guards every day and his training, Bull was a physical specimen. He weighed in at 192 pounds to Saint's 173. Their eyes met once when they entered the ring, but Saint never looked at him again.

The referee, Porter, called the two fighters to center ring. King was Bull's trainer and stood with him to listen to the instructions.

"Now, look, this is going to be a fair fight. Bull, no rough stuff, head butts, or cheap shots. No hitting behind the ear. No rabbit punches. When I say break, break," Porter instructed.

The Mongoose and Cobra stood toe to toe. Bull suddenly pushed Saint down on his butt. The crowd cheered for Bull. Porter pointed them to their corners after Saint got up and Porter wiped off his gloves.

"Bull, it'll get real bad for us if this guy beats you," King said. "Don't hold nothing back."

"I'm-a mop the ring with this ho's blood," Bull said.

In the red corner, Cheyenne gently placed the middle knuckle of his right fist precisely on the center of Saint's chin and twisted his hand. "Enough pressure on these nerves can send the body into paralysis. He will wobble with no defense. It will blind him. You can then kill him. Saint, don't think. Just follow your killer instinct."

That was the first time Cheyenne ever instructed Saint how to hurt a fighter.

The bell sounded. Bull charged at Saint when he attempted to touch gloves. Saint sprang back as Bull chased him. As they moved around the ring, Saint backpedaled, slipped, and parried every punch Bull threw. They clenched at center ring, making body contact for the first time. Bull walked Saint backwards into the ropes.

"Kill 'im!" yelled an old snaggle-toothed redneck in a cap and jean coveralls. "Kill that chicken sumb----, Bull. Don't let him get away. You got 'im, Bull!"

Bull head-butted Saint as if it was legal and followed up with a left hook and another head butt and left hook. The hard left hook broke through Saint's right-hand face protection and he went down on one knee, stunned. Bull punched him again and he fell over on his side. Porter did nothing about the two head butts. The crowd cheered for Bull, who raised his arms in response. Colonel Wall watched from high up in the press box, enjoying the fight attendance. He wanted the arena trashy when the fight was over.

"Breathe deep, Saint!" Cheyenne yelled to his fighter.

Porter pushed Bull to the neutral corner and returned to give Saint the eight count. "*One! Two!*" Saint was lying on the canvas, inhaling deeply. Strangely, he saw his head caught in Boodie's legs in the parish prison. He saw the referee as Walkie-Talkie on his knees, slapping the floor with his hand and counting. "*Three! Four!*"

Saint pushed off the canvas and returned to one knee. He saw the crowd as the clique, cheering against him. As the referee's hand came down with the next count, Saint blocked it with his left wrist. His right hand deployed instinctively, clipping the referee's chin. "*Mbili.*" A left hook followed into the jaw, sending him crashing to the canvas, out cold.

"*Tatu.*"

Bull saw his friend go down and charged Saint, leading with jabs followed by a right. The punches never connected, but Saint turned as if walking away. He then spun back around and saw that his feigned move had worked. Bull was wide open. Going to his right knee, Saint hit Bull in the groin, making him bend over. A left uppercut busted the champ's mouth; blood spewed as he staggered into the ropes. Saint stepped in close to throw a straight right hand, but the bell sounded. Saint instantly turned away but again spun back and forearmed Bull across his nose. The blow knocked him into the ropes and he fell, sprawling face down on the canvas. Saint kicked him in the groin and attempted to straddle him when King yelled and charged Saint with a stool in his hands. "You c---sucker! You hurt my fighter!" he screamed.

As King got closer, Saint crouched, feigning a still target. His arms and hands protected his face, and he peeked at King from behind his gloves. Then he leapt forward and struck King in the nose with a powerful right hand. King threw the stool, causing Cheyenne to dodge it as it flew by him in the red corner behind Saint. King went down on his back. Saint kicked him in the face and regarded him as if deciding if it was safe to leave him alone. Guards climbed up on the ring edge and held the ropes, afraid to enter. Redford stood on the ground, listening to his radio.

"Redford! Stand down. Keep the guards out the ring. Do you copy?" the Colonel's voice shouted over the radio.

"That's a ten-four, Chief," Redford answered. He pointed at two convicts in Bull's corner and told them to go get Saint, who was bouncing around looking at the bodies on the canvas. The first convict ran at Saint, throwing punches. Saint sent the man down with a fractured rib. A kick to his head knocked him out. The second convict came at Saint throwing hooks and trying to grab him. The Mongoose sprang back, leaving the man swinging at an invisible target. He moved in on the man and connected—slamming his temple with ten powerful, jack-hammering, right-hand punches. He followed his target until the man was entangled in the ropes, unconscious.

Saint turned his attention back to the bodies in the ring. He dragged Bull by his braids to the center and slammed his head down on the canvas. The Colonel was watching it all in awe as he now understood clearly what had taken place.

"Niggah, you asked me for a smoke. You didn't ask to use my lighter. I'll kill your b---- a--. Who you think I am? Kufyanza Mbawa Nguruwe!" The flashback had taken Saint all the way back to his first day in jail and the Boxhead Max attack.

Saint raised his right leg to crush Bull's throat, but Cheyenne threw his arms around Saint, lifted him from the canvas, and carried him to the red corner. Saint, unaware it was Cheyenne, tried to kick and punch himself free. "Saint, it's all right! It's me, Cheyenne. It's over! It's over. Ngapi! Time, Saint. The fight is over! The row has been hoed. *Time, Saint, time!"* Cheyenne was saying anything to make Saint snap out of it.

Bull remained unconscious on the canvas for twenty-nine minutes. He was taken to the hospital in Baton Rouge that night. He retired immediately and never fought again.

By the end of spring 1978, Saint had retired every light-heavyweight fighter who entered the ring with him. At first he did what Bull had done, beating fighters mercilessly. Scott stopped him one night after a fight that lasted seventeen seconds where the challenger from Dixon Correction Center had to go to the hospital

Saint and Coleman tie up in the first round.

The Mongoose is on the loose as Saint dances and spares Coleman.

Saint wins! Inmate referee Shamberg holds up Saint's arm after judges score the fight a TKO.

for emergency brain surgery. "Saint! Why do you have to be so abusive and beat them to bloody ruins when you see you have won the fight? Why are you so brutal?" It was then that Saint resolved to never hurt anyone again.

When defending his title against Wallace Coleman, a quick combination from Saint in the first round allowed Saint to retire Coleman. He had clipped him on his chin, which left him open with his arms down ready to be killed, but the Mongoose danced away. When he stopped drawing blood and instead showed mercy by outscoring his opponents under the Amateur Athletic Union rules, the fans turned on him. The heads of security were pressuring trainers of all the fight clubs on the farm to find and train somebody, anybody, who could beat that nigger inmate lawyer from Baton Rouge whom everybody in Angola knew as the Saint.

Chapter 8

Round One: Saint vs. the Criminal Justice System

On June 6, 1978, the United States Fifth Circuit Court of Appeals in New Orleans, Louisiana issued a mandate in an unpublished opinion and remanded Saint's case to the United States District Court, Middle District of Louisiana, in order to hold an evidentiary hearing before the Honorable Frank J. Polozola, U.S. Magistrate. The primary reasoning behind unpublished opinions is that they may not be cited as a precedent in other cases and the cases are of a controversial nature.

> CONGRATULATIONS Mr. Hammond upon obtaining your Capitol High School Diploma through the GED program! It sounds like a Capitol High Lion is ROARING! I love to hear a LION ROAR! Keep ROARING Mr. Hammond. ROAR LOUD! Best regards, Charles Keel. Principal—Capitol High School.

After reading to Martin his court order and the letter from Mr. Keel, Saint showed his aging father his diploma and excitedly explained the order. "I got what they call a 'prima facie case.' This is my boykinization transcript. Nowhere in here shows I pled guilty. I got my questions ready. I got legal cases showing I got no deal because of double jeopardy."

"Well, just remember, Ossie Brown said that you saying you put that gun in Boodie's hand is what incriminated you."

"Well, I won't put the gun in Boodie's hand," Saint replied.

"Boy, it's too late for that!" Martin said. "Now, don't get up on that witness stand and tell a lie under oath. They'll charge you with perjury and throw your whole case out."

"Daddy, listen, they'll charge me with perjury if they catch me lying. The detectives swore on the Bible, then lied saying they read me my Miranda rights at home, remember?"

"M-hmm, them lying bastards."

181

"They played a courtroom con game on us. And what about this: 'You don't have to worry about not going to college. The judge won't take you out of school. We know you're not the triggerman.' Look where I been for the last five years. This ain't about putting your hand on a Bible and swearing under oath to tell the truth, Daddy. This is all about winning! Them good white folks don't care about the truth. That's why they don't tell it. We gonna get 'em, Daddy, don't worry. You want some coffee, Daddy?" Martin nodded. Saint signaled to the concession, and convicts brought coffee and snacks to their table. "We call that black gold up here," Saint said as Martin sipped his coffee.

"Why they bringing all this food? I'm not paying for all that," Martin said, frowning.

"Daddy, it's free. You don't have to pay. I'm the light-heavyweight boxing champion up here. Those men working the concession are my fans. Everybody's scared to fight me. Won't nobody fight me. They scared to even spar with me. I spar with little lightweight fighters all the time. They cause me to move around in the ring fast and quick like them. None of the light heavyweights I see on TV move like I move. I can beat all of 'em." Saint said. "Say, Daddy, do you still eat peanuts while laying on the couch listening to the Astros on your radio? You must think you be at a real game the way you get peanut hulls all on the floor and couch, huh?" Saint laughed as he reconnected with his father. "Teresa and Daisy used to be so mad at you." Martin nodded and smiled his only smile while ever visiting Saint at Angola.

At the end of the visit, they walked to the photo area, where Paul Ceasar took their picture for free before Martin left.

On August 14, 1978, at 7:30 A.M., Saint, escorted by an Angola guard, crossed Florida Street in shackles and entered the federal courthouse building in Baton Rouge. He held a large, gold-clasped envelope as he hobbled up the steps. At 8: 45, when he set foot in court, he felt the same sensations as when he entered the fighting ring. He made it a point to first look at his opponent, the man who had been denying his petitions as if he did not understand how to apply the law correctly and yet had the nerve to call himself a federal magistrate. Frank J. Polozola's eyes met Saint's for the first time. Saint stared at him, but Polozola looked away as though he considered Saint unworthy of his attention. The butterflies Saint felt in 1973 were different today. He felt empowered. He felt like the champ. He was not apprehensive, nor was he the seventeen-year-old

Martin and Saint in August 1978.

nigger boy ignorant about how the criminal justice system worked. Now he was a twenty-three-year-old, penitentiary-trained, fighting inmate lawyer. He was ready for the bell to sound.

Martin and Coach Bates were sitting together in the audience section of the small courtroom, which was adorned with beautiful cherry-wood furniture. Joan Dean Phillips sat on the end as Saint came in. A beautiful little six-year-old girl with an Afro sat on her lap, staring at Saint as the U.S. marshal removed his chains. Saint looked at Joan Dean and pointed his finger at the little girl, then at himself. "Is that me?" he indicated. Joan Dean nodded. "What's her name?" he asked. Joan was thrilled to hear Saint's voice again.

"Angela," she said.

"Angela. Hey, little pretty girl. Hi, Angela," Saint said. He didn't care about the marshal growling at him for speaking to them. That was his little girl.

Murphy Bell, Warren Hebert, and Anthony Graphia sat together talking. When they saw Saint, they assumed an air of innocence, but he read their faces and body language. They considered him as good as dead and buried in Angola with a life sentence. They never believed he would be resurrected.

"Mr. Hammond, I'm George K. Anding. I'm a federal public defender. The Court has appointed me to represent you in these habeas corpus proceedings. I want you to know at the outset that this is the first prison habeas corpus hearing in which I've represented a prisoner."

Saint handed him several stapled pages of yellow legal-tablet paper. "I've already drafted my questions for the witnesses. I need you to follow this list and ask each question in the order they're listed on the pages regardless of how much sense it makes to you at the time. I got a copy and I'll be following you. You can ask any other questions you feel would be in furtherance of my questions and then continue on with asking my questions. I expect Polozola to deny my petition. He's done it twice already. My main thing here is to get everything on record for the Fifth Circuit, because they will overturn his adverse decision. He's arbitrary and capricious. He tried to throw our suits out on the Camp J beatings. He hates prisoners."

"This is good. This is really good. I'm glad you came prepared. This is going to be very interesting," Anding said, looking through the questions.

The clerk calling the matter to begin sounded like a fight bell to Saint. Polozola stepped in to arrange the order of the witnesses who would testify, and Murphy Bell was called as the prosecution's first witness. Saint viewed the move as somehow stacking the deck against him. He didn't trust the good white folks and questioned their intent on everything they did.

Woodson Callihan, the attorney who represented Saint when he was sentenced, died in a 1974 motorcycle accident. The State was using Bell to flood the record with hearsay evidence in the form of the public defender office's policy directives. The directives were being used to show what Callihan likely did to provide effective representation. Anding objected to Bell's testimony as hearsay and Polozola, as expected, overruled the objection.

Anding used Martin's testimony to show that an established relationship existed between Martin and Bell. There was no excuse or reason why Bell did not show up for his son's trial. "When did you get in touch with Mr. Bell?" Anding asked Martin.

"My boy called and told me a young white deputy, ah, Sergeant Daigle, I never forget, had kicked him in his behind with metal-tip cowboy boots and he was bleeding from his a-- and when he fell to the floor he spit chewing tobacco on him and they sprayed him down with that mace chemical. I went to Mr. Bell's office and talked to him about it."

"Did you regularly go to the jail to visit your son?"

"Oh yes, every visiting day I went down to see him when he was in jail, yes."

"Did you ever speak to Mr. Bell following any visits with your son?"

"Yes, I spoke to Mr. Bell one time, I recall, when they beat and stabbed my boy up there in the parish prison. I think a twenty-five-year old man stabbed him. They beat and stabbed him and put him in Earl K. Long Hospital and no official told me my son was there. And when I went to see him, I didn't know him, couldn't recognize him. I went to talk to Mr. Bell about that. I can recall that very well."

Martin testified that Bell said he would take the case and clear his boy. Saint felt that Bell owed it to Martin to stick together as black men and now help his son. The good white folks had interfered. This was Bell's only opportunity to right a wrong he did. However, Bell was helping the good white folks, trying to hang Saint as if it were October 15, 1973, all over again.

Saint offered into evidence a copy of a letter written by Anthony Graphia, assistant district attorney. "Mr. Graphia, let me first show you a copy of a letter you wrote to Richard Crane, the secretary of the Department of Corrections," Anding said, handing him the letter.

"Yes, I wrote this letter. That is my signature."

"Explain for the Court why you wrote that letter."

"Ramsey and a gang of other prisoners had attacked Hammond in the parish prison."

"And you further stated in your letter that Hammond was allegedly guilty under the felony-murder doctrine. Tell us what that means."

"It is the killing of a human being during a felony like armed robbery."

"Doesn't this indicate Mr. Hammond did not actually pull the trigger?"

"Yes, the evidence at trial showed Ramsey killing Billy Middleton with a .38 pistol."

"Tell this Court the extent of the plea bargain for Mr. Hammond."

"The State would accept a plea of guilty and would not prosecute Mr. Hammond under the attempted armed-robbery charge. It would be dismissed."

"As a practical matter, Mr. Graphia, could that capital crime of murder and the noncapital crime of attempted armed robbery be joined together for trial?"

"No. I don't think the law at that time would have permitted it. In fact, I know it didn't," Graphia admitted.

"In the event that he was found guilty at trial for, let's say, murder, could he have been taken to trial on the attempted armed robbery at a later date?" Anding asked.

Graphia appeared somewhat disinclined to respond. He finally said, "Back then it was my impression, ah, at that time, that he could have, ah, you know, I know what you're getting at, the law, that you're talking about, ah, double jeopardy. That the double jeopardy statute didn't allow for a defendant to be tried on both charges in a case like Mr. Hammond's case—that by law he could not have been tried for the attempted armed robbery and for murder."

His answer was detrimental to the State's case. Polozola shook his head. Anding wasn't finished with Graphia yet, though. His next question was his own and in furtherance of Saint's scripted questions.

"So the plea of guilty was being accepted by Mr. Hammond in return or in exchange for what? Since you could only prosecute him on one or the other charge, what was he getting out of this so-called bargain, this alleged deal Mr. Callihan made with the State? What was the concession?" Anding had boxed him in a corner. To observers in the courtroom, it amounted to *checkmate*.

"In return for nothing, to tell you the truth. He got nothing," Graphia answered.

"So you're saying that all Mr. Hammond was getting out of this plea bargain was that he was being allowed to plead guilty by the offer of a false deal used and intended to make him waive his right to trial, is that correct, even though the State could not take him to trial on the attempted armed robbery that was barred by double jeopardy?"

"That's correct."

"And the other bill of indictment for attempted armed robbery was going to be dismissed?" Anding asked.

"That's correct, Counselor," Graphia answered.

There was nothing the prosecution could do to rehabilitate the State's case. There was enough evidence on record with Graphia's testimony alone to grant the habeas corpus writ and a new trial.

Saint finally was called to the witness stand and sworn in as the last witness of the day. "I didn't touch that gun until I got home," he said. "That's when I took it from him—Boodie." He knew he would be pounced on, and it happened. He'd stuck his chin out, telling them to take their best shot.

"Hold up—wait," Polozola said. "Wait a long minute here. Didn't you go to the counter, get the gun, and bring and give it to Ramsey?"

"No sir, I didn't," Saint answered.

"Why did you write a letter to Nolan Edwards, telling him you gave him the gun inside the store?"

"I did?" Saint asked Polozola. He had forgotten about that letter he wrote in 1974. Anding walked to the prosecution table, picked up a copy of the letter, and speed read it.

"Yes, this big long letter you wrote to Nolan Edwards, but it was addressed to Perry M. Johnson, clerk of court for East Baton Rouge," Polozola explained, holding it up.

Saint sat frozen, deep in thought. *How did the State get possession of my letter I mailed to Nolan Edwards?* he wondered.

"Your Honor!" Anding shouted. "That is not what the letter says. I've just read Ms. Castle's copy. Have you read it? It does not say that he got the gun and came back and gave it to Ramsey. In fact, the letter is consistent with what Mr. Hammond has just testified to, that he didn't give the gun to Ramsey. Have you read the letter, Your Honor?"

Polozola hung his head while thumbing through the letter. He shook his head in frustration. "No, I didn't read all of it because it was, ah, just too long, too long," Polozola said. His facial expression betrayed his obvious embarrassment.

Observing Polozola from the witness stand, Saint felt that the Fifth Circuit judges should take points away from Polozola for hitting him like that. Anding resumed his questioning. "So, after nearly four hours in the jury room, what made you decide to plead guilty?"

"I never said I was guilty. I didn't plead guilty," Saint answered. The only authorized pleas in the Louisiana criminal code are guilty, not guilty, not guilty by insanity, and nolo contendere. Saint had never uttered any of those words in court.

Polozola again took over questioning, thinking he had trapped Saint in another corner.

"Did you use the word 'guilty' when the judge asked you how did you plead? What did you say?" he asked, leaning over his bench and glaring at Saint.

"I never did say I was guilty," Saint answered.

"You never used the word 'guilty'?" Anding repeated.

"I don't understand that," a perplexed Polozola said.

"Well, Your Honor, I think—does the Court have a copy of the transcript of the boykinization?" Anding asked. "If not, Mr. Hammond has a few extra copies."

Bunkie High School Charity Fight, 1978. Back row: Al Stokes, Saint, Jerry Chapman. Front row: William "Monster" Johnson, Lee Roquemoore.

"I have a copy," Polozola said, his head still down as he read the transcript. "I don't see how the judge could begin doing a boykin unless he entered a plea of guilty first. I don't see where he says or pleads guilty. I would assume the judge would not have started a boykin unless he entered a guilty plea. If not, we may as well send this case back to state court now, because it's no use continuing. We don't have a conviction here," Polozola admitted after looking through the transcript.

Polozola recessed the hearing at six o'clock that night. He ordered Saint returned to Angola and scheduled the second round for September 6, 1978. Saint had three weeks to train and work on becoming a hard-to-hit moving target in the courtroom.

Colonel Wall transferred Saint to trustee status and began taking him out into the free world, where he fought in charity fundraisers in high-school gyms in places like Simmesport and Bunkie. The boxing-team members fought among themselves in exhibition matches. Since no light heavyweights would fight Saint, he was matched with Conrad Norman from New Orleans, the Angola heavyweight champion. Saint and Conrad put on a good show trying to knock each other out, neither one succeeding.

Before the transfer, Colonel Wall confronted Saint in a meeting in his office. "I've been looking at records. I talked to each convict during my investigation. Each one told me they didn't know who did it and that they had nothing to do with what happened to you in the parish prison. I don't believe them. What you have to say about that?"

"I don't have the slightest idea of who or what you are talking about, Colonel."

Wall stared at Saint as he puffed on his cigar. He shook his head and smiled. "Then it's true," he finally said.

"What's true?" Saint asked.

"The only words you never hear in a courtroom are the words of a silent man."

Chapter 9

Round Two: Short and Sweet

On September 6, 1978, Magistrate Frank J. Polozola sat looking out over a courtroom populated with those who had been in the jury room on October 15, 1973, during discussions with Martin and Saint about pleading guilty. They were there in response to subpoenas issued by Polozola. Warren Hebert was called first as the State's witness. Charles Wood, a white man who had been Pee Wee's schoolteacher, was called as a witness against Saint. Julius Hardy and Warrie Rowley were two black investigators from the public defender's office called against Saint. Rowley, however, testified that Callihan had threatened the Hammond kid with the possibility of receiving the death penalty. Coach Bates and Martin were called.

Marilyn Castle began with her coworker. "Would you state your name and occupation for the record, please?"

"Warren Joseph Hebert, assistant district attorney for East Baton Rouge Parish."

"Where were you employed from April to October 1973?

"I worked for the East Baton Rouge Parish Public Defender's Office."

"During that time, did you represent Forest Hammond?" Castle asked.

"Yes, I do recall representing him. He was charged with murder and attempted armed robbery," Hebert answered.

"Did you file certain motions on Mr. Hammond's behalf?"

Hebert testified that he filed a motion for oyer, a motion to quash, a motion to suppress, a motion for a change of venue, and a motion to quash the jury venire on the grounds of the systematic exclusion of blacks and women. Anding would later kill that testimony by having Hebert admit that most of the motions were drafted but never filed.

"We had a hearing on the motion to suppress the statement Mr. Hammond made," Hebert testified. "I presented the testimony of Mr. Hammond and his father, Mr. Martin. Once the court rules against you on a factual issue, that pretty much locks you out, because the

192 WITH EDWARDS IN THE GOVERNOR'S MANSION

Supreme Court will not reverse unless there is a very clear error."

"Was there any discussion, after the motion to suppress was denied, about the possibility of working out a guilty plea bargain?"

"Yes, there was. I discussed it with Mr. Hammond, and I discussed it—ah, when I say I 'discussed it,' I know that it was discussed in my presence. I don't know if I was the one who discussed it or if it was Murphy Bell in my presence who discussed it with his father," Hebert said.

Hebert, realizing his error, was attempting to edit his words. In 1973, he had only recently graduated from law school and was barred from discussing pleas with a client in a capital case. *Hebert realized that the legal circumstances of Saint's case were in direct contradiction to what he had just said.* Anding would later get him for making that error. Saint observed that even Polozola did not believe Hebert's testimony.

Anding, realizing what Hebert and Castle were doing, plunged directly into the issue. "At the conclusion of the hearing on this motion to suppress, and after it was denied, you reserved a bill of exception then, did you not, after the court overruled the motion?"

"Yes, I did."

"Why did you reserve that bill of exception?"

"Because if you wanted to preserve an erroneous ruling for review by a higher court, you had to reserve a bill of exception."

"Following the suppress hearing, did Mr. Hammond indicate to you that he thought the ruling was erroneous? In other words, he didn't indicate, 'Well, they're right and I'm wrong'?"

"No, he did not back off of the fact that the police promised him that he would still go to college on his scholarship in exchange for his statement. He did not back off that position."

"Did you ever seek appellate review of the motion?"

"No, I did not," Hebert admitted.

"Now, you have testified, Mr. Hebert, that you reserved a bill of exception because you felt that the judge's decision to deny the motion to suppress was erroneous?"

"That is correct, Counselor."

"I show you what purports to be copies of motions, to refresh your recollection."

"Yes, that's my handwriting. I filed these motions. I recognize my signature."

"If you filed these seven motions, Mr. Hebert, how do you explain that they were never actually filed with the clerk of court? There is a difference between filing a motion and drafting a motion, is that right?"

"That's right, but that . . . whatever had happened was . . . I don't recall—it's been five years," Hebert said.

"So, before you advise a defendant to plead guilty in a capital case to a life sentence, with seven motions pending, should you not have exhausted every available means to secure his defense before you begin thinking about telling him to plead guilty or before you sought a plea bargain? So my question is, why did you not seek appellate review of the motion in the early stages of Mr. Hammond's case?"

"At that time, and at the present time, prior to conviction, the only manner in which you can seek appellate review is by applying for a writ of certiorari, and the Supreme Court does not grant writs of certiorari on denial of a motion to suppress the confession."

"And you're saying that as a blanket statement, that they never do that?"

"I've never seen them do it while I worked there."

"Do they have authority to grant a writ?"

"Yes, Counselor, they have the authority, absolutely."

"But you considered it to be a vain and futile effort to appeal that?" Anding asked.

"That's correct," Hebert replied.

Polozola called Coach Bates as a court witness. "As far as you could tell, Coach, did anyone try to force him to plead guilty?" Polozola asked.

"Not with any physical force but with the force of words. It was force through words but not force through physical, you know. So as being a seventeen-year-old boy, he was scared, crying, confused. He didn't know which way to go," Coach Bates explained.

"So, in other words, Coach Bates, during the discussion you said that was going on, was he getting advice both ways on the question?"

"Oh yes, it was about *six of us in there*, so he was getting a little from me, a little from somebody, a little from somebody else, and from his lawyer."

"Was Forest Hammond talking also, or was it just a general discussion?"

"He didn't say too much. He was mostly listening. He would respond, '*But I didn't do nothing. I didn't do that.*' He would respond like that."

"You state it took a long time to make up his mind?"

"Yes. An hour and about forty-five minutes before I got back there; then two more hours. And then a bailiff came in and told us to hurry up because the judge was running late for his lunch appointment."

"Did Mr. Woodson Callihan indicate that Forest Hammond had made up his mind?"

"No. That was the problem. He said that's what's wrong. He wouldn't make up his mind, and Forest needed to plead guilty because that's the best thing for him. He refused to say he was guilty. See, that's the reason why they came and got me. Since I was his football coach, they figured he'd listen to me. They wanted me to tell him to plead guilty, and I told him I couldn't tell him to plead guilty like that. I told them I just couldn't tell him that."

As the hearing came to a close, Polozola began making subtle threats and attempting to intimidate Saint into withdrawing his petition. He implied that Saint could get a sentence even worse than life. Saint knew that Polozola was talking to him as if he was still that seventeen-year-old nigger boy who didn't know a thing about the laws that applied to his case. However, since Hebert had been caught in several lies, Saint felt he had won the case. Saint's final statement on the witness stand was, "I have a strong desire. I want to be free."

"Boy, there is either a lot of misunderstanding or a lot of perjury going on in this case, but I'm going to get to the bottom of it, whether it's a lawyer or a defendant, or whether it's a witness or a schoolteacher," Polozola said. "That's nothing related to you, Mr. Hammond, but there has been a direct contradiction all the way through this case. If I have to get the U.S. attorney to stay with the grand jury for fifty years, I'm getting to the bottom of this. If I've got to call every other witness and retry this case, I'm going to do it, with the transcript. I am going to take it line by line in this case. I want everybody to understand, you may know some of these witnesses, you may not; but I was very upset by the fact that there were extreme conflicts in the testimony presented in the trial. I mean, there've been some absolutely direct contradictory statements made that I just can't ignore. Don't be surprised when the FBI goes out and interviews every witness. If it's memory, that's one thing. If it's deliberately lying to me, it's something else. So, Mr. Hammond will be returned to Angola. Court is adjourned."

PART II

Chapter 10

Leaving That Place, Angola

Out on the trustee yard at 5:30 A.M., the figure of a lone runner moving along the illuminated fence line between the night prison lamps was not alarming to the guards. The figure stopped under each lamp and then moved in a tight circle. His bending forward at the waist was accompanied by a spring in his step as he danced his in-and-out moves. He bobbed and weaved, then circled in the opposite direction. He would throw countless combination punches, then take off sprinting to the next lamp along the fence line, disappearing into the fog. There he repeated his drills.

This was my ritual each morning after running my usual five miles. I loved running and breathing the fresh Angola air.

The week of Valentine's Day was humid and foggy. I continued to get up at 0500 hours and ran my five miles with my hands wrapped. *"One of these days gonna be the last time I strap this gear on,"* I found myself saying every morning as I dressed for training. I didn't have to train as hard, since I hadn't had a fight in eight months, and no upcoming fight was scheduled. I had reached my peak condition and just maintained it by running either in the morning or at noon. Even though this was Angola, I had to admit that the air we breathed here was ever so fresh. Training for me now had become therapy that I needed.

"Keep going, Fats, keep going. You can make it," I implored. Fats dropped the leg end of the military stretcher. I carried the head end, straining to keep it up as the other end dragged on the ground. Still 250 yards from the hospital, I saw the end coming and wished for a miracle. Finally, I turned the stretcher around and pushed it from the head end as if it were a football sled.

I could hear Coach Bates yelling, *"Keep your legs moving! Pump 'em! Pump 'em!"*

The front handles hit a seam in the concrete, stopping the stretcher abruptly. I swung Graveyard around and pulled him over the seam, dragging him towards D-Block.

"*I can make it. I can make it,*" I kept telling myself. I was wearing my boxing training clothes, and my hands were wrapped. Stepping in blood, I slipped and dropped the stretcher to the concrete. The impact accelerated Graveyard's death. I tried to stay on my feet but staggered and fell into the security fence. I was tired and winded, and everything hurt. I couldn't get up. I saw the same glassy look in Graveyard's eyes that I had seen in Edna's eyes. I crawled to my friend and held his head in my hand. Graveyard's body arched, his back lifting off the stretcher. He grimaced as his body slowly sank back down. A thick bubble came out of his mouth like chewing gum. It continued to enlarge, stretching to the size of a basketball before bursting and covering his face as his body lay flat and motionless. He died looking at his friend. I was unable to help or save him.

My body coiled up as I watched the guards and three trustees rush out of the cellblocks. They picked up the stretcher and ran off with Graveyard. Fats lay forty feet away, vomiting on the walk. I sat with my back against the fence, then slowly lay down, gasping. The control-center gate buzzed open. Two teams of convicts carrying another stretcher came through. Leonard Turner and his sidekick, Black, were both dead. They had ambushed Graveyard thirty seconds after the door was opened for chow, stabbing him in the back, but Graveyard killed them both with their own knives and twisted Turner's head nearly off. He now lay on the stretcher on his back but with his face down.

Angola, Angola, I thought as I lay gasping. *I gotta get outta here.* I could feel the nearby presence of the Death Angel as I recalled Graveyard's friendship.

Johnny Frank, a young black freeman from Moreauville, stopped in the aisle at the foot of my bunk. He stood there a moment before making any sound. "Hammond," he said, softly at first. "*Hammond!*" he said louder and with more urgency.

I sat up quickly, brushed my face with my left hand, and focused on Frank through one eye. He had never done this before. "What can I do for you, Mr. Frank?"

"I got a call to have you at the A Building for seven o'clock this morning. You being transferred to the state police barracks." He was out of breath from rushing over to deliver the good news.

Leaving Angola was the most important news a convict could receive. Even the freemen didn't like to be in Angola, and they only worked there.

"Let me see," I said, reaching for the thin strip of paper that was my gate pass. With both eyes now opened so as to not misread anything, I read it twice, then backwards to make sure it said what I thought Frank said. "Now that's what I'm talkin' 'bout! Kiss my black a--, Mr. Frank. Ah, not you but Angola—ah, you know what I mean. I'll be ready as soon as I get out my bunk. To hell with making this motha' up. Let me brush my teeth and wash my face and I'm ready *rat now,* Mr. Frank!" I shouted. Johnny Frank smiled. He liked me as a friend.

I was ready in less than five minutes. I grabbed my six-year-old breadbox with all my personal effects and hit the big green door, headed up the walk.

"I'm outta this motha', y'all!" I shouted when I entered the law library.

Victor leaned back in his chair, smiling. His arms lay across his big stomach as he held a cup of coffee in his left hand. I gave Shorty and Sioux Dog all my cases, case-file log, and deadline sheet. Rufus claimed my desk for himself.

"Say, Saint, when I win that big case, boy, you ain't gonna be able to just walk into my office," Shorty said, smiling. "I'm-a have young female receptionist, female bodyguards, female stress counselors, female secretaries, drivers, nurses, and cooks—all in bikinis."

Sioux Dog was next in line to wish me well. He had been here since 1960 and was still able to rejoice for anyone who left Angola. He promised to keep filing suits and writs. All of the law-library crew had hopes of winning the Herbert Hatcher class-action civil-rights suit filed against Warden Maggio for the Camp J beatings.

Victor came up and firmly put his hands on my shoulders as if preparing to hug me. "Now, Saint. You take good care of yourself, you hear? You're going someplace in life—just keep that attitude. Remember, there are four things that come not back: the spoken word, a spent arrow, time past, and a neglected opportunity. Don't forget that."

"All right, Victor Linkletter. You take care of yourself too. I enjoyed working with you, old man, and I won't ever forget the blitzkrieg you taught me in chess."

Burke, with tears, offered to carry my breadbox to the A Building for some last-minute words of advice. I had trained him for disciplinary-court cases. We embraced. "I'm-a miss you, Saint. I can't help it, brother," he said.

"Burke, stay away from them drugs and get outta this motha', you hear me?" I turned to see black Mississippi coming out of the A Building. He had worked at the governor's mansion but had been sent back. The hospital-gate freeman stood watching us. "Mississippi, I'm going to the police barracks," I said.

"That's fine, that's fine," he replied. "Come here, Youngblood," he added. With his arm around my shoulder, he walked me out of earshot of the freeman. "Don't trust nobody, *anyone! Do you hear me?* And keep your name away from the ears of Detective Joe Whitmore. He's State Police Intelligence. If you do anything, he will find out and you're back up here like me. Now listen at me! *Listen! Are you listening?*" Mississippi asked, his voice conveying a clear urgency. "Whitmore will crawl on his hands, knees, and on his belly in the mud, rain, sleet, or snow at night in freezing weather under a house in a brand-new suit to bust you. He and Detective Bob are like twin brothers." He stared to see if I fully grasped the gravity of what he was saying about Detective Whitmore. Thus assured, he said, "Take care, Youngblood," and departed towards the control center.

A freeman was waiting for me on the visitor's side of the A Building. It was 0630 hours. I was early. "Can I load up now, Chief?" I asked. The old redneck guard behind the cage looked over his black-frame glasses and asked if I was Hammond. "That's me in the flesh, Chief," I said, grinning. With the press of a button, he released the lock. I pushed the iron gate with my breadbox, making it swing open to allow me to walk through. "Do I have to sign out, Chief?" I asked, as if I was checking out of Hotel Angola—California.

"Naw, go ahead. We got the orders," he growled, waving me through.

"You're Hammond?" a short white man in plain clothes asked. I dropped my box in front of him and extended both my hands together so he could shackle me in cuffs. "Oh, no!" he said. "You're a trustee. You're going to the police barracks."

I was smelling freedom on the other side of the front gate. As long as I was still inside here, though, the Death Angel had its talons fastened tightly to my mind and I knew it. Death is always present in Angola.

The freeman opened the rear tailgate of the station wagon. I put my breadbox in and got in the backseat, as if he was my driver and I was the boss. We made a quick stop at the front gate to clear security and then drove away for the first time in six years. It felt really good.

"Freeman, you mind if I roll my window down for a second?" I asked.

"Go ahead," he said, a little curious.

I stuck my head out the window and for one brief moment, I could see myself standing at the front gate on November 8, 1973, weighted down by a life sentence. Turtle and the other three prisoners were behind me as we all baby-stepped up the long walkway and AU convicts stuck their heads out the upstairs window yelling at us. The station wagon rocked after hitting a dip in the road. It brought me back to the reason why I asked to roll the window down.

"*Goodbye, Angola! Kiss my black a--, you bastard,*" I yelled. As the car sped off, we cleared the summit of the hill. The front gate of the Louisiana State Peniversity disappeared from sight as my words still echoed through the thickly wooded Tunica Hills. I had graduated and was moving on to further my education.

I noticed the freeman shaking his head chuckling as I pulled my head back into the car. The Death Angel seemed to have lifted off my back and out of my mind as we drove away. "How much time do you have?" Grandpa asked. Convicts always give nicknames to those they have to spend time with—even if it's only the driver during a brief ride to town.

"Natural life," I said to him instead of at him.

"How long you be incarcerated?"

"Five years and ten months," I said without thinking.

"You're one of the lucky ones," he replied. "Yeah, you're lucky."

The distance from Angola to Baton Rouge in terms of miles is short. If you have been sitting on a bunk covered with sweat in a hot dormitory, or in a six-by-eight-foot cell, or on the concrete floor of the dungeon, with tons of time to serve and thick layers of judicial red tape stretching before you, that journey can become equal to the distance between Earth and the most distant star— light years away.

We drove into the front entrance of the Louisiana State Police headquarters on South Foster Drive. I immediately recognized Capt. M. L. Hugh in the guard shack as one of the officers who sprayed me with mace in the city jail the day I was arrested. For a brief instant,

I saw the flash of recognition in his eyes. He remembered. He said nothing to me and I said nothing to him. All communication was through our eyes.

The station wagon slowly moved along a narrow black asphalt street and came to a stop in front of a military-type barracks building. Grandpa checked me into the barracks office. I could feel the eyes of the other trustees on me. I had lived this scene before.

Chapter 11

Voices and Echoes at the Mansion

I was here and couldn't believe it. Deep down, however, I knew that if the general public ever found out about my presence in town, they would protest. I had to be mouse quiet and stay away from the news media. I became suspicious of everyone.

I wasn't sure how I got here. The fact that I had never pled guilty was clearly on record. But maybe it's the boxing that got me here. Billy Roth said he would see what he could do after he saw me fight Tom Landry, the ninth-ranked contender in the United States in the A.A.U. light-heavyweight division. So many possible explanations went through my mind, but I could not settle on a single one.

When Grandpa checked me in with my LSP identification card, I thanked him and shook his hand. He started to tell me something but caught himself. "Well, you've made it this far," he said. "You know how to make it. You know what to do. Keep doing what you've been doing." Then he left.

All of the barracks' corrections officers were dressed in plain clothes. Fred Kennedy was the first Louisiana state trooper I met. I thought it strange when he made it a point to come and shake my hand and introduce himself. He looked like Warden Maggio's twin brother.

Mr. Williams, a short black freeman, led me through double doors into a dormitory. He gave me a top bunk on the corner. From my bunk I could see through the windows of the swinging double doors into the activity room. Williams then walked me around the barracks, showing me the points of interest. "Just relax. You'll be all right," he said.

After making my bunk, taking a shower, changing into white pants and a short-sleeve shirt, and getting settled in, I was led by a tall, blond, blue-eyed state trooper to a barbershop in the barracks complex. *There goes my Afro,* I thought, watching my hair fall to the floor. Next, he drove me to Independence Boulevard, where I got my driver's license. Our next stop was Goudchaux's Department Store on Main Street, where he purchased black dress socks, lace-up shoes, and a pair of white Chuck Taylor All-Star high-top shoes for me.

"Forest, are you hungry?" he asked after we got in his dark-blue unmarked unit. "Do you want anything to eat? Whatever you want, just name it."

This is special care, I thought. "You'll get me anything I want?" I asked. I wondered who told him to do this. Whose orders was he following? Who was he working for? *Okay, how about a taste of freedom,* I thought.

I began eating as soon as we received the food at the drive-thru window. I was starting to feel human again. I had forgotten I could feel this way. I sat back in the state police unit, eating and enjoying the scenery of the city, especially the fine women. *Hmmmm,* I thought. *I'm dressed in all white; I got a haircut, a driver's license, and new shoes; and I'm eating a Big Mac, French fries, and a hot apple pie and washing it down with a large Coke. I'm doing real good. I wonder if he could fix me up with a good piece of p---- and a cold glass of water. Damn!* Thinking of this sitting next to the state trooper made me want to laugh out loud. He saw me acting funny, unaware that I was trying to hold it in. I thought, *Well, maybe I'm crazy now, all the s--- I've been through.*

"What's the matter, Forest? Are you all right?" he asked, seeing I'd kept my head turned away from him.

The car beside us had several women passengers who saw me with both cheeks full of food as I chewed. I crossed my eyes and must have looked like an idiot to them. They were all laughing at me. I was smiling with a mouthful of food. I finally swallowed. "Ah, I was just thinking about something, that's all."

For the next two weeks I was assigned to operate the drink machine in the Department of Public Safety and Corrections cafeteria.

You are working in this place that the public is accessing. Be aware that you are being watched. They want to transition you and see how well you work with the public. Watch how you greet people, serve drinks, handle the money, and respond to requests for refills. Smile, be nice and diligent about helping them, and be as friendly as you can.

I couldn't afford to be caught staring at any of the women's behinds, regardless of how delicious they looked. Those watching me might think I was a sex maniac. The good white folks knew what Angola could do to a man's mind after a period of time. I wouldn't look at any behind directly, but my peripheral vision should have burned their clothes off. A woman would come to my counter and get her drink, and when she turned back around, her sensuous gluteus maximus would be staring me square in the face as if grinning and daring me to take a much-needed peek. I knew if I looked, I might be history. I felt I would be locked in, mesmerized and unable to turn away once their curves captured my attention. The women's perfume only intensified my desire to be close to them.

I made an extra effort not to bump into any of the women working behind the counter with me. It almost seemed that they wanted their breasts to touch my arm, shoulder, or back as they moved about. I ducked and dodged to keep from making any contact with them, all the while thinking, *I could use these moves in the ring in my next fight. I could turn this into a workout.*

If I were still in Angola, the thoughts occupying my mind would be fine. But now it was different. I saw each woman customer as a challenge to my willpower. One day during a particularly difficult inner struggle, a voice in my head had me considering diving over the counter and bulldogging them as if they were steers in the Angola rodeo. I bit my tongue to keep from smiling. I bit it harder to keep from laughing. The voice was coming more and more frequently, taunting me and telling me all kinds of crazy things.

I was afraid that if I accidentally touched a woman or one touched me, the chemical reaction would be so devastating that I would lose all self-control. I hadn't made it this far to sell out for sex. Fresh air from the Mississippi River made my sense of smell as acute as an Angola bloodhound's. If push came to shove, I could just walk out on the balcony at breaktime, inhale deeply, and smell all the females in the parish.

After I cleaned my workstation each day and ended my shift at 5:00 P.M., I sat at a table in the barracks activity room, playing solitaire until late at night. Fourteen convicts who worked at the governor's mansion always came into the barracks around that time. They were exhausted and relieved to be back. When they came into the main lobby, the older men went straight to bed, while the younger ones walked around looking for something to do that would allow them to claim part of the day for themselves. They eventually followed the old men and collapsed onto their own bunks. None of them ever talked to other inmates, nor was there ever a word spoken in the barracks about what went on inside the governor's mansion.

Early in Governor Edwards' first term in office (1972-76), he experienced a lot of stomach problems. His physician told him it was the food he was eating, which at that time was being catered to the mansion. Elaine Edwards then hired a chef to cook the food at the mansion, but the governor's stomach problems persisted. The first lady fired and hired chef after chef. Mississippi, an assistant chef who had witnessed the governor's gastronomical illnesses, told her that there was a convict in the cellblock lockdown who was a really good cook.

"Why is he in the cellblock lockdown?" Elaine asked. "Is he dangerous? Has he killed anyone since he's been in Angola?"

"Oh, no ma'am," Mississippi replied. "He was selling food out the kitchen. The inmates be hungry in the dormitory at night and he'd bring food to the dormitory and sell it. Just some eggs, bread, peanut butter, jelly, sometimes a little ham and sausage and pork chops. He'd bring it after the last meal, but he's a chef, a real good chef, ma'am."

The first lady got on the phone, called the warden at Angola, and told him to have Bobby Turner shaved, showered, barbered, and issued new clothes, because she was sending the state police helicopter in one hour to pick him up. On its return, the chopper landed on the front lawn of the mansion. Bobby got out carrying a pillowcase with his personal effects and an old raggedy transistor radio. He was interviewed by Mrs. Edwards and told that he would be pardoned at the end of the governor's term. Governor Edwards never had any more problems with his stomach. The promise of a pardon was broken when Edwards was reelected in 1975 and Bobby was retained at the mansion another four years. During the first term, Bobby tried to be a model prisoner, but when he wasn't released, his attitude soured somewhat.

Bobby knew everybody who was somebody in the state: every senator, state representative, district attorney, sheriff, and police chief. He knew wealthy businessmen, all the big-time lawyers, bankers, offshore-drilling contractors, and everyone who visited the mansion as an invited guest for any type of function. If there was a function, premium food was served and Bobby cooked it. Scheduled guests ate in the state dining room. Others ate in the private rear dining room, five steps from Bobby's workstation.

A stool in the corner by the window gave him a clear view of every car passing in front of the mansion going west towards the

State Capitol. If a car turned in coming from the State Capitol, Bobby couldn't see it, but one of the butlers saw it for him. A butler was at the front door to offer every visitor coffee, tea, soda, juice, or water. When the butler went to the butler's station to prepare a guest tray, Bobby found out who the guest was. Guests always announced their name and purpose for being at the mansion to the security intelligence officer at the front desk. The butlers heard it all. If they didn't, Bobby would inconspicuously walk into the foyer to see the guest's face. Everybody who came to the mansion represented potential dollars for Bobby. These wealthy people kept bankrolls in their pockets, and Bobby fed them all very well. They fell in love with Bobby's likeable and witty personality. It was common practice for them to tip him fifty or one hundred dollars.

Panhandlers were as common at the mansion as on the downtown sidewalks. Everyone wanted something. Members of the governor's cabinet stopped by the mansion daily for a free cup of coffee and to see what news they could get on the "Silver Fox"'s activities. They always sought Bobby out for a heads up. "What's the governor up to?" "Is the governor in town?" "For how long?" "Who's been over here to see him?" "How long did they talk?" "When is his next scheduled out-of-state trip?" "Where will he be going?"

Bobby began charging them for the information they sought, and he upped the price of lunch in the private dining room when the governor was out of town. They gave him twenty dollars and got twenty dollars worth of information. Fifty dollars got fifty dollars worth. For one hundred dollars, Bobby gave them "a big hot baked potato," which was information they could only partially verify. They paid him because of vanity. They simply had to know something that others did not.

On weekends, when the first family was out or at LSU football games, the mansion had only three security personnel. Bobby would ease into the scheduling secretary's office and read her list of upcoming events. A few feet from the elevator was the entrance to the governor's office. Before he made his move on the governor's office, with its correspondence and files, he made sure the coast was clear. Bobby fed mansion security well so they would be full and more than likely take a short nap on the sofa in the lounge at the back desk and not go on routine patrol inside the mansion. A butler was stationed at the front and back desks, and a butler or cook would always be in the basement getting supplies. If mansion security started walking, the butler in the basement rang the butler's station on the first floor, alerting Bobby to get back to his station.

When George Fisher, head of the Department of Transportation and Development, would ask about the governor without paying the proper tribute, Bobby would go into his *Amos 'n' Andy* routine, pretending to have lost his memory. He would act like the stupidest, most uneducated nigger on the face of the earth. When George tipped him, Bobby would serve him a big lie. Bobby would say when he departed, "F--- 'em! They a bunch of lying bastards, anyway. I just give them what they deserve. All the people they lie to, you think I care?"

When an information seeker attempted to siphon information out of Bobby without paying, he would open the hot oven and sprinkle cayenne pepper inside. The rising heat carried pepper particles into the eyes of anyone around. "I'm purging the kitchen; I'm purging the kitchen," Bobby would announce. In less than a minute there would be nobody around but the convicts. Everybody else ran out with eyes burning.

Bobby had a practical hand in raising the governor's children. He taught them like a street hustler. The penitentiary wisdom he imparted to them was unavailable in the state universities. Steve and Victoria got the message; Anna rejected it outright. David was receptive in his own big, childish way. The entire family loved Bobby. Of course, some did not express their feelings openly, like Mrs. Edwards and Anna. But Steve, Victoria, David, and the governor, or "Pops" as Bobby joined his kids in calling him outside his presence, loved Bobby Turner and showed it openly.

The legislative session always began unofficially at the governor's mansion. The Senate president, House speaker, businessmen, key lobbyists, and others gathered there to get a head start by conferring with the governor on important legislation. At 7:00 A.M. on the day of the first 1979 pre-legislative meeting at the mansion, equipment was delivered to the public parking lot across from the rear drive. Long tables, folding chairs, waste containers, plastic bags, large ice chests, butane gas tanks, huge boiling pots, and cardboard soft-drink cartons were moved and set in place by butlers. Bobby was easily recognized in his white chef's jacket and chef's hat. He gave Francis, his assistant, last-minute instructions for boiling the crawfish and shrimp and frying the catfish. Bobby then went back inside to continue preparing his huge lunch menu.

Slim, the tall, dark-skinned driver of the Krewe of da Mansion van, and his sidekick, BigOne, washed the first couple's vehicles. By ten o'clock that morning, the mansion grounds were covered with vehicles. Inside, the mansion was packed. Some guests huddled in groups. Others saw the governor briefly and left.

Damon Robicheaux drove a country-squire station wagon up the mansion drive, making his way through the line of new vehicles parked on both sides. He was slowly pulling a double horse trailer. Robicheaux was just returning from Governor Edwards' ranch in Junction, Texas, bringing a young colt and Diamond, a beautiful Arabian cutting horse, to the mansion for Edwards to inspect before taking them to the governor's new home being built on Highland Road. A makeshift stable had been built near the public parking lot on the mansion grounds to keep the horses.

After Robicheaux unloaded and saddled Diamond, Governor Edwards got on the horse to exercise its skills. He rode it hard on the long strip of the mansion lawn. He stopped him suddenly, cutting on a dime. Diamond shifted left and right, pivoting on his hind legs. A small crowd of guests applauded the governor's riding skills. Paul Fontenot, the best-dressed bodyguard, hovered at the edge of the lawn with his suitcoat opened to allow him quick access to the weapon in his shoulder holster. He kept a watchful eye on passing vehicles as well as all activity around the governor.

Inside the mansion, Mrs. Edwards walked Laura through the foyer, sitting room, and drawing room, showing her all the draperies she wanted changed. Meanwhile, those who wanted face time with the governor jockeyed for position to convey their requests to the first lady. It was her role to screen the requests. She casually made her way through the crowd, pausing to speak with businessmen. One man appeared to be listening in but quickly stepped aside when he thought she saw him. She caught his move out of the corner of her eye, however, and turned to shake his hand. As she did so, he leaned forward, whispering in her ear what he needed to say in his precious few seconds of allotted pitch time. She smiled, acting as if the man had just told her a funny joke before continuing on to the next guest.

State Police Capt. Gene Jones seated a hardworking shrimp-boat fisherman, his wife, and their attorney in the foyer by the governor's office. They would be seen first. Jones and another bodyguard, Butch Miley, fine-tuned a list of all the people who would see the governor and the order in which they would see him. It was a daunting task.

When the elevator opened, Paul Fontenot got off first, followed by Governor Edwards, who waved at the guests as he walked towards his office. Edwards noticed the small box of preserves resting on the lap of the fisherman's wife.

In the kitchen, Mike Mix, head of mansion functions, was in constant communication with Bobby. As the number of people who would be staying and eating lunch changed, Mike relayed the latest number to Bobby, who in turn would instruct Francis and Sally, the dishwasher, on what to get from the supply room in the basement.

Everyone always wondered how Bobby was going to pull off each function costing thousands of dollars. They never seemed to have faith in him until the event was over, the mansion drive and parking lot were vacated, and the butlers were resetting the state dining table for the first family's evening meal—all without incident.

"Governor, this is his second misdemeanor drug conviction," the attorney said, reading from his client's file. "The thirteen disciplinary reports in his Department of Correction file were basically involving fights where he acted in self-defense." Edwards sat at his desk, listening to the attorney plead the case of the Cajun fisherman's son. The man and his wife sat together on a leather sofa as the wife poured creamer and stirred their coffee. They both watched the lawyer. Edwards saw them squinting, as if the lawyer was not saying what he had promised them. The governor raised his left hand, cutting the attorney off. He turned to the old man and asked him in Cajun French, "How much did you pay this attorney to represent your son?"

"Ten thousand dollars and twenty sacks of live crawfish and live shrimps each," the old man answered in French. His wife nudged him but he ignored her at first. Then he leaned to hear her whisper. He straightened and continued. "He wanted twenty thousand, but that's all the money I have. The hurricane weather gave us a bad harvest this season. He wanted more crawfish, but the season just started. I told him I was bringing the crawfish I had and he wasn't getting no more," the old man said, his wife nodding approvingly. The butler, Devold, waited patiently as the wife finished mixing the creamer into her coffee. The lawyer didn't like the expression on the old man's face as he spoke.

Edwards got up, walked around his desk, and stood before the couple. "A rotten sack of crawfish," he said, still speaking French. "Look, I'm going to make him refund you half of your money.

Your son will be home before the next Pecan Festival. Put him to work on your shrimp boat." The governor twisted open a jar of muscadine jelly from the box the wife was holding, stuck his finger in, and tasted it. "Boy, that's so good, so good!" he exclaimed. "I love muscadine jelly." The old woman smiled.

The governor shook the couple's hands and opened the door for them as they exited. He then whispered to the attorney, who nodded and gave a weak, embarrassed smile. The lawyer followed the couple into the foyer, through the crowd of people, and out the front door.

As the governor went to his desk, the main door behind him opened, causing him to turn. Before Capt. Gene Jones spoke, however, Mrs. Edwards appeared in the foyer doorway. The governor turned his head to look at his wife. The captain, who did not see the first lady, spoke first. "You better come see," he said. "Damon says he thinks the colt has colic. I called Dr. Chat Kleinpeter. He said he's finishing another call and will be here in ten minutes." The governor nodded.

Mrs. Edwards beckoned with her index finger at her waist and tilted her head towards the elevator. She walked out of view and pressed the elevator button. The governor left his study and got on the elevator with his wife. The door closed behind them.

Joining the Krewe of da Mansion

Every time I see him, something's up, I thought when I saw my friend the blond, blue-eyed state trooper enter the cafeteria. It was one o'clock and lunch was over. He asked me to come take a ride with him. I didn't ask questions. The managers and supervisors were nodding when I turned to tell them I had to go. They all smiled and waved.

"Let's see, haircut, driver's license, tennis shoes, black shoes, and socks—I think that's it. Do you have any idea where we're going now?" he asked as we drove off in his unit.

I did good, so y'all bring me to get some poontang, I thought but didn't say. "No sir, I don't," I answered, "but I know you're going to tell me, right?"

He chuckled. "Look, you're going to have an interview with the first lady."

"You talking about Eve?" I asked.

The trooper fought to keep a straight face but couldn't hold his laughter. "Now, tell me that was a joke. You got to tell me that," he said.

Joke, my a--, I thought. I was serious. The good white folks had gone to the moon. They might have figured out a way to go back in time and bring Eve back.

"No, that's the governor's wife, Elaine," he explained. "She's the first lady. She's a strange woman, so make sure you are very courteous to her. You can make it. You've made it this far. You'll be all right. Look, I hear things. I can't really tell you about it now, but I've heard things. Who have you trusted to get this far?"

"I've trusted me." He wouldn't believe me telling him about the voice of my invisible friend.

"Well, don't trust anyone over here except the old man. Besides him, 'anyone' means 'everybody.' Don't trust nobody over here," he repeated.

I accepted his warning as a token of genuine concern for me. I recalled what I had observed of the Krewe of da Mansion when they came into the barracks late at night.

The state trooper got on his unit radio and said, "107 to mansion security."

"Go ahead, 107."

"I'm, ah, two minutes from the back desk, with, ah . . . " he paused and thought a second, then continued, " . . . ah, with Mrs. Edwards' package."

I began to feel butterflies. I was a "package." Why didn't he say my name so it could be heard over the airwaves?

"That's a 10-4, 107. I'll see you when I see you. Over."

"Hammond, I want to tell you something, so listen to me good," the trooper said. "You know we first met a long time ago." It wasn't so much a question as a declaration.

"No, I didn't know that."

"I'm going to make you remember the first time I saw you, okay?" he asked.

"Okay."

"Do you remember ever being at Earl K. Long Hospital on Airline Highway in 1973?"

"Ah, no sir. I don't remember ever being over there," I answered truthfully but with a degree of uncertainty. The year 1973 was not a good year for me. I turned to read his eyes, but he looked straight ahead.

He described to me the condition I was in when he first saw me being rolled into the emergency room on a stretcher and later, as I sat handcuffed to a wheelchair. Scenes began bouncing inside my head, like a slide projector malfunctioning at high speed. There I was being wheeled to the emergency-room entrance by EMTs. My head, face, and hands were stitched, bandaged, and throbbing with pain with each heartbeat. When I heard the voice of someone I knew from Capitol High, I managed to look up. It was Shine, ol' Black Shine, and as always he had a hat on, this one purple. He was talking to people about me but didn't know it was me.

"Hey, Shine, give me cigarette," I muttered through swollen lips. He didn't understand or even turn around. "Hine! Hine!" I said louder. The pain was excruciating. Someone told Shine I was talking to him.

"Who, me? You talking to me?" Shine asked. "Do I know you? What's your name?"

"*Oris. Oris. Oris Ammon!*" I managed to mumble.

"Forest Hammond! Forest, that's you? What happened? Who did this to you?" he asked.

"Hib he higarette, a higarette!"

"You want a cigarette, Forest?" Shine took a Kool out, lit it, and stuck it in my mouth. He held it while I took a draw on it. "Forest, who did this to you?" Shine asked again. "We gonna get 'em."

Talk was extremely painful. Then a gold stripe on the blue pants leg of a Louisiana state trooper stepped into view in front of me.

"Sir, I'm going to have to ask you not to ask him any more questions. It's hurting him to speak," the trooper said. He had been standing to the side, listening as I named everyone in the clique. I never saw his face, but the voice talking now was the same voice from 1973.

"You were beaten and stabbed in the parish jail," he said. "I first saw you on the hospital loading dock."

I just let him describe what he saw while I quietly relived it all. The hatred and desire to kill welled up inside me again. Now I was closer to getting those who had set the whole thing up: Ossie Brown, Judge Lear, Warren Hebert, Sergeant Daigle, Capt. M. L. Hugh, the deputies who threatened to lynch me, the cop who called me a nigger, and lying police detectives Bob and Jimmy. Even as the thoughts raced through my mind, *something* told me not to do that.

Seeing the governor's mansion come into view made me remember years ago when Paul and I drove past it first as little boys, then later as teenagers, riding in the fire wagon with Michael and David to go clean offices. We always wondered what went on inside that place. Now, I was actually going there and would soon find out.

Once we arrived at the back of the mansion, the trooper continued his warnings. "Don't forget. She's a strange woman. Answer her, 'yes ma'am' and 'no ma'am.'"

I got out and followed him to the back desk in the basement. Inside the back office, I noticed a white man sitting at the desk, observing us. "Mrs. Edwards said to let you know she'll be upstairs on the second floor in the bookroom," said Lt. Danny Hart, a trooper in his late thirties. He was dressed in a nice suit with a yellow shirt and a tie that featured the Looney Tunes characters.

"Hell, I don't want to go up there and see her," the trooper replied. "Get one of the butlers to take him." Turning to me, he said, "Well, I'll see you, my friend. They'll take care of you from here. I'm very glad to see you are doing all right and made it this far. Take care now."

"Thanks for everything," I said, never thinking to look at his name badge. I thought I wouldn't talk to him again, although I expected to see him in the course of going back and forth to the barracks.

Capt. Gene Jones rushed off the elevator into the basement lounge. "What are you doing?" he asked me. From my white-pants uniform, he knew I was a convict. I was wearing what the Krewe of da Mansion wore each night when they came back in.

"Captain, this is the new guy. Just arrived," Hart said quickly.

"Come with me," the Captain ordered and went out the back door. I followed him up the ramp and to the stable, where BigOne was holding a colt. "He hasn't tried to lie down, has he, Ellis?" Captain Jones asked, using BigOne's real name.

"No sir."

"Look, he's coming to relieve you," the Captain said. "Go finish helping Slim and Vic with the parking. Give him the reins." BigOne gave me the reins and left. "Now, look, whatever you do, don't let him lie down. Keep him up on his feet. We think he might have colic. Dr. Kleinpeter, the vet, is on the way. Let me know when he gets here, okay?"

"Yes sir," I answered, securing the ropes around my hand.

As the Captain was leaving, he decided to avoid the ramp and went instead towards the front door. Governor and Mrs. Edwards were walking up the ramp together, engaged in conversation. The first time I had seen Governor Edwards was when DMB and I attended his inauguration on the steps of the State Capitol, and the last time I saw him was on TV answering reporters' questions about a federal grand jury investigating him. He and his commissioner of administration, Charles E. Roemer II, were being investigated for their alleged connections to Carlos Marcello, purportedly the head of the New Orleans mafia.

The wind began to blow as the first couple stood near the colt's head. She talked while he listened and looked in the colt's face, brushing its neck with his hand. Governor Edwards alternately shook his head in disagreement and nodded in agreement as she made her points. He covered his mouth with his right hand or looked straight down at the ground, so his lips were hidden when he talked to her. Anybody watching from a distance couldn't read his lips. He did it naturally each time he spoke.

I stood at end of the length of the rope, about ten feet away, so I couldn't hear. Mrs. Edwards occasionally became animated in her conversation. The governor looked towards the mansion now and then as if he recognized arriving vehicles. He walked alongside the colt and stood on one side of the animal facing his wife, who stood on the opposite side. I was behind her. While listening, Governor Edwards continued to stroll and now stood directly behind the colt. I wondered if he knew he was standing behind a horse. I was somewhat uneasy, because even though I was only a convict, I knew it was not wise to stand behind horses. They kick.

Whack!

"Oh, Edwin! Are you all right? Does it hurt?" his wife shouted. The kick sounded like a hard plastic cup thrown against a brick wall. Hearing the kick and Edwards' grunt, Mrs. Edwards had dashed away a few steps before stopping. Her instinct of self-preservation had kicked in when the colt kicked the Cajun crap out of the governor. His right hind hoof had struck the governor's left shin. The colt then swung his head around and looked at the governor in a manner reminiscent of Mr. Ed, the talking horse. He looked as though he was asking, *"What did you expect, Fast Eddie?"*

The first lady was now trying to cover for her reaction, but I had seen it all. That fact suddenly became a dire threat to me. For the first ten seconds, the governor couldn't say a word because of the pain. It was as though his mind was searching for an adequate response before he could articulate it. He grimaced, blowing air out through his nostrils and mouth as if he had been holding his breath underwater for several minutes. Sounds that mimicked those made by a hog emanated from his nose and mouth at the same time. Edwards bent over, grabbing his left shin with both hands. He then began bouncing on his right leg. He held his head up to the sky, wearing an expression that said, *I didn't know I could feel like this!*

The governor's tongue was poking in and out repeatedly like a snake's, but faster. As I observed him, his tongue developed a unique lengthwise fold that curled up towards the end, as someone does who knows exactly how to suck on crawfish heads.

Nigger, I dare you! was written all over the first lady's face as she glared at me. I turned my head towards the governor. He was messed up. I started feeling that I better show this lady I didn't have anything to do with this colt kicking him. Her stare looked as though she was trying to find a way to pin the blame on me rather than Governor Edwards because he was distracted by whatever in hell she was telling him. Realizing my helicopter ticket straight back to the front gate of Angola was about ten feet away, watching and waiting for me to crack the slightest smile, I bit my tongue hard, feeling *pain.*

Does it hurt? What a very intelligent question she asked. She must have read a book where somebody got kicked by a horse and it didn't hurt. Damn, Saint. What you think? It makes me think that maybe a whole horse can kick and it won't hurt or cause any pain. I tasted salt in my mouth and realized my tongue was bleeding.

Say, Saint, I sho' hope she don't ask any more of those intelligent first-lady questions. I can't stand it! I began wondering how long I could last. *Man, go ahead and laugh. That's some funny s---. She gonna laugh at it later on, I bet. Stop trying to hold out. Look at her good. She's biting her own tongue. Look at that! The governor's bouncing is original. I'd give him a ten plus if I was judging.*

Realizing that the first lady was still glaring at me, I began looking at the colt to see if I could tell if something was wrong with it. Maybe colic meant muscle spasms. "Ma'am," I said. She rolled her eyes, as if I didn't have permission to talk to her or offer my unsolicited analysis. "Maybe it's the colic, ma'am. One of the men from inside the mansion said he thinks it has colic."

Yeaaaah, you're a smart nigger. She's gonna thank you for that—watch. She never would have thought it was an involuntary reaction by the colt. It did it in response to the position of the moon. The moon affects a lot of thing animals do. Remember the werewolf?

The full moon turned a man into a werewolf, Saint. Remember how Lon Chaney, Jr., turned into a werewolf? She's over fifty; she remembers that. Tell her the moon made that colt kick his a--.

I got the feeling from her expression that I'd better shut up. But I furthered my own convict's diagnosis as if I were an inmate horse doctor. I attempted to give the appearance I was examining the beast to see why it malfunctioned. I *sho' nuff* didn't want her to see me fighting to keep from laughing at the governor out here entertaining me by hopping on one leg, poking his tongue upwards, and acting as if he was sucking on an invisible crawfish head hanging down from heaven. I bit my tongue harder in a new spot.

See, Saint, the colt didn't mean to do it, but it had to kick him for standing directly behind it, because that's what horses do when you violate their law of nature. Everybody knows that! Damn, Saint! Even you know that, and you only got a GED diploma."

"*Ow, ow, ow!*" Edwards began chanting once he finally found his voice. After the pain became bearable, he went hopping back up to the big house with Elaine at his side, helping. I remained with the prizewinning colt. I made sure they were in the mansion, well out of earshot, before I turned in the opposite direction and laughed.

Now, Saint, really bro, I don't care if you was the governor of the universe, you still wouldn't stand behind a horse unless it was a statue, or it didn't have any hind legs, huh? He needed to be kicked, standing behind that colt—like that colt knew he was the governor. I bet he won't stand behind another one.

I stood there thinking. If he's the governor of Louisiana, and he didn't have sense enough to not stand behind a whole live horse, then I could be the governor. I have better sense than that.

I was glad they were finally gone and the comedy was over. My tongue would be sore for the next two days. The vet Kleinpeter came and took the colt away in a horse trailer. I walked down to the back desk. It was about 1:00 P.M.

Chapter 12

Louisiana's Slavery Not Abolished—Just Hidden

The back-desk officer directed me up the stairs to the first floor. When I arrived on the top step, I went through a door that opened up to a hallway with white marble flooring. A tall swinging door was closed to my left. To my right were two white swinging doors. Opened and locked in place, they led into the kitchen. Two chefs were in the kitchen wearing tall white hats. Bobby was one and Francis was the other. Bobby had been sitting, but when he heard the stairwell door open, he stood quickly so whoever was coming would see him working. When he saw it was only me, he retook his seat.

Sally was dressed in all white, operating a steaming-hot, pressurized, commercial dishwasher. He stood with his legs crossed, arms folded, and a toothpick stuck in the left corner of his mouth that he moved to the right side. As soon as Sally saw me, he turned his head away, giving the impression he was unconcerned with who I was. He was already running me through his penitentiary database to determine what kind of problem niggah I was.

"You here to see Mrs. Edwards?" Bobby asked.

"Yeah."

"Say, Phillip, Mrs. Edwards waiting for this dude. Take him up there," Bobby ordered as he studied me. Phillip led me through the door to my left. We then passed the men's and ladies' restrooms and made a quick right turn to enter the elevator foyer. This area had a small antique loveseat, a set of twin chairs on both ends, and a table with a phone, lamp, and vase with fresh beautiful red roses that filled the air with their aroma.

Everything's real over here, a still small voice said. I logged it into my long-term memory.

"How is she?" I whispered after the elevator doors closed. Phillip rolled his eyes up as if to tell me, *"Don't talk in here. The elevator is bugged."* "Gotcha," I said.

The door slid open and I followed him around a corner to a

bookroom. Mike Mix stood leaning against the wall, listening to the first lady. She was sitting on a stool in the doorway of the bookroom, wearing a red long-sleeve sweater and black tights.

"Thirteen thousand dollars!" she exclaimed. "Oh, my gosh. That's too much. Why is it costing so much for one month?"

"Mrs. Edwards, Forest Hammond," Phillip said as Mix left. Phillip was extremely well mannered. He spoke softly, and his eye contact with her was brief as he introduced me and then focused on the floor. He left immediately. She quickly gave me the impression that she had to look at me before I had permission to speak.

Laura walked up from the elevator. The first lady reached inside the bookroom, grabbing a gold envelope. "Laura, you did say $15,733, correct?"

"That is correct, Mrs. Edwards," Laura answered as she took the envelope.

Two black maids in white uniforms walked by carrying towels.

"Betsy, please make sure there are enough extra towels available in the guestrooms," Mrs. Edwards said. I recognized Betsy as Mrs. Vaughan, who lived down the street from us on Washington Avenue. It had been a long time, but I was sure it was her. I tried to concentrate on being sharp for this interview. I knew how to clean from Daddy's janitorial business. I was ready to tell her about all the houses and offices I had cleaned.

"Here, Scott, place this one in that box against the wall," Mrs. Edwards said to her eight-year-old grandson, daughter Anna's son. She stood and pointed to where he should place the book. I stood seven feet in front of her, both arms hanging to my side in a semi-parade-rest stance. Scott took the book from her, making eye contact with me as he did so. Judging from the titles on the spines of the books I saw inside the room, most of the books were on Louisiana history, Southern culture, and, to my surprise, life in the South during slavery. She had books on art, antiques, antebellum homes, Southern cuisine, Louisiana politics, sharecropping, and how to have better master-servant relations.

I stood watching the first lady, while she in turn used her peripheral vision to watch me. *She could live on the walk watching like that,* I thought. After several seconds, she finally turned, folded her arms loosely across her diaphragm, and gave me a soul-piercing stare. She was the boss, and she knew it.

"So, you're Forest 'the Saint' Hammond, I take it," the first lady stated more than asked, sassily tilting her head to the right, towards the doorframe. It was her way of telling me that she knew more about me than I could imagine and that I had met my match.

"Yes ma'am," I answered after a short delay. I wondered if she detected it. She was obviously in control of the situation, but with my brief pause, I wanted her to know that I was in control of me. *Dare not allow her an opportunity to think you have misunderstood her, thus indicating she does not articulate herself well enough. Allow her to know your ability to respond to her most indistinct sigh,* I had been instructed.

"I'm Mrs. Elaine Schwartzenburg Edwards, the first lady and the governor's wife," she said. "I have scrutinized your prison file and I know everything there is to know about you—even things you don't think I'm supposed to know. Nevertheless, I have selected you to come and work here at the governor's mansion as my butler." She never blinked an eye.

My eyes did not blink either. "Yes ma'am." We were having a meeting of the minds.

She broke our eye contact momentarily. I looked at Scott staring at me, then returned my attention to her.

"You will be working here inside the mansion waiting on the first family. You shall address the first family, mansion security, employees, and mansion guests as sir and ma'am. Address male children as master and females as miss. Is that understood?"

"Yes ma'am."

"I want you to clearly understand that the first family comes first and foremost, above and before anyone else that may be present. That is to say, you shall never put anyone before them, is that understood?"

"Yes ma'am."

"Never at any time initiate any greetings, conversations, or questions to the governor. The governor has enough to be concerned with in dealing with the business of running this state to be entertaining your trifling concerns. Is that understood?"

"Yes ma'am."

"Speak when you are spoken to, answer when you are questioned, be present when you are summoned, and leave when you are excused. Is that understood?"

"Yes ma'am."

"You are to wait on and serve our mansion guests and, last but not least, mansion security. Whatever the family wants or needs as your service to them, you are to promptly provide it, no questions asked. Is this clearly understood?"

"Yes ma'am. Clearly understood."

"Mrs. Clemons, the mansion activities scheduling secretary, quite frequently schedules functions here at the mansion for senior-citizen teas, debutante balls, and small to average settings for crowds numbering from 50 to 300 guests. These functions are regularly held on weekends. Sometimes we operate on short notice, which may give you not a lot of time to set up. You are to make sure that all silverware and the tiny teaspoons are cleaned, shining, and free of tarnish. All mansion brass is to be cleaned and polished daily. The silver trays, ice pots, and all silver dining utensils are to be cleaned at least three times per week. Is that understood?"

"Yes ma'am."

"We will occasionally require your presence at center court until the games are over."

"Yes ma'am." I would find out what she meant by that later on.

"Your primary duties are to keep the mansion clean and spotless at all times. I will do unannounced periodic inspections. Each butler is assigned a specific area of the mansion to maintain and care for. You will not have any specific area, as they are already taken. You just help out as needed by the other butlers, and in the kitchen, help Bobby, the governor's chef, with whatever he needs." She looked up. "How am I doing thus far?"

"Yes ma'am. You're doing all right, ma'am. I understand you clearly."

"Good. We're going to get along just fine. I can tell already. When I'm finished with you, go down to the back desk and have security make arrangements with the tailor to have you outfitted today with your butler's suit and everything you will need. You will start at five thirty in the morning when you first arrive here. Shower and take care of your personal hygiene and be dressed and on the first floor in the butler's station by eight o'clock to answer the service phone. I allow absolutely no hair growing on your face—no sideburns, mustache, and the little goatee thing around your mouths and under your chin. Is this understood?"

"Yes ma'am."

"You will remain in the butler's station ready to serve the first family until everyone has eaten lunch or dinner before you clean up and leave for the day. No one ever eats breakfast. If the majority of the family has eaten and the governor hasn't made it in yet to eat, you shall remain in the butler's station until the governor notifies mansion security that he is or is not going to have dinner. Have I lost you? Do you understand?"

"I understand. Yes ma'am. You haven't lost me."

"Now, if you ever fail to carry out any of these duties, or if you violate any mansion policies or procedures, or cause any undesired disturbances, or fail to politely welcome and greet our mansion guests, or serve and make our mansion guests feel welcomed by any degree, or you are caught acting rude, and fail to respect any members of the first family and their friends, regardless of their ages, or you're caught drinking alcoholic beverages or caught under the influence of alcohol or drugs, or if you answer the service phone improperly, or you are caught fighting with the other inmates working here at the mansion—I absolutely have no tolerance for fighting—then you will, without any hesitation on my part, be sent back to Africa—Angola, no questions asked. Understood?"

"Yes ma'am. Understood."

"Now, on the other hand, if you remain here until the governor finishes his term in office, he will pardon you and you will be free to go home, a free man. Understood?"

"Yes ma'am. Understood very well, ma'am."

"Are there any questions?"

"No ma'am, no questions."

"After going to the back desk, go on the first floor to the butler's station, watch the other butlers, and do what you see them do. Okay, you may leave now."

"Thank you, ma'am." As I walked away I recalled how Scott moved around in the room behind the first lady, staring at me as she spoke and listening to my answers. I felt she had her grandson there as a lesson to watch her humble a great Angola-African warrior. I thought, *What the f---? Slavery wasn't abolished. It was just hidden!*

Chapter 13

Convict Chefs and Butlers—Louisiana's Best

From field niggah to house niggah? Man. After being measured for my butler's suit, I sat on a green stool in the corner of the butler's station by the coffeepot 'and observed the other butlers. I felt I was watching the slaves who had been in America long before I arrived. They knew the white man's language and habits. I was fresh off the slave ship, having just come from Angola.

"The governor's not eating dinner. Mrs. Elaine said y'all can go," Mike Mix told Bobby as he walked into the kitchen at six o'clock that evening. Bobby took his apron off and rushed downstairs to the locker room. Everyone followed, changing into white pants, shirts, and sneakers. As the Krewe of 'da Mansion van drove us away from the house, my real orientation began. It was as though they couldn't wait to get me into the van.

"Don't never say anything in the mansion about Mom or Pops," Roy Lee told me. "That's the governor and Mrs. Elaine. His kids call 'im Pops, so we call 'im Pops."

"Since he gonna pardon me, I'll call him Jesus Christ!" Slim cried from the driver's seat. Everybody agreed.

"Don't talk about nothing till we get here. This the 'conference room,'" Roy Lee said. "Slim sweeps it daily for bugs. Don't say nothing to nobody at the barracks. It's full of rats." Roy Lee and I were the only two butlers from Baton Rouge.

"And you can forget about all that inmate lawyer stuff, too. These good white folks don't play that 'round here," Phillip chimed in. "They know you think you F. Lee Bailey," he added, laughing.

"He ain't gonna have time for that anyway, huh, Sally?" Tommy Mason asked.

"*Pooool!* One hundred twenty-five hours a week," Sally said, "and forty-eight hours straight Christmas and New Year's. These good white folks love to party at Christmastime. I wash more glasses in two days than I wash all year. They love that booze." Sally was laughing like a maniac.

"And don't let them catch you looking at the fine white women either," Phillip said. "Them bodyguards be watching us like hawks."

"And Mr. Bulldog Butch, he's a drug specialist. He knows every kind of drug on the market. Can tell you who make it, what effects it has on the human body, the street value, anything! You get high, he gonna get you," Slim warned.

"Is that why he's always looking at us?" Sugar Bear asked.

"I thought he be watching us to see if we gonna do Pops something like a Nat Turner insurrection where them niggahs killed all them white folks," Mason said.

"That's Bobby's cousin that killed all them white folks," Frank stated. "Bobby, you better watch out. They really be watching you, making you think they watching us." Bobby listened and chuckled in the backseat.

"Sally must be Joseph Cinque, who killed the whole crew on the *Amistad,* huh, and tried to drive that ship like a car and ran a red light and got pulled over by the water police?" Phillip asked jokingly.

"They looking at the wrong ones," Slim said. "I don't want nothing to happen to Pops. I'm already scared he'll die and we'll have to work four more years for this new Republican governor, Dave Treen." The van became silent as Slim's words sank in.

"Is y'all through warning me, massa, suh?" I asked. "Ya'suh, massa, suh. Ya'suh, boss. I'z gonna be'z a good house niggah, suh." Bobby and Sally burst into laughter, but the others didn't find that to be very amusing.

On my first full day at the mansion, I was fully dressed, sharp and clean, in my new butler's suit. It was the day the 1979 Louisiana legislative session began. Guests arrived to meet with the governor before he opened the session at the State Capitol.

At 8:00 A.M., I sat on the green stool in the corner by the coffeepot. With the service phone constantly ringing, Bobby had butlers delivering grits, biscuits, eggs, bacon, ham, sausages, hash-browns, juice, and coffee to the front- and back-desk mansion-security personnel.

"Phillip speaking. May I help you?" He listened. "Yes sir," he said and hung up the phone. He prepared a coffee tray and exited through the elevator foyer door. Roy Lee hit the basement stairs going to the locker room. Bobby was making pies. Lunch was cooking. Devold made more coffee. Sally prepared the salad bar with fresh veggies. Mason, Sugar Bear, Frank, and Devold set the dining-room table

Saint at the governor's mansion's rear parking-garage area, 1979.

with utensils and napkins. Francis hit the stairs with a list of items to get from the supply room. I sat watching everybody. With every butler preoccupied with work, the phone was ringing off the hook.

"Saint, the phone's for you!" Sally yelled from his dishwashing station.

The phone was within easy reach from my stool. It hung on the partition wall in the kitchen between the double doors. "Ah, hello, kitchen. May I help you?" I asked.

"This is Sappington down at the back desk. I need a Coke on ice and send it to me by the dumbwaiter. Thanks." State Trooper Ira Sappington hung up the phone.

"What's wrong?" Bobby shouted.

I shook my head and quickly got a tray and glass, filled an ice dish, got a bottled Coke from the cooler, and exited, passing Phillip as he returned from a service.

Sappington waited by the steps for the dumbwaiter. I jumped three steps to the floor going to the back-desk door. "Ah, here I am— that's for me. Thanks. You didn't have to do all that." Sappington took the tray, entered the back-desk office, and sat down.

Francis was inside the supply room. Roy Lee came around the corner from the locker room and went upstairs. I followed and caught him in the stairwell. "Roy Lee," I whispered. "Look here. That back-desk man, Sap—something, he calls the kitchen and said, 'I need a Coke on ice,' right? He said, 'Send it by the dumb waiter, okay?' I take him a Coke with ice, then when I give it to him, he say, 'You didn't have to do this.' What's wrong with these white folks? They just talk bad to a niggah in his face, huh?"

Roy Lee couldn't close his mouth for laughing. I followed him up to the butler's station. "That's the dumbwaiter," Roy Lee explained, pointing. It was a mini service elevator used for sending things up and down in the mansion.

Everyone at the mansion found out what had happened in ten minutes. "You a dumb mothaf---a," Phillip whispered, quietly laughing.

By 10:45 A.M., the twenty-four-foot state dining table was fully set for twenty-four. Roy Lee spread out the *Morning Advocate* newspaper on top of the closed salad bar and read.

We never knew how many visiting guests would stay for lunch until fifteen minutes to eleven. Late appointments always stayed to eat, not daring to pass up that opportunity. Governor Edwards brought home about fifty mouths to feed every day from the State Capitol. That number could climb to eighty by 10:55. The minutes just before eleven o'clock, "show time," were the most critical and dreaded by us convicts. Within that window there existed the threat that the service phone would ring. The convicts watched and waited.

It was 10:56. The service phone rang. Phillip grimaced and then answered. "Kitchen, Phillip. May I help you?" he asked. Bobby cringed. "Yes sir." Phillip hung up. "That was Mrs. Betsy. She said send her and Mrs. Ruth's plate on the dumbwaiter."

Every butler sighed, visibly relieved. Bobby and Sally didn't relax until one minute to eleven.

"Go, banquet! Go, banquet!" Mason cried, entering from the elevator foyer. "Fifty more guests are coming with Pops from the Capitol, per front desk."

Roy Lee grimaced, closed his newspaper, and placed it under the sink in the butler's station. The butlers worked together like a symphony orchestra, transforming the state dining room in minutes so that the twenty-four-seat table could accommodate forty-eight.

Without disturbing the lunch setups already in place, they removed leaves from the long table, thus creating several smaller tables. Additional dining chairs bloomed from locations throughout the mansion. The settings rivaled those of the finest restaurants in New Orleans. Glasses of iced tea and water sparkled. The shiny caps of crystal salt and pepper shakers provided additional twinkle to the room. Little baskets of hot glazed rolls resembled small piles of gold nuggets beneath white linen napkins. The smell of fresh yeast and melted butter permeated the dining room.

Mason applied the finishing touch by placing an urn of red roses in the middle of each table. It was one minute to eleven. Phillip turned off the radio that rested in the window over the sink in the butler's station. Roy Lee and Devold lifted the top off the salad bar and put it to the side.

When the double doors were swung wide open at eleven o'clock, the governor entered first, followed by his entourage. Women guests were directly behind him, with men bringing up the rear. Rainbow colors twinkled throughout the room as light reflected off and through the prisms of the crystal chandelier that hung like a miniature star in the center of their dining galaxy.

French antique dining chairs became thrones upon which each ruler descended and declared business, justice, and judgment. From the convicts' viewpoint, the good white folks felt they were living out the state motto, *Union, Justice, Confidence*, but in reality, they practiced *We Take Care of Our Own.* The large mouth of the pelican stood for the volume of quarry it took to satisfy her greed, which she then shared with those in the nest with her.

Bobby always seemed to cook enough food to feed a multitude on unreasonably short notice. He never got caught short, and he never cooked too much either. When some political and business stragglers came in, Bobby said, "Say, Forest, make eight lunch setups in the back for me."

"Like out in the front?"

"Yeah."

After I copied what I saw out front, I made my way back into the kitchen. I walked where the workbench had a blind spot and stood there. "Say, Bobby, you know Mississippi?" I asked.

Bobby turned around as if he were working. "Uh huh, uh huh," he replied quickly.

"He said for me to tell you to look out for me."

"Uh huh, uh huh," Bobby answered again. He spun back in front of his stove to see who may have noticed us talking. Francis and Sally were of no concern to Bobby. It was the guys I was working with that he watched for. Bobby entertained his guests in the rear while the governor entertained his in the front. When guests shook hands with Bobby, it was common for them to press folded cash into his palm.

Bobby was now turned on and operating like a machine. He roasted two huge mounds of premium beef and two mounds of equally premium hams. He prepared several casseroles with crabmeat, crabmeat dressing, and jumbo Louisiana shrimp. Dishes of freshly steamed zucchini, yellow squash, broccoli, cauliflower, and spinach were covered with a sauce of light butter, melted cheese, and half-and-half, exactly suited to everyone's taste buds. Green peas and green beans were steamed and mixed with Campbell's cream of mushroom soup. Bobby always kept his larder stocked with premium rib-eye steaks, T-bones, New York strips, sirloins, and filets, for the governor and any of Bobby's special guests. The bottom drawer of his stove was always filled with hot, foil-wrapped baked potatoes. The back of his counter was laid out with all the fillings for the potatoes and all the dressings for sandwiches. Each morning he replenished the bacon bits, chives, onions, tomatoes, lettuce, and pickles.

Sally, as always, handled the lettuce and was in charge of the salad bar, ensuring that the ranch, bleu cheese, Italian, and thousand island dressings were filled and surrounded by ice. Francis was the master chef's runner. If a dish was running low, Bobby had Francis go downstairs and load the dumbwaiter with what he needed to make it through the feeding period.

Governor Edwards entered the butler's station with his train of guests and pointed at the salad plates on the salad bar. It was his signal for them not to follow him into the kitchen. Bobby saw him as he approached and waited. All the butlers stood ready to perform. Their first contact with guests would be to pull out the chairs for the women, who were seated first as they came to their table with their salads.

Governor Edwards entered the kitchen. Bobby watched him and pulled out the overhead grill just enough for the governor to observe the rib-eyes, T-bones, and filets. They were all ready just the way he loved them, medium well and still sizzling under the fire. "Bobby, *what'cha got?"* the governor shouted in his Cajun-French accent. The women, watching from the salad bar, giggled.

Bobby went into his best African-slave act, reciting his menu for the day and intentionally mispronouncing each item on the stove, but close enough to be understood by the "government," as Bobby referred to Edwards. Bobby always kept a pot of gumbo that he made on the back burner of the stove. It had crabs, oysters, premium gulf jumbo shrimp, sausage, ham cubes, and drumsticks. A small pot of sautéed crabmeat sat ready as a garnish for the gumbo.

The governor pointed to some items and poked at the smallest baked sweet potatoes to indicate his choices. He cut into the salad line, then went to the head of the first table just outside of the butler's station. The governor waited for everyone to sit before he entertained them with a joke or two.

The first lady was always the last person to be seated. She watched and waited until the butlers properly seated guests. Five seconds after the first lady was seated, Bobby had her daily avocado peeled and on a plate in front of her. She maintained her weight and health obsessively.

" . . . and so, the priest invited the beautiful young woman upstairs to his hotel suite. She goes up and the priest locks the door with his key. She goes into the bathroom and gets undressed and gets in the bed. While the priest is in the next room, the woman notices huge boxes all along the wall of the room. She lifts the top of one and then two and several more and sees severed body parts of women—hands, feet, heads, and all—in plastic bags. Her heart starts beating frantically. The monsignor comes out of the room with a large butcher's knife and approaches her. The woman jumps back in the bed, pulls the cover up to her neck, and backs against the headboard. 'I'm going to rape you!' the monsignor tells her. The woman says, *'Oh, thank God!'"* The room roared with laughter.

"Works every time," Phillip said.

In the course of serving lunch, the butlers were allowed but two mistakes. The first mistake was the actual mistake. The second mistake was to let Mrs. Edwards see you make the first mistake. She always sat to the immediate left of the governor. A buzzer was placed at the head of the table near the governor's right foot. If he or a guest wanted anything, the governor would press the buzzer and it would ring in the butler's station. A butler would appear at the governor's side as if he were summoned by the governor's thought.

Guests were always amazed at this mystical ability of the governor.

When I first found out about the buzzer, all the butlers were in the dining room serving guests. I was on standby on the green stool, looking around at the dumbwaiter, cabinets, wall, floor, coffeepot, and kick plates on the two dining-room doors. I heard a noise that sounded as if the dumbwaiter door wasn't closed. I checked it and the sound stopped. It then started again. I began looking up at the wall and ceiling, like the Beverly Hillbillies did whenever their doorbell rang.

"Go to the governor! Go to the governor! Hurry!" Sally cried in a low but urgent voice. I stepped through the door and stood at his side. The first lady's silent stare said I was late.

"Go to my study and look on my desk and bring me that open jar of muscadine jelly."

"Yes sir," I said. I did as he asked and returned to my stool.

The double dining-room doors would stay open until the main course was served. The butlers exited the kitchen with full plates in each hand, served the guests, and returned to the kitchen for more until everyone was served. Mrs. Edwards watched everybody at once, including her husband. She listened to him and the guests while furtively examining each plate the butlers carried through the door. If she saw something out of order, the butler never made it past her. She would twirl her right wrist and index finger to direct the butler back to the kitchen to make it right.

With the main course served, the double doors were closed, and first-class service began. Each convict butler had to be all things at all times. The tea and water levels had to be watched and maintained at every table. The ice server had to keep the glass full with a mini scoop of ice. Never could the ice server or tea and water server make a mistake and drop an ice cube on the table or bathe a guest in water or tea. Even if ice fell at the most distant table from Mrs. Edwards, she would hear it like a Colt .45 pistol discharging in an empty school gymnasium. She knew what sounds to listen for—the sounds of a mistake.

To serve ice, the metal scoop had to be fully loaded the first time and its lip skillfully placed on the rim of the thin, fragile glassware, which was already partially full. The server couldn't overfill the glass, causing tea or water to run over onto the table and getting the linen napkin wet. The convict had to use some system of "add and subtract" by looking at the fluid level in the glass, filling his scoop, and, with a quick flip of his wrist, allowing the ice cubes to slide quietly down through the narrow mouth of the glass, all without disturbing the guest's conversation.

Any response from the guest, such as an animated gasp caused by a splash of water or tea on their breast or face or in their food, and it was back to Africa, no questions asked. The governor's guests came to eat, not take a shower. Yet servers couldn't be too slow by being overcautious. That made the guest uncomfortable, and the servers would fall behind too. When they finally got to the last guest, the glass might be empty. This was not what the first lady had in mind, and she had no tolerance for sloppy service.

Every butler had to be prompt and courteous. The tea-, water-, and coffee-toting butler had to make sure the levels were one-fourth of an inch from the rim of the glass or cup. He quietly inserted his invisible arm to reach the glass, poured, and then disappeared in search for the next guest needing his service. No guest ever had to hold up a hand to be served. The pickup butlers stood quietly to the side after inconspicuously entering from the butler's station. They silently patrolled the tables in search of the "signaling fork." The fork could not be lying face down for over ten seconds. Once a signaling fork was located, the convict made sure his approach to take the finished dish did not disturb the discussion between the guest and governor. After the pickup butler left with the plate, another butler filled his post. The empty plate would make its way to Sally, who by now was working feverishly as he stacked all his dishes. The governor, when finished, lifted his hand just above his plate—turning his palm upwards in the middle of a conversation. He only did it once. This meant that all butlers should keep their eyes on the governor, ready to take his plate within three seconds of his signal.

When Governor Edwards finished his main course, Roy Lee held a large silver dessert tray to the governor's side. He selected his favorite: fresh, hot apple pie. The governor knew everything already, so Phillip didn't have to list each dessert. When Roy Lee held the tray to the guests, Phillip pointed to and announced each dessert.

"Excuse me, ma'am, would you care to try our desserts? Everything is made fresh daily. We have pecan brownies, chocolate-chip cookies, pralines, Boston cream pie, apple pie, cherry pie, blueberry pie, lemon meringue pie, cheesecake, and French vanilla, chocolate, and Neapolitan ice cream." Phillip's white-gloved finger maintained an acceptable distance when pointing out each item.

The fact that Mrs. Edwards had the ability to be involved in everything at once kept the butlers in check. At no time while on the floor would a convict dare look at women's cleavage or become mesmerized by their sensuous beauty. There could be no running into each other or dropping and breaking a stack of the state's china or glassware. Mrs. Edwards didn't want the Three Stooges on the state dining-room floor, embarrassing her and the chief executive officer of the state of Louisiana. It was essential to be extremely efficient and flow like a current of water. We had to make the first family look good at all times, which was something we would always seem to fall short of. But actually, we made them look better than good. We made them look like what Tony the Tiger would say: *"Grrrreat!"*

The Fear of Elaine

Once everything was finally over with and we reassembled the table as one long piece, replaced all the chairs throughout the mansion, and set up the daily twelve dinner places for the first family, the last two things to do were done by me. I vacuumed the state dining room thoroughly as if I were doing it for Martin's Personal Janitorial Service. *"I want all them chairs pulled out and vacuum underneath the table and put the chairs back,"* I could hear Martin say. The last thing I did was turn the lights off and close the doors.

Sally reset his salad bar while we straightened out everything in the butler's station. With the top replaced on the salad bar, Roy Lee quickly went under the sink, got his newspaper, and opened it back to the sports section. "Now, let me finish reading my baseball sports like I was doing before I was so rudely interrupted."

Phillip turned the radio back on and all the first-floor workers ate whatever they desired. Before eating, Devold made a fresh pot of coffee, and he and nervous Frank went to the basement to smoke. Sugar Bear went to take a nap in the bomb shelter, a part of the basement set up with bunk beds for when convicts stayed over or took authorized breaks. Sally, as always, worked alone at the dishwasher, rocking and rolling with a toothpick in his mouth and his eyeglasses steamed up as he placed all the dishes, glasses, and silverware back in their respective places, never saying a word to anyone. He was at peace just working by himself, handling his business. Afterwards, he and Francis eased to the rear dining room, sat upright at the table, and closed their eyes, grabbing a quick nap. Bobby sat at his station on a stool, looking out the window and listening to the old raggedy radio he'd brought from the cellblock seven years ago. It was still working fine. I sat on the green stool in the corner sipping a cup of Community coffee, thinking about my writ in federal court and what the first lady told me. I found that staying on the first floor in the station was my official duty, regardless of what anyone else did or how tired I was. If Bobby didn't leave, I wasn't going to leave. Mrs. Edwards said be here. If I was going to be sent back to Angola, it would be for something I alone was chargeable for. I would never hang out with or follow another niggah the rest of my life.

The sneakiest of all butlers was Phillip. He would gently push open the door to the state dining room to see if the first family and guests were gone. He would not allow the door to close all the way as he listened. He had the keenest hearing in the mansion. He knew when Mrs. Edwards would be walking through the mansion to surprise the convicts and even mansion security personnel. He would be leaning over the salad bar reading the newspaper when suddenly he would perk up and busy himself at some chore.

Whenever things were slow, Phillip knew when a door was opened anywhere in the mansion, which meant someone was moving around somewhere in the building. He would deploy himself to find out who and wouldn't stop until he had run into the walker. Since he could discern the silent footsteps of Mrs. Edwards, everyone else was a piece of cake. Phillip knew the location of all mansion security as soon as he arrived in the morning, and he would monitor all activity throughout the day. He had to know so he wouldn't be surprised while in the governor's office, looking through the stacks of pardon-board files. While reading a file, he could tell when a vehicle turned into the driveway. He knew when the phone was ringing downstairs at the back desk. He could tell when a door or window was opened—he felt a change of pressure inside the mansion. He would know if someone was coming in or going out. He did not feel safe until he knew exactly where they were, who they were, and what they were doing.

The first family left the dining room that night without telling Bobby. Roy Lee, Phillip, Mason, Devold, Frank, and Sugar Bear all cleaned up, clearing the table and polishing it. I vacuumed the carpet and killed the lights. Angry because they kept us late and left without telling us, Sally scrambled to place the dishes inside the washer, talking to himself in French.

Bobby cleaned his area in the kitchen and carefully placed everything in order for the next day. After killing the kitchen lights at 2330 hours, we rushed downstairs to the locker room, where we changed into our whites, marched past the back desk, got into the "conference room," and rode across town to the police barracks, exhausted.

Each day I made mental notes on the modus operandi of all mansion personnel for my personal benefit. I studied everyone I saw. Bobby provided information. Our work habits were a testimony of our character. After Bobby and I established a solid convict-to-convict relationship, he talked with me about everything. I shared with him details of my case in federal court and the history of my boxing career. I had been hearing things from the other butlers and sought verification from Bobby, because if it was true, he would know. Bobby did not want either of us to be hauled away and end up before a federal grand jury investigating Governor Edwards. For that reason, when the subject of Pops came up, Bobby always spoke to me in parables.

It did not take long before I noticed an undercurrent of strife among the butlers. Roy Lee took me on as a friend. Everyone else was from New Orleans or somewhere else. They never revealed their feelings in the mansion, but in the conference room they murmured, griped, threatened, cursed each other, pointed fingers, and rolled their eyes. I managed to remain neutral in the simmering disputes.

When activity was slow on the weekends, I practiced my greetings to the point they no longer had any emotional effect upon me. "Mr. This." "Mr. That." "Mrs. This." "Mrs. That." "Ma'am, may I offer you a cup of tea, soft drink, coffee, or water?" "Oh, thank you, sir." "Thank you, ma'am." "The restroom is this way, ma'am," "Please don't forget to flush the s---ter, ah, I mean, toilet, ma'am." "Ya'suh, suh, massa, suh." "Noooo suh, massa, suh." "I beg ya poddon, suh?" "Tank ya, suh, tank ya, suh." "Oh ya'suh, I go set da table up, suh. How mainey peas in the pot coming you tink gonna yeat with the governor, suh?" I trained myself to say these things without having to bite my tongue. I didn't realize I hated the good white folks, and now I was working in the midst of them because they all came to the mansion daily.

All but Bobby wanted me to stop my slave talking. Even Roy Lee got nervous. Since I had them on the defensive, I ramped it up. "And everybody treats Pops like a don, like, ah, a Cajun godfather," I said when all the butlers were in the station. Phillip turned the radio up a little.

"Man, you better cut that out," Mason advised.

"Don't tell him nothing," Frank said. "Let him find out for hisself. When they ship him back, he'll learn. I don't want to work with you, because you dangerous. Y'all can work with him, but I ain't. My nerves too bad." He scratched his balding head and brushed his face with his hand.

"Everybody that comes here treats him like a don. Y'all can't see that?" I asked. "No, you just a buncha ignorant niggahs, hell. I'm calling him Don Edwards from now on."

"Man, you better stop talking about the governor like that," Devold said. "Mrs. Elaine gonna hear that and send you back to Angola, and you ain't never getting out."

"How she gonna find out unless one of you niggahs go rat and tell her? I don't see her standing in here now," I said.

"Now, what y'all gonna say about that? Huh?" Bobby asked, laughing.

Instead of the fear of God, they had the fear of Elaine in their hearts. I was glad, because all but Roy Lee had begun exploiting me. They had me doing their work, as if I was their employee. But now I could go into my slave-and-master act, and they all would say, "Man, I ain't working with you. You's dangerous!" They knew this was their only shot to get out and were scared to death I would blow it for them.

One night I stayed up late calling everybody I knew and ended up calling Julia Hines, a girlfriend of mine from Capitol High. She was the finest girl on campus, with a beautiful copper complexion. At 0800 hours the next morning, I was resting on the green stool as Governor Edwards was getting coffee and talking to two guests in French. I was dreaming of hearing men speaking a foreign language. A sudden silence roused me. I wasn't dreaming. Governor Edwards, wearing a gray suit with a black leather patch on the left breast, was speaking French to a short Cajun man with black hair, wearing a checkered sports coat, white pants, and white shoes. I continued sitting on the stool, looking around, while every other butler stood at attention. Governor Edwards was holding a plastic jar of honey in the shape of a bear. He stirred three spoons of honey in his coffee and one spoon of creamer, placed the spoon on a saucer, took a sip, then faced me. I looked at his ugly suit fifteen inches away. He turned and walked out through the elevator-foyer door, with the men following him.

"Boy! You just wait until Mrs. Elaine hears about this. You didn't stand up when the governor came got his coffee," they all seemed to say at once.

"You gone, bro. Bye-bye," Frank said, close up in my face.

The elevator-foyer door opened, and Captain Jones rushed in and got a cup of coffee. Everyone acted normal until he left. Then Frank resumed his attack, elated at my predicament.

"Ain't nobody told me anything about standing up when the governor comes in," I said. "Matter of fact, this the first time I've seen the governor get coffee since I been here. Mrs. Elaine might want to know why ain't nobody told me about this yet when y'all know that's normal procedures." No one responded.

"Now what'cha gonna do? Take that!" Bobby said. He and Sally laughed in the kitchen.

Chapter 14

The Setup

While Laura was inspecting the work of her employees, who had replaced the drapes in the mansion, I sat on the green stool at the salad bar, eating lunch with the other butlers. Governor Edwards entered the butler's station and stood at the coffeepot, going through his coffee ritual: three spoons of honey and one spoon of creamer. Crowded around and hiding him were his bodyguards, Captain Jones, Butch Miley, Paul Fontenot, and Jeff Bordelon. Each of the butlers stood up except me. I was the only butler with my back to the governor and hadn't seen him, and when I turned, Fontenot's tall, broad frame was blocking him from sight. I did notice all the shoulder holsters filled with automatic weapons and revolvers. Butch frowned at me, but I ignored him. Roy Lee tried to say something, but I kept eating. None of the other butlers said a word.

From the elevator foyer door, Damon Robicheaux slowly entered the butler's station, looking around. He was six three, long haired, clean shaven, and dressed in brown boots, blue jeans, and a plaid long-sleeve shirt. "Hey, Mr. Damon Robicheaux, long time no see," Bobby said. "Where you been, in the basement again?" he added with a laugh. I didn't turn around, but I noticed that Bobby got no verbal response. Damon entered the kitchen, got a brownie off the counter, and disappeared through the rear dining room.

Governor Edwards placed his spoon on a napkin, sipped, and saw me sitting and eating. He walked over and asked, "Are you the boxer?"

I turned around surprised, noticing his Cajun accent. "Oh, yes sir. I'm sorry, I didn't see you! My fault," I said, wiping my mouth with a napkin. I was eating another rib-eye Bobby had grilled for me. Ever since I told Bobby that Mississippi said to look out for me, he fed me everything he fed the governor. The other butlers didn't like it. I stood up, still chewing and wiping with the napkin.

"How many fights you had?" Governor Edwards asked.

"Ah, about forty-five, forty-seven."

"How many you lost?" he asked.

"I lost my first fight," I said, thinking. "Yes sir. I think I was disqualified."

"You ever got knocked out?" Governor Edwards asked.

"No sir," I said, shaking my head. The bodyguards looked on, smiling and listening as the governor questioned me.

"How many knockouts do you have?"

"I don't know. I think I knocked all of them out except three or four of them."

"How you move? Let me see you throw a combination."

"Right in here?"

"You need more room?"

"No sir. I can do it here." I took my butler jacket off and laid it on the stool. The bodyguards moved back, giving me more room.

"Let me see if I can hit you," Jeff said, also in a Cajun accent. He was the most dangerous bodyguard Governor Edwards had. He took his suit coat off, exposing two shoulder holsters with black automatic weapons. He took them off and gave them to Fontenot. He took his pistol off his hip, bent down, and took a pistol out of his ankle holster. He then raised his hands like a fighter and came at me. The Mongoose began slowly bouncing back and forth. I deflected every punch he threw, while throwing two or three jabs in a counterpunch at his face. I didn't hit him but came close enough for him to know he would have been hit if this were a real fight. Jeff tried to box me in, but the Mongoose didn't allow it. Jeff got tired and stopped before he got sweaty. I bounced to and from each bodyguard, throwing combinations half-inches from their faces. Even in the dress shoes I had on, my footwork was quiet. They froze, afraid to move. Governor Edwards sipped his coffee, watching. Butch and Jeff, hearing the wind popping as I threw combinations, became concerned for Governor Edwards' safety. I sprang in as he sipped, threw a three-punch combination—*"moja, mbili, tatu!"*—within a quarter-inch of his face, and sprang back.

"Hey, hey!" Butch yelled, drawing his weapon. It was too late. I stood by the salad bar with my guard down, letting the governor know I had finished the demonstration. Governor Edwards smiled. The butlers smiled. Bobby, Sally, and Francis were grinning.

"You know it's against the law to be that fast?" Jeff asked, still a bit winded. He turned to the governor. "He's good. This is a bad son of a gun you got here!" Fontenot gave Jeff his weapons back.

"When we leave here, you come ride with us," the governor said, then walked out, followed by his bodyguards.

Jeff rushed back through the elevator foyer door into the butler's station, as if he'd forgotten something important. "We'll get back in touch with you, okay?" he said to me. He looked at each butler before leaving. *"This is the governor's nigger!"* he seemed to be saying.

"Pops ain't never did nothing like that," Bobby remarked when he left. "Pops likes you. He likes boxing."

I put my jacket on and sat in the kitchen next to Sally with the rest of my lunch. Damon Robicheaux walked back in. "They say they got a boxer around here," he commented as he got a Coke out of the cooler. He pulled up a seat between Sally and me as if joining a poker game. "Is that you?" he asked. I nodded, my mouth full of food. "So, you're the boxer everybody's talking about?"

'That's me," I answered.

"Well, you don't look like a boxer," he said.

"Well, looks can be deceiving."

"All right, but I mean, you used to actually box up there in Angola? For real?" he asked. Bobby stood behind him, cueing me with his facial expressions.

"*Used* to box? I *still* box. I'm a fighter," I replied, frowning as if to make him think I was offended.

"Well, I mean, do you think you can still box? I mean, you know, you haven't been fighting and training in what, let's say, three or four months?" he asked. He had rolled his eyes to the ceiling when calculating how long I'd been at the mansion. I was surprised at his accuracy. I sized him up as a mathematician, since mansion security intelligence officers were specialists. Those figures were reached too quickly for just a casual conversation. "Do you still think you can fight, I mean, like, right now, how you did in Angola?"

"Did you see the Mongoose a few minutes ago in there?" I asked.

"No, he wasn't in there," Bobby said as he set to work making pastries. "He didn't see."

"Did you know the governor loves boxing?" Damon asked.

"No sir. I didn't know that," I said.

"Hey! Come see. Let's go!" Butch shouted, rushing in from the elevator foyer to fetch me to go with them.

"I'll get back in touch with you," Damon said, nodding.

I stuffed the last chunk of the thick, tender rib-eye in my mouth. Roy Lee, Bobby, Sally and Francis were all smiling. I had suddenly become a commodity, rather than just a butler. The others were mere house niggers, with nothing to offer the good white folks but a "yes sir" and "thank you, ma'am."

Butch led me to the elevator foyer, where the governor and his bodyguards caught the elevator to the garage and got in three different vehicles with tinted windows. The blue Oldsmobile Regal turned left, followed by a blue Olds Ninety-Eight, heading for the State Capitol. The white Olds Ninety-Eight also turned left but got on Interstate 110 to Interstate 10, then I-12, before exiting at Airline Highway. Butch drove while Governor Edwards read a file. I sat in the backseat, sightseeing.

We drove to the governor's new home on Highland Road. It appeared to be about half-completed. After the governor went inside and checked the progress of the construction, we drove to his office on the Airline Highway service road, where Jefferson Highway merged into Airline. Governor Edwards and Butch went into the office for five minutes and came back to the car. Butch brought the Olds Ninety-Eight to a stop in a service-road exit lane, waiting for an opening in the lunchtime traffic on Airline Highway. I saw opportunities that Butch could have taken to enter the street, but he didn't. Governor Edwards didn't like being a sitting duck on any street. He always preferred to be on the move. Pops was on a schedule.

Butch missed another opportunity. Governor Edwards, still reading the file, released an inaudible sigh of frustration. *Pops wanted to be on the go*, I told myself.

"Boxer," the governor said.

"Yes sir."

"Come get behind the wheel."

Butch turned to him, then laughed, thinking the governor was kidding. Then he realized he wasn't. "Sir, are you sure? I mean, it's my job to look out for your safety, sir."

"Let him have it—apprenticeship." the governor said.

Butch and I got out and exchanged seats. I was wondering if the governor was a little crazy or just a fearless white boy who loved taking chances. I adjusted the power seat, the steering wheel, and then all the mirrors.

"When was the last time you drove, Boxer?" the governor asked.

"In 1973, sir."

"You see that service road across over there?" he asked.

I squinted to see the service road a quarter of a mile away and nodded.

"Yes sir. I see it."

"When the traffic light changes, turn right behind the last car in this first wave, and get in the left lane, and turn left at the first median. When that red van at the end of the wave of traffic coming from Siegen Lane passes, turn left and come back this way, get in your right lane, and turn right on the service road. Now tell me, can you do that?"

"Sir, your safety is my responsibility," Butch said, unfastening his seatbelt. "I think I better take the wheel back."

"Yes sir," I told the governor. I hit the gas, but the car was still in park. The engine revved. Governor Edwards resumed reading the file.

"It's not in gear! Put it in gear!" Butch yelled.

I burned rubber while turning right, blowing the horn with my left hand and rolling the steering wheel with my right. Feeling the power under the hood gave me a rush. I put the left signal on, checked the driver's-side mirror, and moved into the left lane. Butch, fumbling to fasten his seatbelt again, kept his eyes on the road. The Olds Ninety-Eight approached the median, but a Bano Produce truck cut in front of me. I checked the mirrors, signaled a right-lane change, and accelerated past the truck. I signaled a left-lane change and accelerated again, but the median was upon me. "You're not gonna make it!" Butch yelled. I hit the brakes and turned, causing the big vehicle to slide sideways. It was resting in the street with the nose partially in the median.

I punched the gas. The big Olds Ninety-Eight thrust into the median as the truck moved in behind us. The governor was cool the whole time, still reading his file. I thought he was some type of maniac, like Cheyenne. The red van passed us and I followed the traffic flow, turning right onto the service road and disappearing into a subdivision. During the drama, I had kept rolling the wheel and inadvertently honking the horn.

"You like blowing that horn, huh?" Pops asked.

I smiled. "Sir, that's how we use to roll in '73," I answered.

"See, Butch. I gambled and won. He's a good man. Most people don't like to take big chances. That's what makes life fun and worth living, especially when you win."

The white Ninety-Eight coasted into the courtyard of a townhouse complex and came to a stop. Pops dialed a number on his car phone, then picked up the receiver. "I'm twenty-five steps from your door," he said and hung up. Pops got out and ran up the stairs. The door opened as he approached, and he disappeared inside. Laura smiled and waved at me. My eyes nearly popped out of my head. *Damn, that's the lady Mrs. Edwards gave a $15,000 check to,* I thought.

"Some things you see you don't ever talk about, you understand?" Butch said more than inquired.

"Can I ask you something?"

"Yeah, go ahead," Butch answered.

"If Governor Edwards thought I was a rat, tell me, would I be here?" I wanted to say more, but this was no laughing matter.

Butch became extremely angry, but I knew he wouldn't tell the first lady. He leaned forward from the backseat. "Get out of here," he ordered.

I propelled the Olds Ninety-Eight forward, throwing Butch against the backseat the way police like to do with violent criminals. The engine's surge of power was intoxicating. I wasn't used to it yet.

"No, no, stop!" Butch yelled.

"You sound like one of them freemen in Angola," I said and hit the brakes. The car stopped on a dime, throwing Butch forward halfway over the front seat. I was not used to the brakes yet, either. I thought about speeding off then hitting the brakes hard again, sending him through the windshield for hollering at me. *Say, Saint, you could just use the gas and brakes to beat him up without ever laying a hand on him,* my inner voice told me.

Butch was furious. "Now, put it in park, turn it off, and get out," he said, hanging over the front seat.

I did as ordered, walked around to the passenger side, and waited between the front and back doors. "Which seat? Back? Front?" I asked, unsure.

"Get in the back," he commanded. I knew if he was a real police officer, he'd say the back.

On the way back to the mansion, Butch and Captain Jones spoke over the radio and switched me at the Government Street exit ramp. Captain Jones took me back to the mansion. That night when the Krewe of da Mansion got back to the barracks, we all stopped at the office to see if we had any mail. Bobby and a couple others received letters. I didn't. I was expecting to receive notice from the clerk of court that my petition for writ of habeas corpus had been granted and a new trial ordered.

Back in the Ring

"Come take a ride with me when you finish." Damon had found me vacuuming the state dining-room carpet. We got in his unmarked state police unit and left the mansion from the rear drive. "Here's the deal," Damon said. "Some very wealthy businessmen want to invest a lot of money in you. They want to promote you as a professional boxer after you get out. The governor leaves office in March, the twenty-first, 1980, I think. You are going to be matched in a fight at the Centroplex Coliseum with a guy from Fort Polk military base. The investors want to see if you can really fight as good as everybody says you can before they put up all that money." I thought Damon's long, dark-brown hair made him look like an undercover narcotics agent.

Damon drove to the Athletic House sports-equipment store. "All we have to do is get everything you need to get back and stay in shape. Anything you want, you got it."

Inside, we loaded three shopping carts with a 100-pound black-leather heavy bag, a 70-pound white-canvas bag, a professional speed bag with rack, a double-end speed bag, half-pound mini handweights, two leather jump ropes, two plastic running suits, two sweat suits, a burgundy warmup suit with double white stripes on the shoulders, a pair of leather work shoes from which I would immediately remove the heels, a pair of white boxing shoes, bags of socks, sets of jockey straps, mouthpieces, a dozen sets of hand wraps, a long upright mirror, and a sit-up bench. "I just have to get everything I think I need," I said, pushing two of the carts while Damon pushed one. As I looked around to see if I missed anything, I rammed my carts into a small cart pushed by a young woman.

"Oh, my God, *Saint!*" she said.

"DMB."

"How long have you been out?" she asked, grinning.

"I'm not out, DMB. I mean, I work at the governor's mansion. He brought me here to get some equipment." I pointed at Damon, who stayed a respectful distance from us, thumbing through a magazine near the register.

"What, boxing equipment? You're a boxer now?" DMB asked,

excited. Her eyes were wide. "Saint, you look so good, so healthy."

"You do too, DMB."

Damon knew it was a friend and allowed me to talk to her. He was super. He watched DMB hand me a card. I nodded to her that I'd call her, and she left for her car. Damon acted as if he didn't see a thing. As I came to the register, he glanced at DMB's car as she pulled away. He did it so quickly it nearly got by me, even though I was looking right at him. After paying for all the equipment, which cost over a thousand dollars, we loaded it in his car.

"Where are we going to put all this stuff?" I asked.

"Let's set it up in the boiler room," he suggested. "Nobody goes in there for anything. It's not in Ross's way when he's doing the laundry. It's hot and good for sweating and losing weight."

"Sounds good to me," I said, grinning. Together, we set up shop, turning the boiler room into a mini boxing gym. A land route was mapped out for me to do my road work. It was in front of and next to the mansion. Coming out of the drive, I turned right and ran to the bridge, turned around, ran back past the mansion, and turned left at the corner traffic light on Capitol Access Road. I ran to the end of the mansion property line and backtracked.

After an hour of running in my plastic suit, I'd do my exercises on the grassy area by the bridge next to Capitol Lake. In the mornings, I watched white herons wade in the water near the bank, slowly leaning forward, resembling long slender reeds being blown by the wind. They stabbed their long beaks into the water, catching small fish or frogs.

I sat on the ground doing stretching exercises. As I watched traffic drive by on the interstate and people walking or riding bikes through Capitol Park, my mind drifted back along the path I had traveled over the last six years. I felt that there was a force causing all this to happen—and it wasn't EWE.

It was not acceptable for a convict in my position to ask pointed questions. When Damon popped up out of nowhere and told me he had arranged a fight for me in two days at the Baton Rouge police athletic-league gym on Laurel Street, what could I say? He and Billy Roth had been working to arrange a fight for the benefit of the investors he had told me about but whom I had never seen.

"The guy's name is Darryl Sampry. He's A.A.U.-ranked seventh in the U.S. Do you think you're able to fight this man without having any sparring and with two weeks of training?" Damon asked. His face betrayed his concern.

"I'm the one fighting. Why're you looking so worried?" I asked.

"There's going to be some pretty wealthy people there watching you who're interested in promoting you if you do all right," he said.

When it came time for the fight at 8:00 P.M., I rode to the academy with Damon. My co-workers had already made it there and were sitting in the bleachers. Governor Edwards and the first lady were sitting in an area at ringside where several good chairs had been placed.

The referee, a middle-aged Italian, checked my gloves, cup, and mouthpiece with great professionalism. The way he talked to us while giving instructions indicated he had done this for a long time.

The bell sounded and I took the fight to Sampry, because he was in inch taller than I. I sized him up as a counter-puncher. We tied up a couple times and the referee separated us. My jab was working well, I thought, judging from the blood coming from Sampry's nose and mouth. He wouldn't be able to fight long if I put pressure on him and tired him out. The first round was easily mine. In the second round, Sampry caught me on the ropes, but I grabbed him and shook my head to the crowd, indicating that he didn't do any damage. I started dancing and scoring blows to the stomach as I moved in and out like a mongoose. Sampry tried to counter me with uppercuts but kept missing. I continued my attack, scoring points. Pulling out, Sampry caught me with an uppercut. He had clipped me with his long reach. I stumbled and fell back on the canvas. My hearing was fine, but I couldn't see anything. I did deep-breathing exercises to get oxygen to my brain so my vision would return.

"Stay down; don't get up," the referee said, pressing his hand on my chest and pushing me back down.

"I'm all right; I'm good," I told him.

"You're all right, but just stay down," he whispered, still holding me down on the canvas. I figured because of the new A.A.U. ruling that prisoners were not allowed in A.A.U. competition, he was making sure I didn't get hurt. He kneeled and asked for my mouthpiece. I poked it out. He checked my eyes.

"Why you didn't let me get up? I was all right," I said.

"Don't worry about that. You're in good hands. The board slapped and it was loud. It sounded like you went down harder than you did. They told me don't let nothing happen to you. I just wanted to make sure you're all right."

"What happened, Champ?" Governor Edwards asked, smiling, when I stepped down out of the ring. "You're all right?" The first lady stared at me, holding on to her husband's arm like a teenage girl with her boyfriend.

"Yes sir. I'm all right—a little disappointed. I'm a little off. A little slow. I need sparring and to lose some of this weight I've gained."

"You're a good man," he said, cutting me off. He turned, shook his head, and gave a thumbs-up to a group of white men standing across the ring.

Arrangements were made immediately for Damon to bring me to the police academy three nights a week to train when the gym was open for boxing. I became acquainted with the fighters Billy Roth brought to Angola for tune-up matches before tournaments. Tony "the Tiger" Williams was a black, 132-pound lightweight, and the two James brothers were black lightweights. Pat and Steve Burleigh were two white brothers in the 147-pound welterweight class. Their father, Gene, was their trainer. Alvin Vessel was a black heavyweight.

Michael Bryant, the former defensive back at Capitol, was there on my first night and greeted me. He had played football in college and the NFL. I hadn't seen him since 1973. He gave me a good workout that night. He was glad to see I was all right.

I was earnestly trying to revive the spirit of the Mongoose that I had in Angola, which gave me quickness and hand speed. Each morning, I got dressed at five thirty, and after dinner, I put on my plastic sweatsuit, strapped on my work boots with my wrapped hands, and ran for an hour, carrying two mini weights while throwing punches. I fought an invisible man, pushing myself through the burning pain in my shoulder, arm, and leg muscles. I did 200 reflex exercise drills. I did fifteen rounds on the heavy bag, ten rounds of jumping rope, 200 sit-ups, and 150 pushups. I was soaking wet and exhausted when I got into the ring.

Tony, Pat, Steve, Mike, and Alvin beat the crap out of me, taking turns whipping my sluggish butt. But I loved the chocolate-pecan mansion brownies that Bobby baked. Wearing a thick sweatshirt under my sweat suit made me bulky and uncomfortable as I tried to execute punches—missing my target and getting hit by their counterpunches. They all talked trash to me in the ring, saying they were punishing me for having gained all that weight. I caught jabs, hooks, and body blows.

One night I stumbled and tripped. Alvin sent me down to the canvas, where I coiled up and gasped for air. Gene offered his hand to help me up. I refused it. Gene wanted me to take a break, but I wouldn't. Cheyenne would never let us stop when we complained of pain and fatigue.

I went back to the barracks bruised and sore from the punishment. The next day when I served lunch to guests and the first family, Mrs. Edwards cringed at the bruises on my face. "It just doesn't make any sense to me at all to get in that thing, that cage thing, and be thrashed so severely," she remarked to her husband and children during dinner later. That night I washed my face with my own urine, the way Cheyenne told me. The next day the bruises were gone and cuts were healed. The first lady stared at me in disbelief, wondering where the bruises had gone.

After three weeks of sparring, I urged Tony, Pat, Steve, and Alvin not to lighten up on me. "If I think you're easing up or feeling sorry for me, I'll beat you up," I threatened.

"If they're kicking your a—, just how are you going to beat them up?" Billy Roth asked, laughing with the rest of them. "Forest, if you don't stop eating all that good food at the mansion, you're going to have to fight heavyweight."

The fighters swore that they were not taking it easy on me. Without my realizing it, my little friend the Mongoose was stirring up in its burrow. I pulled my punches on Tony and the Burleigh brothers, not wanting to hurt them. I opened up on big Alvin, burying him in a barrage of combinations. He was seeing cross-eyed when he came off the ropes. I didn't want to hurt these guys. They were my friends. If Cheyenne were here, he'd be yelling, "If you pull when you spar, you'll pull in a fight! You fight the way you train!"

I was rematched with Tom Landry, the light heavyweight from Lake Charles who was A.A.U. ninth-ranked in the U.S. My weight was down to 178. Tom weighed in at 190. He was six feet tall and built like a rhino with big shoulders. His specialty was aggression. He charged at me as though he had a football helmet on. We fought from bell to bell. Tom was a slugger and I was a boxer. He was set on throwing punches at my waist to deaden the nerves in my hips, which would slow me down and keep me from dancing. He wanted me to stay still. It was a Friday night, and the governor and his wife had their seats at ringside, along with friends and bodyguards. All fourteen of my co-workers were seated high in the stands.

Tom was a better fighter than Sampry. We threw hundreds of punches in the first three-minute round. We pushed, tried to trick and set each other up, wrestled, and fought in the corners, along the ropes, and in center ring, manhandling each other. We were still throwing punches after the bell rang, causing the same referee to break us up.

"*Stop fighting!*" he yelled, stepping between us. He swung me around him to the middle of the ring, pushed me into my red corner, and pulled Tom out of the ropes. I didn't know where I was for a moment. Neither Tom nor I had heard the bell. The police-academy gym was filled to capacity, and the crowd was on its feet, shouting and cheering as if they had won the lottery.

Damon placed the stool in my corner. Darrell James took my mouthpiece and gave me water, which I spit into the bucket he held. "I'll take that b---- out," I said.

Damon was laughing. "Damn, Saint, you wasn't lying. You can really fight. They loved it! They loved it!" he said, speaking of the investors and the governor.

It was just the first round. We fought another four, throwing hundreds more punches in each. It was an exhibition with no winner, but the contest gave me status at the police academy and mansion. Everyone treated me as if I had already won the light-heavyweight championship title of the world.

Train Hard

On Saturdays, when traffic at the mansion was slow and the first lady was out of town, anyone was liable to show up. At 1600 hours the day after the fight, Damon came and stood on the front steps, waiting for three other men to exit their cars. Two were state troopers, and the third was a blond man wearing tan slacks, a sports jacket, and a tan shirt with no tie. He chewed gum and stared at me when they all walked into the butler's station. I was the only butler on hand. The others were down in the bomb shelter, either shooting dice or asleep. Bobby sat in his window, pretending to be working on something but watching us. I stood at the salad bar playing solitaire.

"Saint, I want you to meet Billy Wright," Damon said. "He owns Wright and Percy Insurance Agency. He's one of the investors I was telling you about who're interested in promoting you as a professional fighter once the governor pardons you. I brought him here so y'all could meet and talk."

"Saint! How're you doing?" Mr. Wright asked. He extended his hand, flashing a wide grin that creased his face, especially around his mouth and eyes.

I placed the card I held on the salad bar and shook his hand. His grip was powerful and solid, as was mine. "I'm all right, sir. I'm good," I responded.

All three men studied me, as if to see what kind of nigger I was out of all the niggers they'd ever met. Mr. Wright introduced his two state trooper friends. The taller, older officer wore glasses and outranked the other one. I shook hands with both troopers, but the younger man's grip forced me to grimace. It felt as though I had placed my hand in a vise.

"This is our muscleman here," the older trooper said. "Whenever we need something done, he gets the job done. We call him 'Done.'"

"You could work for Don Corleone," I said. They all laughed.

"Boy! I thought you were gonna knock that son of a b---- out the godd--- ring last night. Why didn't you?" Mr. Wright asked. He clenched his fist, raised his guards, and threw a punch at me. I instinctively deflected his punch and countered with a right and left hook to the chin, pulling them before impact. Surprised, he jumped back, showing his palms in surrender. Everyone laughed again. "Wait a minute," Mr. Wright said. "I'm on your side, Champ."

I just smiled. Without their realizing what I was doing, I turned and looked at Bobby. He was nodding and rubbing his thumb and index finger together, indicating these people were wealthy. I turned back, picked up the deck of cards, and shuffled it.

"Saint, seriously," said Billy, as Damon called him. Billy stopped smiling and was now chewing his gum a little slowly. He looked me in the eye and stood toe to toe with me, almost as though he was challenging me. "Do you think you can beat all the fighters out there in your weight class? What I want to know is can you bring home the cheese—the world title?"

I had seen that when Governor Edwards was asked questions that put him on the spot, he would look down and then back at the person, eye to eye. I did the same. "With my trainer Cheyenne in my corner, with him training me, with the proper rest and sparring, and if I can lose all this weight I've gained since I've been here at the mansion, can't nobody beat me," I said, staring back in his eyes, expressionless.

"Well, that's not a problem," Damon replied, shaking his head. "That's not a problem. The governor can take care of that. I got the perfect solution for you to lose the weight. I'll tell you about it later. Where is this Cheyenne guy at?"

"He's in Angola doing life for rape. He said he didn't do it and—"

"That's what they all say," Billy interjected. Everyone laughed.

"I believe him," I said. "He used to train boxers in New Orleans."

"Well, don't worry about him for right now," Damon said. "What Mr. Wright wants to know is can you beat all those professional fighters out there in the light-heavyweight division?"

"See, Forest, what we want to do is promote you as a professional as soon as possible," Billy said. "We have all the money we need to push you up through the ranks. We're ready to start making some serious money. Are you ready to start making some money?"

"Yes sir. I'm ready to start making millions," I replied.

"Yeah, yeah, that's right," Billy said, caught somewhat off guard. They all laughed but it was a nervous laugh. "What we want to do is get you as many qualified matches as possible while you're here at the mansion, so when the governor cuts your time at the end of his term, we can just step you up right into the professional arena. How's that?" Billy pulled a big bankroll of $100 bills from his pocket. He sorted through a few hundred and handed them to me as if they were napkins. "Sugar Ray Leonard is fighting here in a few weeks. Go buy you a couple suits. We are all going and we want you looking good sitting up there with the governor and us."

"Thank you very much," I said. I tried to avoid saying "yes sir" as much as possible. This man was hustling, so I got away with it.

"You just keep on training real hard and running and practicing and everything, and we're going to get this thing together, all right, Champ?" Billy asked, extending his hand. We shook hands on the deal.

"Take care, Champ," the younger trooper said. "Train hard." He offered to shake my hand again. I declined.

"All right," I said. When they left, I walked into the kitchen, counting the money.

"What he gave you, a grand?" Bobby asked, guessing. I was still counting.

"Damn! A thousand two hundred dollars. Twelve hundred!"

"*Booooy*, them white folks is serious about you," Bobby said, shaking his head. "Anytime them white folks fork out C-notes like that, you better believe they see making a hundred times more than that, but they don't want you to know it."

"That's why I told them I was ready to make millions. I want them to know up front that I'm not a stupid-a-- niggah who don't know what he's worth. Every fighter I read about died or retired broke. I want them to know where my level of thinking is at."

Chapter 15

The Amazing Ball Runner

It was 10:00 A.M. on a Sunday, and the convict staff was congregated in the butler's station. No guests were expected in the house until lunch and then an afternoon tea scheduled for 300 senior citizens. The service phone rang. I noticed that the butlers were very apprehensive about answering it. When Devold finally answered it and hung up, he looked at us as if he had just been notified by the Grim Reaper that it was his time.

Outside on the tennis court, Mrs. Edwards wore her white tennis suit. Two butlers came out and stood by to serve as ball runners. Whenever one ran up to her with her balls, she would extend her racquet and expect him always to place them there. Pops, on the other hand, wanted the butler to bounce his balls to him, so that he could catch them with his hand. The butler's throw had to be perfectly timed and at the correct distance. The governor would catch each ball and place it in his pocket.

The butlers ran hard for the first forty-five minutes in a cool breeze. As the sun strengthened, however, it was quite another story. It looked as though the out-of-shape butlers were about to have a coronary. They crouched on one knee at the net post, trying not to get sent back to Angola for delaying the tennis game. The good white folks hated to wait for anything, especially getting a ball for their next serve.

As the game progressed, the runners were sweating and gasping for air. They stumbled and fell on the court like drunks. Their legs were weak from running across the tennis court and bending to pick up those little light-green balls. The scene resembled a slapstick comedy, with tennis balls bouncing over Governor Edwards' head and him jumping up to grab at them in the air. He also swung at the wild balls with his racquet as if he were swatting butterflies. The first lady looked on with irritation as she waited for him to make his next serve.

In his own cool way that always made people like him, Governor Edwards stood squinting as he patiently waited for the convicts to collect the overbounced balls. When the first couple or other tennis players felt like playing several sets, they alternated runners to keep us fresh. That's why on weekends, the butlers dreaded picking up the phone when it rang.

This would be the first day that I ran balls for the first couple. It was after lunch, and my partner was Phillip. The governor always let Mrs. Edwards serve first. When her first ball failed to clear the net, Phillip took off from the net post like a crop duster on a dirt runway. He scooted across the court, bent down, grabbed the ball, and ran to my side. "Make sure you hurry and get it and run to the other side, you know?" Phillip told me, gasping. He hadn't run forty yards and was already panting like a dog.

"All right," I said, waiting for the next miss. The first lady's return again failed to clear the net, and I shot from my position, grabbed the ball without breaking stride, and made it to the other side, spinning around ready to go again. I kneeled and looked at Phillip across the court. He smiled, knowing I was showing off. I turned to look at the first lady. She was stunned, letting me know how impressed she was in her own executive, first-lady way.

After watching her play for a while, I realized the first lady was missing a lot of balls on purpose. My speed and accuracy never diminished. The first couple waited for me to miss a ball, but it didn't happen. I turned it into a game—a challenge to never miss a ball. I was playing against them.

Mrs. Clemons walked out to the court and spoke with the first lady at two o'clock. Phillip was ordered into the house to clean up prior to the tea guests' arrival. That left me alone to chase balls, and my clothes were soon soaked with sweat. But word of my performance got around the mansion, and soon everybody who played tennis there wanted me as their ball boy. David and Jenny, Anna and her husband, John, Victoria and one of her girlfriends, guests, and mansion security all called for me. After a while, I figured that they just sat around looking for something to do and decided to call the kitchen: *"Hello, kitchen. Yes, ah, we want to play a few sets of Run, Forest, Run; see da niggah run dem balls. So, tell Hammond to get his eyes, hands, a—, and legs out at center court."*

Alone, I'd retrieve balls four hours straight for different teams of players. No one ever came to relieve me. When the huge drapes moved, Mason, Phillip, Devold, Frank, and Bobby could be seen watching me from inside the mansion.

The governor and first lady wanted to play after I had run three hours for Anna's kids during their private lessons one day. At the beginning of the first couple's set, I had to perform as if I had new batteries. She revved me up a few times, intentionally hitting the ball into the net. The first lady always wanted to see a few test runs first, to make sure I was still working before she began playing in earnest.

After an hour of running, I broke fast out of my imaginary starting blocks but tripped over my shoestring. I pushed off the green-painted court with my left arm, grabbed the ball with my right hand, retracted my arms to my chest, and went into a roll. I came up on my feet at the other end of the net, looking as though I did that stuff for warmups. The spot where I rolled was stained dark green from my sweat. The asphalt was so hot that the wet stain disappeared before our eyes. *I think they know I'm playing against them*, I thought. They saw my determination to never miss a ball.

In the state dining room before a game one time, John bet David that he could make me miss a ball. I knew nothing about the bet until after the game was over. At first, when they were just practicing, there was no need for all-out recovery efforts on my part. Then in the first set, never was a ball missed. In the second set, after I had gotten soaked with sweat, John put a wicked spin on the ball on one of his serves. It went into the net and then fell to the court, taking a crazy bounce. I was already reaching for it but grabbed air. I continued to the other side as if I had picked it up, as basketball players do when they still go through the motions of a layup even though they have lost the ball.

I ought to let that motha' stay out there, I thought, standing at the post. John was a professional, I'd heard. David was just eighteen years old, real big and fat. I heard him complain to John that his serve was illegal.

The first family comes first. Whatever the family wants or needs as your service to them, you are to promptly provide it, no questions asked, I thought, recalling the first lady's words during our interview. I took off as if nothing ever happened and snatched the ball up like always. David lost the fifty-dollar bet but never held it against me.

As the first family's tennis frenzy continued, I lost weight, but I continued eating like a horse. I couldn't help it. I would change clothes several times a day. Sometimes I would have time to take a shower before returning to the court. Normally, pitchers of ice water and Gatorade were placed on a table under a tent for the family and their guests. Before long, David instructed the butlers to bring my own pitchers. When I ran for David, he allowed me to have the butlers bring me things from the kitchen, too.

"Hey, Forest, you want something from the kitchen?" David had asked one day. He, Jenny, and their guest were sitting at a table under a huge umbrella on the patio, talking.

"Ah, yeah, sir," I answered, not quite saying "yes sir."

"Sugar Bear!" David yelled, calling him just before he could reenter the mansion from the patio doors. "Go let Forest tell you what he wants and bring it to him."

Sugar Bear walked up to me frowning, unhappy at the idea of having to wait on me. None of us had ever seen this occur before. I instantly felt special and privileged.

We were far out of earshot of the patio. "Ah, nigger boy, I'll have you bring me, ah, let's see, two fully dressed double cheeseburgers, eight pecan brownies, a pitcher of orange juice, and an ice-cream Coke float," I told him. "And look, nigger boy, you better not spit in my drinks or on my food. Tell Bobby to seal it."

I did this to all the other butlers except Roy Lee. They were so angry that I always checked my food.

Now, the first lady didn't play that food and water game with me. She was strictly 1800s. I could just imagine her reaction: *Oh no, nigger! You better get your black a-- back out there on that court and run those darn balls. How dare you ask for snacks and refreshments? We're the good white folks, not you. Have you been talking to David lately? I think we need to interview about this.*

As I huffed and puffed and ran after those darn little light-green balls, I began analyzing the importance of my functions in connection with the game of tennis. I had questions. *Why do the players get all the glory at tennis matches? Why not honor the ball runners like me, s---. After all, I'm out here scrambling across this hot court in this hot sun to scoop up* your *ball that* you *missed! I'm fixing your mistake with zero downtime. Share! Let us get some of the glory sometimes,* I thought. I knew I was hallucinating, but they were running me without remorse.

Say, Saint? Man, you need to tell these white folks you're not a horse; you're not an animal. You are a man, *a human being. They running you like you're a machine, brother,* my invisible, unwelcomed friend added. *You the most important motha' out here! They need to change the name to CTC All-Star Tennis, 'cause that's what it's all about, you running your butt off in them Chuck Taylor Converse.*

And why they wanna call you the ball boy? Why you can't be the ball man? All the running you do, they ought to call you the ball godfather. And tell the first lady you need refreshments! It's hot out here. If she thinks a horse can kick you and it not hurt, she might think a niggah can run all day and not get tired.

One day I had been running balls all morning for David, John, and mansion security. It was the day before the governor was leaving for one of his annual trips. Now running for the first couple, I was exhausted. Once, after I collected the first two balls and bounced them to the governor, he caught and placed them in his pocket. When I bounced the third ball to him, sweat was burning in my eyes, and I inadvertently bounced it too close. The ball hit Pops directly in his executive testicles.

"*Ow!*" he gasped and doubled over, dropping his racquet. Butch ran to his aid.

"Aaaaw, s---!" I exclaimed, but low enough that Mrs. Edwards couldn't hear. The governor heard me, though. I looked around quickly. The first lady stood eighty feet away, her racquet hand on her hip and her other hand acting as a sun visor.

Damn, Saint! That's gotta hurt. You delayed answering the first lady. You beat Butch up in the car. Now you done hit the whole governor *of the whole* state of Louisiana *in the whole* nuts. *What's wrong with you? She won't be screaming, 'Laissez les bons temps rouler'* tonight in the first bed in the first bedroom! They were out here getting this last game on to build up for a good climax before he left, but now you done tabled her sausage jambalaya. Niggah, your a-- is toast.*

"Are you all right, sir?" Butch asked while glaring at me.

"I'm all right," Governor Edwards said, straining to talk as he waved Butch off.

Now, niggah, you need to stop backing up to your post at the net. Turn around and walk back to it so you can face Mrs. Elaine. You know she's looking at your a--, huh? You're acting like you don't want to see her. She's still back there, niggah, waiting for y'all's eyes to make contact. I mean, you gonna have to run up to her and give her the balls anyway. Man, that ain't your fault, Saint. All this running you been doing all day. What they expect? You a human being. You ain't no machine. You gets tired. They should have had two runners out here anyway. Saint, man, you shoulda hit him from day one. Then they would have never kept bringing you out here. But no, you want to show off. You're a Capitol High Lion and all that crap. She gonna get you and Lion your a-- back to Angola. Just watch.

When I made it to my post, backing up all the way, I thought it proper to update her. *"He's all right, ma'am! He said he's all right!"* I yelled. The first lady must have thought I had a crick in my neck and couldn't turn around, because I was facing the governor as I shouted at her. I wished I had a rubber arm I could stretch forty feet to politely place her balls on her extended racquet. That way I didn't have to walk over there and face her.

When I finally did go over to her and give her the balls, she had this look in her eyes that said, *"I saw what you did, Hammond, and I have been waiting for you to turn around and face me like a convict so I could reprimand you about the careless handling of my goods over there, but you wouldn't dare look my way."* At the same time, I didn't read anywhere in her eyes that she was mad at me. The long stare and roll of her eyes seemed to be telling me that, strangely, I wasn't in any trouble. After all, my invisible, unwelcomed friends made some good points in relieving me of any fears.

When she rolled her eyes looking away from you, that meant, "Now, Hammond, next time, I want it where if I can't have it, they can't get it neither. I want him down! I want him flat on his back, not just bent over, Hammond. Take him down—ambush him! Put the Silver Fox on his a--, Hammond. That's why I got you here. I studied your file. If anyone can do it, I figured you could, Saint. Do you copy me? Darn it!"

While I squatted at the post, it looked as if they were at war. Governor Edwards would jump off the court and put all his power behind his serves. I thought he might have been trying to induce a heart attack in his wife as she tried to make the return. Occasionally, she would ace him and he would get mad. He would try to ace her time after time, but she would politely airmail his serve back over the net, stamped *return to sender.*

"Damn! I can't see how she keeps sending it back," Pops muttered each time he thought he had gotten a ball by her.

Chapter 16

Boxing, Tea Parties, Chess, and Football

Damon drove me to Cohn Turner, a formal-clothing store where Daddy bought his expensive suits. With Billy Wright's bills, I got a black three-piece pinstriped suit. Then at Montgomery Ward, Deborah Lafayette, a classmate I took chemistry with, bought me a lovely shirt and tie.

The night Sugar Ray Leonard fought Marcos Geraldo, I was sitting ringside with the governor and feeling like a gangsta. Before the fight, Damon made arrangements for me to spar with Sugar Ray at his training headquarters, the Capitol House Hotel in downtown Baton Rouge. A ring was set up and I met David Jacobs, Sugar Ray's actual trainer, though Angelo Dundee was his trainer for publicity purposes because he had been Muhammad Ali's trainer. After Jacobs saw me warming up in the ring, he decided not to let Sugar Ray spar with me, saying I was too fast for a light heavyweight and Ray might get cut before the fight. "You move like Ray," Jacobs said. "You can spar with Roger, Ray's brother. He fights professional and this would be good experience for you."

A friendly sparring session with Roger Leonard for five three-minute rounds turned into an all-out fight, which is what sparring actually is. He was trying to knock me out. I took pleasure in frustrating his attempts, utilizing everything Cheyenne taught me. Roger threw everything he had during the first two rounds as I danced to loosen up. In the third round I went into the Mongoose mode, scoring points. The fourth round I worked on inside fighting, where Roger caught me with a powerful left hook that jarred me. I blitzed him with several combinations and backed off. In the fifth round, I danced and jabbed him, bloodying his nose and mouth. At the end of the fight, I felt like going five more rounds. I was addicted to fighting.

Billy Wright, Billy Roth, and the other investors were impressed. "This is my fighter," Billy Wright said, introducing me to one of them. He gave me several more $100 bills. They knew it was a matter of time before I would be light-heavyweight champion of the world.

A lot of guys I knew from the hood had come and cheered for me as I sparred. They were surprised that I had become a boxer, after having always seen me as a track star and football player. They thought I was free, asking me, "Say, Forest, when you got out?" Damon was always in earshot.

Jacobs came to the mansion the following day and met the governor and the convicts. He gave me his phone number and address in Palmer Park, Maryland and told me to come see him when I got out.

The Sugar Ray fight was my first time seated at ringside at a professional fight. Geraldo was much taller and bigger than Ray, but Ray worked him over throughout the fight. Geraldo got frustrated because Ray was a moving target that was too hard to hit. Sugar Ray won the fight.

A rematch was arranged between me and Coleman at Angola. As Damon, Captain Jones, and I walked past the cellblock approaching the control center, I saw the spot where Graveyard had died. Captain Jones asked what was wrong with me. I told him nothing. Once the iron gate slammed behind them, Damon and Captain Jones turned and looked back at their only way out.

"Now, Captain, look, you ain't gonna have no problem because you're an old man," I said. "Damon, if any of them big white convicts walk up to you and look at you, just say, 'I'm Saint's ho'. I belong to Saint.' And ain't nobody gonna mess with you, okay? I'm not kidding. You gotta say it." I barely finished before bursting into laughter at the expressions on their faces. Damon was scared out of his wits. I saw it in both their eyes. The Captain was having second thoughts. After all, they were still Louisiana state policemen who were coming inside the state penitentiary. By coming down on the big-yard walk with me, they were taking a chance on actually being killed.

At the law library, it was good to see Shorty, Victor, and Sioux Dog.

A huge crowd of convicts stood at the big-yard snitcher gate by the machinegun tower as we approached. "Y'all better watch your backs," I told Damon and Captain Jones. "Half these dudes down here are packing knives, so I hope they don't recognize y'all as being the one that sent them up here. I'm not playing this time. This is for real; watch your backs and each other's back. They'll be looking at you hard to see if they recognize you, okay?"

They nodded. Captain Jones lit a cigarette, then realized he was holding a lit cigarette in his hand already.

In the first round of the rematch, Coleman brought the fight to me. I got on my bicycle, but I needed more speed. The entire big-yard population had gathered around the ring, which was out on the big yard on this bright Fourth of July holiday. It reminded me of boxing films I'd seen of Jack Johnson back in the early 1900s when they fought in the sun.

I played *catch me if you can* with Coleman the first round. The second round, Coleman was getting better, and I saw he had become really good. He was sharper than when I'd first fought him. He trapped me against the ropes. He had learned how to cut the ring off now. I slipped his overhand right just a quarter of an inch from receiving full impact. My weight of 180 was still hindering me. The blow brushed the front of my face. At the end of the round, my mouthpiece wasn't fitting securely in my mouth. In my corner I talked to Damon about it.

"Take my mouthpiece out. It ain't fitting right. I can't bite down on it," I said.

"Damn, Saint!" Damon exclaimed. "He done knocked your two front teeth out of socket. They're leaning back against the roof of your mouth. I'm gonna throw the towel in."

"No, man! I'm all right. It's just teeth! I can still fight. I can still knock him out and win. We're Vikings down here, captain. Whores throw towels in. We do or die in here. They been expecting and wanting to see this fight. Let us fight. Win or lose, I don't care. Are they completely out or just leaning back against the roof?"

"They're leaning against the roof," Captain Jones said.

"I think we ought to throw the towel in, Captain," Damon reiterated. "Too much is at stake, Captain," he pleaded.

"You think you can take him down, Forest?" Captain Jones asked, squinting and drawing on his Camel cigarette.

"It's take him *out*, Captain. Take him out. I'm-a try. Can't let him know I'm hurt. Y'all acting like I'm hurt and his corner gonna tell him he hurt me. The secret to fighting is to never panic when you suffer a disadvantage. All these convicts down there ain't pulling for me. Lot of 'em spies. They try to get close and listen and go tell his corner what they heard." I looked down into the faces of convicts I knew.

"One of these convicts has probably found out and gone over and told his corner," Damon said, looking around. I looked around, too.

"No way," I said. "I see now that everybody down there are friends. They wouldn't let a rat get close to my corner."

"All right," Captain Jones finally said. "Whatever you say. Don't let him hurt you, now. Watch him close. He's good."

Because of my teeth, I couldn't bite down hard if I went into a mix-up with him, so I avoided getting into any punching exchanges. A hook would easily break my open jaw. I continued boxing on the balls of my feet. Coleman chased me all around the ring trying to knock me out. He never landed or scored any clean head or body blows. When he got in, I tied him up and pushed him off, which frustrated his attack because he had to catch me again and that wasn't going to be easy. But in the end, I just could not fight my fight.

Many guys lost money betting on me. The big-yard crowd that was cheering for me wound up booing me—except for my friends.

"Man, that niggah Saint ain't fighting!" one convict shouted. "That niggah too fat to fight. I thought that niggah was a Saint." It was obvious he had lost lots of money on me.

"Saint, you're still the champ," Keith Muhammad said as he shook my hand. "You still won by giving Coleman a chance to be the champion up here now. They had been wishing for this fight. You're on your way out. Now it's his turn to be king of the river."

"Y'all see that guy back there that told me I was still the champ?" I asked my escorts.

"Yeah," they said.

"That's the Muslim that was one of the leaders in the January 10, 1972, shooting on North Boulevard, where police killed four Muslims and their own officers. Y'all remember that?" I asked.

"Uh huh," they both responded quickly, in a hurry to get out of Angola.

They contacted mansion security, who made arrangements for a dentist to be waiting for me when we got back to town. Damon's wife, Tara, worked for Dr. William Tuttle. At the time, Dr. Tuttle was enjoying his Fourth of July holiday, sitting around the pool with his family. He left immediately for his office on Goodwood Boulevard, where we met him. Dr. Tuttle popped both teeth back into place, performed a root canal, and gave me some pain pills. He was intrigued as Damon told him the details of the fight.

Captain Jones was Governor Edwards' main driver, and he said he would tell Pops about what went down when he came back from his trip out of state. "He'll be really impressed with your courage."

In the meantime, inside the mansion we continued serving various groups. On weekends we mostly waited on old white ladies who socialized during tea parties as if they were class reunions. They boasted about how well they could speak, read, and write Spanish, French, and German. They took pleasure in talking with the butlers, recounting how their instructors were really hard on them back then, but they were glad and proud their parents instilled discipline. They were old and generally disregarded by present-day society, but in my mind, they were the personification of what winners really are.

During a tea function, half the butlers set up the state dining, drawing, and sitting rooms. Some set out nuts and mints. Bobby sent out huge silver trays with stuffed eggs, crabmeat dip, tuna dip, sour-cream dip, chips, and Hi-Ho, Club, Waverly, and Ritz crackers. Sally made the tea in one of the sides of the huge coffee unit. As we brought cups to the back, Mason would pour any remaining drops of tea from each cup into an empty half-and-half carton. He would light a candle in a small pocket-size bowl and place it in his locker. He would then pour all the tea drops he collected into the bowl, surrounding the candle as it burned. As the wax melted and dripped down to the tea, whoever left that drop of tea in the cup tipped us. Devold and Sugar Bear were afraid of Mason's magical ability to make the women tip.

Mason collected the tea in a plastic medicine bottle and poured it into the vat after the first batch ran out. After Sally made the first batch of tea, he went to the rear dining room and took a nap. Mason made the second batch. By the time the second batch was gone, the 300 elderly women were so jolly that they finished tipping us and began tipping each other. Big, tall Ira Sappington, the state trooper who I thought called me "the dumb waiter," would come from his post at the front desk, stand in the middle of the foyer, and stare through his black-framed glasses to see what all the chatter was about. The scene was a far cry from when the tea got started. The old ladies would be cackling like yard hens. Seeing that everything was all right and the ladies were enjoying themselves, the state trooper would go back to his seat at the front desk. During a tea function, mansion security didn't have to be on the spot, watch-dogging us, because there was nothing during a nice little old-fashioned tea party that the convicts could screw up.

"Oh, here, boy. This is for you," the ladies would say. "Would you freshen up my cup of tea, please, darling? Girl, I'll take care of this one. You did the last one. Here, sonny boy, and bring me another one, will you, please, and bring my friend one also?" Some of them even started calling us sir: "Sir, would you please bring me another cup of tea? Thank you, sir." Nobody knew what had gotten into them. Mason always said his voodoo was working on them and bragged that it was the reason we were being tipped so much.

Mason and Phillip would show the old ladies where they could hang their coats and where the restrooms were and give them a peek into the governor's office. They were all in the grannies' faces as they hugged and walked among them. We grinned and were charming, and the ladies rubbed their bodies against us while we carried their trays. In the end, each of us collected, on average, $200. Sugar Bear laughed and smiled as he collected his tips. Roy Lee tried to be slick and not let anyone see him take any money, but his hand kept going into his pants pocket as if he had an itch. I started getting scared after I had collected over $200. One time we collected nearly $900 each.

On some rainy days, David Edwards played chess with Phillip and Mason in the rear dining room. Jenny, his wife, was always with him as a witness to his prowess in kicking convicts' butts on the chess board. I heard her one afternoon expressing her excitement over a chess game between her husband and Mason, an intelligent and educated convict. Mason had been the assistant editor of the *Angolite*, the nationally renowned prison magazine. Wilbert Rideau, who served on death row from 1960 to 1972, when the U.S. Supreme Court abolished the death penalty, was the editor and had won many national awards.

When I walked back there, Sugar Bear, Roy Lee, Devold, Frank, and Phillip were shaking their heads, saying, "Mason had him and let him get away."

"Forest, can you play?" David asked.

"Ah, not really," I answered. That turned out to be the wrong response. David was young but intelligent. He read between the lines.

"What do you mean, not really? You can either play or you can't play. Come on, sit," David ordered. "Mason, move and let Forest have that chair." I tried to decline.

"You want me to go tell Mama you don't want to play chess with me?" he asked. He wasn't serious but just liked calling a technical foul on me to get me to cooperate. He began reminding me how the pieces moved. Victor and I played chess so much in the law library back at Angola that I would never forget how they moved.

"I tried to warn you," I said, after beating him two games straight.

He loved a challenge, so he wanted to continue playing. It was July and playing chess with David turned out to be a good way for me to escape running tennis balls. If mansion security, Anna, or the first lady called the kitchen, they were told that I was occupied in a game of chess with David, and they got someone else to run the balls. They kept walking by us with their racquets in their hands. Boy, was I glad! I would boast to David how I was going to beat him the next time. That way he would keep me at the table, inside the big house enjoying the air conditioning and ice-cream floats.

I began beating David fairly regularly. I would brag of whipping him with the blitzkrieg technique, which Victor Linkletter had taught me at Angola. I loved it. He had explained to me that the term meant "lightning war." It was an attack maneuver employed by Germany during World War II, based on speed and the element of surprise.

"The blitzkrieg. It's the blitzkrieg, Master David, sir. The blitzkrieg. There is just absolutely nothing you can do to defend against it. It's unbeatable."

"*Damn it, Forest! I want you to tell me there is no such thing as a blitzkrieg. You're just making that up!*" David shouted one day, taking his nickel-plated .357 magnum off the table and sticking it in my face at point-blank range. "*Tell me there ain't no blitzkrieg!*"

Jenny was frightened and moved back against the wall. She had never seen her husband this furious. "Tell him there's no blitzkrieg, Forest," Jenny pleaded, fearing that David would pull the trigger.

"Mr. David," I said, "it's not 'ain't' like you said, but isn't. You should say, 'Tell me there isn't no blitzkrieg.' Oh, but yes there is. Want me to show you? Look right there." I pointed at the marble chessboard, where my black pieces had checkmated his white king. "That's it right there. Take another look. Checkmate. That's the blitzkrieg."

"*There ain't no damn such thing as a blitzkrieg. This blitzkrieg better win, damn it, or else your a— is going back to Angola*," he promised. "*I'm-a tell Mama. I'm serious. You better win, Forest, and save yourself.*"

"Ya'suh, massa, David, suh," I said.

"Let's go," he said, picking up his pillow and the set. He ordered me to follow him as he went stomping through the elevator foyer hall. He entered the governor's office. "*Sit there, damn it,*" David ordered, pointing at the governor's chair behind the desk. David stood staring me in the face. At this proximity, I saw that his eyes were the same as his father's.

"But that's the governor's chair, Mr. David. I don't think I better."

"*Sit down, damn it!*" he yelled again.

"All right. All right. I'm-a let you win, okay?"

"*No you're not either! Sit down,*" he ordered again. Deep down inside, I knew he was angry because I was a niggah and a convict that he couldn't outthink. Somebody must have told him or taught him or he read it somewhere in a book that a niggah couldn't or wasn't supposed to be capable of thinking, especially since chess was a thinking game. I had been whipping his butt and talking Angola trash to him while enjoying ice-cream floats.

"Well, Massa David, suh, dis here gonna be one of dem good old Angola convict whipping I'm 'on have to put on ya here, suh. So prepare yo'self to take dis here beatin' here, suh."

I picked him apart with my knights. David was infuriated as I made his moves look ridiculous. I would whinny like a horse before I picked up his piece. "I t'ink," I said, sounding like Sally, "I want to go on an Easter egg hunt on a golf-course green." My knight captured his pieces as though they were gifts. My invisible, unwelcomed friend was having a ball. My listening to it and repeating its words was what had gotten David mad as hell. I tore David a new one, with Jenny right by his side. He played as if he was supposed to win by Divine Right. "Ah, this is Captain Kirk," I would say before I made his chess pieces disappear. "I'm getting ready to beam your queen up, Mr. David." He would get up, stomp out of the office, and come back looking like a mad Angola bull. Jenny got frustrated and left at times but always came back.

At one point, David noticed me taking too long to move and turned around.

"Aw, Mom," he said, "leave him alone. I made him sit here. He didn't want to. He's already scared. I have to beat him when he's not under pressure. Will you leave, Mom?"

"Come here, David," the first lady said softly to her son. She moved out of sight towards the elevator. David followed her. The sound of the elevator door opening made me realize she was going back upstairs. When David came back in, he called the kitchen and had Roy Lee bring him an ice-cream float.

"You're not in any trouble, so don't worry," David said, assuring me.

"Mr. David, the only thing I was worried about is whether or not you were gonna let me have a float too. That's unfair pressure for you to have one and me not have one."

Football on the Lawn

It was August 1979, the height of hurricane season. When it rained, there was no tennis, which meant no ball running. On one such weekend, the butlers were standing around in the butler's station reading the newspaper, listening to music, eating snacks, and just relaxing when Bobby announced that David's car was coming up the drive. Five minutes later, Phillip answered the service phone and said, "Yes sir, Mr. David." He hung up and walked towards the stairs. "Mr. David told us to get dressed. He wants to play football. You too, Mr. Boxer," he added with a smile, knowing I had not yet been exposed to this page of the mansion's program.

"Phillip, are you serious?" I asked. "Does he know it's raining cats and dogs out there?"

"That's the only time David likes to play—when it's raining," Roy Lee explained. "The wet soggy ground helps cushion his fall when he's tackled so he don't break his big a--."

"Let's get it over with," Phillip said, shrugging.

I looked at Bobby. He was laughing. "Are you going, too?" I asked. Bobby shook his head. "Man, we's dry and comfortable. What's wrong with him?" I asked anybody who would answer. Suddenly, I realized I hadn't played football in a long time. *Why not go play some football out on the front lawn of the governor's mansion with the governor's son?* I got over it.

The grass was so thick it was almost like running on a mattress. On the first play of the game, David caught a pass and somehow broke a tackle. He looked to his right as Phillip and Devold tried to tackle him. He stiff-armed Devold into the water-soaked lawn. Phillip was too smart to try to bring David down to the ground. David dragged Phillip until he let him go. Coming from my coverage of Mason, I caught up with David from the left—his blind side. He was looking right and didn't see. He then saw me running beside him. I was looking straight ahead, pretending to be a jogger just running my daily course. We had a ways to go and he couldn't outrun me. David tried to slant away from me. That's when I dumped him.

Onto the grass we both went. David was sliding on the grass on his stomach, kicking up water like an eighteen-wheeler when it passes a car in the rain. I was lying on his backside, as if riding a surfboard, when he finally stopped sliding. All the butlers looked at me when I turned around, then simultaneously they glanced towards the mansion's second-floor window. I hopped off David's butt like a spooked Texas jackrabbit. It would have been my luck that just as Mrs. Edwards was moving around in her upstairs room, she decided to check on her son. *"Oh, my God! Edwin, come see, quickly. What is Hammond trying to do? Is that how they play football in Angola?"*

I got a lot of pleasure out of my tackle. David wasn't hurt, but just the idea that I slam dunked him on the grass did me all the good I needed. What counted most of all was that David loved it. He didn't want the convicts to keep babying him. He wanted to play football. He wanted us to be rough with him. He wanted to experience everything about football, including the force of a real tackle.

After receiving the ball for our possession, I attempted to run a quarterback sneak, but I felt like a car spinning its wheels in the mud. I slipped and fell down. My face and hair were covered with mud and grass. I looked up and there was David, flying through the air. When he came down, he landed on top of my head and chest. I knew it was payback. "Aw, shucks. David, man, I was down!" I yelled. The butlers thought I had lost my mind.

"I had to touch you, though, Forest," David answered.

"Touch me? You almost broke my neck! David, you dived on top of me. You know, like skydiving! That was not a touch, man."

"Well, Forest, I'm sorry. I didn't mean to hurt you."

"It's automatic, David! It's automatic hurt. Do you see what I'm saying? Forget about it. Let's go. Let's play ball," I said as we lined up for the next play.

In early October 1979, the campaign of Democrat Louis Lambert against Republican Dave Treen to succeed Edwards as governor was plotted at the mansion nearly every weekday. Lambert came to consult with Governor Edwards and Camille Gravel, Judge Edmund Reggie, and other political supporters. We were feeding at least 120 guests per day.

"Next month it's gonna get worse, right up to the time Pops goes out of office," Phillip said. "According to Mrs. Clemons' schedule, that cross-eyed b---- got us booked with parties at night and old folks' teas and balls in the daytime every damn weekend and some through the week."

For the first family, all of this free slave service would be coming to an end. Such royal service would have to be paid for, and even then they wouldn't get their money's worth. No five-star restaurant or hotel in the free world could outwork us convict butlers. Another group of convicts could only tie the game.

In the middle of October, Governor Edwards started jogging with me after he ate dinner. He was fifty-two years old at the time, so I would run step for step with him and then tell him I had to go. "Go ahead, Champ," is all he would say. The exercise made him feel great, and he continued running until it began getting cold. Paul Fontenot was always his bodyguard, floating in the general direction he was running, with his eyes on I-110.

Because of my morning and evening training schedule, I worked harder than any other butler. Damon appeared on many occasions just to pull me out of the mansion. We had become really good friends. He would take me riding around through town, running errands for himself. Damon had become involved with the governor's daughter, Victoria, and was catching a lot of heat from his wife, Tara. Victoria had a strong hold on him. He always seemed as though he wanted to tell me something but couldn't. Each time, he changed the subject. I sensed it wasn't about Victoria.

The rear floorboard of his unit was covered with magazines addressed to Governor Edwards. At first I thought they were women's fashion publications. "The governor sure likes his fine-dressed women," I said one time.

Damon showed me an arsenal of handguns and rifles he carried in the trunk. There were more than twenty different pistols and several rifles and electronic devices. He quickly closed the trunk so that I would not see anything for long.

Chapter 17

Serious Underlying Ramifications

At approximately two o'clock on a hot autumn weekend afternoon, Damon walked in from the stairs. "We got to talk," he said, moving quickly. I was the lone butler in the station and was playing solitaire on top of the salad bar. Damon got a Coke out of the cooler, opened it, and moved towards the dining room. I gathered the cards and headed to the stairs. He entered the dining room, calling, "Let's go in here, Saint!"

We usually talk in his car when he's moving like that, I thought. When I turned the corner by the dumbwaiter, the dining-room door was closed. I entered, and Damon was already seated in the sixth chair on the right side, with the double doors that led to the foyer behind him. The fifth chair was pulled out a little for me to take. Something about Damon's eyes made me wary as I sat in the chair he indicated.

"I got some pretty bad news for you," Damon said. To me, pretty bad news would be that Daddy was dead.

"Bad news?" I repeated. "I've been hearing bad news all my life. One day, my mother's living; the next day she's dead. One day I have a scholarship to play football in college; the next day, I'm in jail with a murder charge. I'm used to bad news, Mr. Robicheaux. What is it?"

"Billy Wright's dad. He's the one that owns the Wright and Percy Insurance Agency, not Billy, and he would be putting all the money up. He was a friend of Middleton y'all killed. Other investors knew him too. Neither Mr. Wright nor the other investors will allow their money to be used to promote someone charged with killing a friend of theirs. As it stands now, the boxing deal is dead. It's like it never existed. Gone," Damon explained.

I was wondering, *That's all? If that's as bad as it gets, that ain't nothing. When I get out, I'll go play pro football with the Saints if I have to.* I shuffled the cards as I listened. My head was hung a bit as I began to realize I was working with something more serious. I began to feel butterflies. I wondered if I might be overreacting.

"You know, just maybe, and I'm just saying maybe, I could win Mr. Wright and the other investors back over on your side," Damon said. "I mean, we got—they got too much invested in this thing already. You can tell these people are serious about spending money to promote you. I think what I need are some mitigating facts about your case. I got to have something to go back and hit them with. Billy wants to promote you, but it's his dad. Tell me, Saint, now, you didn't kill Middleton, did you, and blame Ramsey for it, or something, huh?"

"Oh, no, I didn't kill him," I answered truthfully. I knew he was reading my body language. I made direct eye contact when I answered. I exhaled deeply, tired of talking about what happened in the drugstore. I continued shuffling the cards slowly. As I talked about the events of the crime, Damon looked at me with an understanding and friendly face, one that I knew I could trust. He had helped me with boxing and had become a personal, caring friend of mine.

"So when I opened the door, I, like, halfway called out to him. I said, 'Hey, Boo.' I didn't finish because to the right I saw Boodie wrestling with the man. I yelled, like, 'Hey, Boo'daaaay!' He turned to me. The man pushed him over the center shelving, then fired a shot in his face. I don't know why it didn't hit him. I hit the floor and heard shots, then a clicking noise. I saw Boodie pointing a gun at the man, pulling the trigger. I yelled, like, 'Boodie!' and he snapped and threw his arms in front of his face, seeing the man pointing the gun at him. He turned in a circle then ran out, and I ran through the glass. So I run across Plank—"

"Wait—hold up, Hammond," Damon said.

I detected a hint of anxiety in his voice. His body language betrayed him. I was visited by the same sensations I felt on April 12, 1973, when Detectives Bob and Jimmy interrogated me. *Hmmmm, you've never called me Hammond before. Am I being interrogated?* I wondered.

"Didn't you go to the counter, get the gun, and bring and give it to Ramsey?" Damon asked.

Still shuffling the cards, I turned to answer him, but noise from the kitchen interrupted me. I turned to my left to see Phillip just as he pushed the door open from the butler's station. He saw we were in a serious discussion and backed out. Looking straight ahead and still shuffling the cards, I tried not to betray myself. I stared at the new drapes, studying their length and width as the silence built. In spite of my best efforts, I gave an involuntary and indistinct gasp as realization set in. I divided the deck and shuffled it, hoping Damon didn't detect it. *But he had to,* I thought. *He's sitting here watching me.* The butterflies turned into a full-blown adrenaline rush. I had to control it. *Damn,* I thought. I suddenly saw the big picture. I knew who Damon really was, but he didn't know I knew. I had to continue to act as though I didn't know who he was.

"Well, Saint, what? Did you?" Damon asked again, a bit impatient this time.

In the ten seconds that elapsed between Damon's telltale question and Phillip's lifesaving intrusion, I blinked my eyes calmly as I tried to remember what I thought I'd heard, seen, and experienced somewhere in the past. I recalled Bobby's strange greeting to Damon the first day we met in the kitchen, when he asked me if I could still fight.

"Hey, Mr. Damon Robicheaux, long time no see. Where you been, in the basement again? Ha, ha, ha."

"I didn't touch that gun until I got home. That's when I took it from him."

"Hold up—wait. Wait a long minute here. Didn't you go to the counter, get the gun, and bring and give it to Ramsey?" Polozola asked at the evidentiary hearing.

Why you called me Hammond when you asked me about the gun? I wondered now. *What? You're doing police work? I'm not your friend Saint, the boxer, anymore? How you know Ramsey was my codefendant? And most of all, how is it that you just asked me the identical question Polozola asked me in federal court during my evidentiary hearing?*

"Boy, there is either a lot of misunderstanding or a lot of perjury going on in this case, but I'm going to get to the bottom of it. . . . If I have to get the U.S. attorney to stay with the grand jury for fifty years, I'm getting to the bottom of this. . . . Don't be surprised when the FBI goes out and interviews every witness. If it's memory, that's one thing. If it's deliberately lying to me, it's something else."

Within a nanosecond I had total recall. I stopped shuffling the cards and turned. Damon and I stared into each other's soul, it appeared, glaring eye to eye, our faces twelve inches apart. *You're undercover, aren't you?* I tried asking with my stare. *You're wired up. You're wearing a wire, aren't you?* I wanted to ask him so badly,

but I couldn't. "Oh, no, Mr. Robicheaux," I said. "I didn't do that."
I hate to disappoint you, podnah, I thought.

Since I didn't take the bait, Damon got up. "Well, I'll see what I can do with that," he said. "We can get other investors. Just keep all the stuff you have and keep training."

Why don't you ask me some related questions? I wondered. *You mean to tell me you're finished?* I looked up at him as he stood over me. I saw no reason that he would be feeling worse than I over the news of the boxing deal being dead. *You must be working for the feds and ratting on Pops too,* I thought.

Damon exited through the double doors. I got up and immediately reset the two chairs to the table, just as I learned working for Martin's Personal Janitorial Service. I was surprised to see Damon's Coke untouched and picked it up. Seeing that it left a water ring on the dining table, I entered the butler's station and got some paper napkins. When I came back, Damon was half-turned and walking out the doors again. "You got my Coke?" he asked. I nodded. He closed the doors and left. It had taken over six months for them to set this up, with all the promises of a professional boxing career, to ask me that one question. It all reminded me why my friend, the state trooper who brought me to the mansion, warned me not to trust anybody over here.

I saw the fifth chair was askew even though I had just pushed it up to the table. I pulled it out, looked under the bottom of the table, then tore a napkin and saw where adhesive residue made the piece of napkin stick.

"Why talk in here where it's so quiet when we've always rode and talked in your car, Mr. Robicheaux?" I whispered. *"How can you ask the same question Polozola asked in federal court? Why you moved my chair just to look for your Coke? Why you had to enter the room? You could see that the Coke was gone after opening the door. And the answer is,"* I said, sounding like a game-show host, *"because you're undercover. Damn, those bastards are serious about getting my a--!"*

During a dinner service, I was late making it to the first floor because of an appointment with Dr. Tuttle to make sure my teeth were healing correctly. I got back to the mansion as the desserts were ready to be served. I put on my bowtie, prepared the dessert tray in the kitchen, and headed to the dining room.

"I think it's a shame I'm being asked not to pardon him. He's a good man," Governor Edwards said to Polozola. He had invited himself over for dinner with Pops to discuss my case. "We saw him fight at the police academy one night with the ninth-ranked fighter in the United States. I think of all the hard work and training this young man had to go through be so good. He fights like a young Muhammad Ali—never a dull moment. Captain Jones took him to fight in Angola on the Fourth of July. Over a thousand convicts came to see him fight. He got his two teeth knocked out of socket in the second round. Damon wanted to throw the towel in and stop the fight, but he said no, he had three more rounds to fight. He told Damon, 'They been wanting to see this fight. I can still fight.' It just makes me feel, ah, I don't know how to describe it. Bad."

Roy Lee burst out of the dining room with two dinner plates in his hands. "Say you, Hammond boy," he whispered, "I don't think you better go in there." He stood between the salad bar and the cooler. I stood two steps from the door and across the salad bar from him. "I bet you'll never guess who's in the dining room talking to the governor about you." He couldn't wait for me to ask. "Polozola. I just picked his plate up. He's talking to Pops about your case. Pops told him you're a good worker and does your job and that he intended to pardon you at the end of his term."

Roy Lee put the plates on the counter and took the dessert tray out of my hand. Lieutenant Hart walked in from the elevator foyer and stood between the coffeepot and dumbwaiter, as if he knew something was going down. I saw Roy Lee's eyes focus on somebody behind me. I grabbed the plates, went to the window, and washed my hands. Officer Sidney Scott walked up and stood with Lieutenant Hart. It made me wonder what was going on. They had never done this before. As Roy Lee followed Phillip into the dining room, he tilted his head to the right, telling me Polozola was seated on the right side of the governor. I turned right as the door was open and saw Polozola wearing a light-blue suit and talking to Pops. He wore gold-frame eyeglasses.

The mansion security walked out as quickly as they had walked in. Other guests had come with Polozola, and a few butlers got upset that I wasn't picking up plates and servicing them. I saw several people leaving, but Polozola was not among them.

"Look here, Phillip," I said as I carried several glasses to the kitchen from the empty dining room.

"Yeah, what'cha need?" he asked.

"I need your expertise. I need you to find out if Polozola is in the governor's office. You know who I'm talking about?" I asked.

"Yeah."

"He's wearing glasses and got a blue suit on," I added.

Phillip burst through the elevator foyer door with the giant tablecloth wrapped around his arm as if he was looking for someone to give it to. I gathered all the dirty silverware and began cleaning.

"He's in there along with two other people, a district attorney dude from Baton Rouge and a fine chick. I never seen her before," he said when he returned.

"For a bill, go find out what they talking about. Can you do that?" I asked.

"Are you kidding?" Phillip smiled. "For $100 I'll tell you what color panties she wearing, strip search the DA, and take one of these coffee trays and whip that Polozola off state property." I couldn't help chuckling. If anyone could find out, Phillip could. "I'll be right back," he said. He quickly put a coffee tray together with four cups and left.

We got word to go home, and everybody went to the locker room and got dressed except me. After putting the finishing touches on the dining room, I vacuumed and turned the lights out. I saw the coffee set up on the counter and knew that Phillip had made it back but left with the Krewe of da Mansion at 7:45.

I did my daily workout and called Slim to come pick me up at 2200 hours. When I walked into the barracks, Phillip was in his usual place, on the phone talking to one of his many girlfriends. He saw Slim come in and knew I was behind him. I stopped by the office to see if I had any mail from the federal clerk of court. Mr. Williams was smiling as he approached me with a letter. It was DOC inmate farm mail. I had received a letter from an old friend in Angola. I sat at the table in the activity room among all the other convicts. The letter was short and sweet and said what I needed to know. It primarily consisted of instructions.

Adisaa, I hope this communication finds you doing well and still training hard. Word got to me about your fight on the big yard. You did what I would have done with the injury you had. It's takes a Giant, with a capital *G*, to fight like that. Don't forget to do all your reflex exercises and your parry and right-hand slipping drills. Nobody will ever hit you with a right hand as long as you dance like Mongoose. Always remember, don't throw just one jab. Throw three and four jabs to keep your man off balance. He won't see the right hand when it is time for you to throw it. When you are working your bag, keep moving and dancing around it the entire three minutes per round you are training. When you train, do your 200 sit-ups and 100 pushups. Do your neck exercises and jump ten two-minute rounds of rope. Don't worry about power. It's speed. It is Mongoose speed that frustrates Cobra. A moving target is hard to hit! Don't forget clip.

Baki na heri, rafiki (Remain in peace and stay with blessings, friend),
Cheyenne

I felt tears welling up, rushed to the darkness of the dormitory, and got in my bunk. I couldn't let anyone see the tears I cried. I looked over my life and saw all the fights I had ever been in. I felt now that I was involved in a fight for my life.

Phillip ended his conversation when he saw me reenter the activity room and joined me at the table. "Hey, bro, what do underlying— underlie ramiscation—let me see. I been thinking about this all night. He could force an appeal and delay it, or some . . . I don't know what he was talking about. Polozola said he was afraid of the underlying ramiscation of granting 'his writ.' Who he was talking about? You?" Phillip asked.

"I don't know. I didn't go in there. You did. That's why I'm paying you."

"He was telling Pops something about granting a petition, a writ. Oh, yeah, Pops told him a man shouldn't serve time in prison if he wasn't convicted. Pops was saying that when I walked in on them. That was it for me. I had to leave. I didn't want them to catch on to me being in there. That was a fine white b---- in there too. That ho' looked good! You seen her in there before?" Phillip asked. "Mike Mix and Bulldog Butch was in the foyer. I could have waited there and heard more, but I got all that from when I first went in with the coffee. They shut down after I was in there."

"All right, bro, now tell me again," I said. "Start from the time you first went in there."

Phillip repeated what he had heard several times before I paid him. I was trying to squeeze more words out of him. I couldn't drill him too long because of the rats at the barracks. They would report anything out of the ordinary to the good white folks, especially two niggahs who worked at the mansion talking like we were.

I figured Phillip heard Polozola say something about underlying ramifications. I had read the term in law books hundreds of times. "A man shouldn't serve time in prison if he wasn't convicted," the governor told Polozola. I lay in my bunk thinking about the conversation until I fell asleep. What did Polozola want to know about me and why? Would he deny my case and force me to appeal back to the Fifth Circuit? What are the underlying ramifications of granting a writ petition like this?

Chapter 18

The First Couple on Trial

Louis Lambert lost the gubernatorial election to Dave Treen. The governor-elect immediately started assembling his cabinet. During the campaign and the ensuing transition, we never had a dull moment, but our daily routines didn't change one bit. We were little different than pots and pans in the kitchen—no emotions, and you never had to say thanks to us because we weren't alive. We were inanimate objects that were treated like, well, property.

With Thanksgiving over, there was a change in attitude around the mansion. The convicts operated with a heightened level of sensitivity, as if they knew trouble was approaching and they didn't want to be the ones to get the ax. I thought I had left that feeling of impending danger at the front gate of Angola. Not hearing from Damon since our encounter in the dining room led me to conclude that something definitely was not right. Most troubling of all, a whole year and two months had passed and I still hadn't received a decision on my case. It was unprecedented to not get an answer on a writ of habeas corpus, pro or con, after an entire year.

Governor Edwards went on hunting trips to Canada and would be gone for weeks. Bobby always knew what to cook for the governor when he came back: a rib-eye steak, baked potato, steamed green lima beans in cream of mushroom soup, salad, iced tea, and fresh, hot apple pie—his favorite dessert. The fact that the governor had been running hard showed in his face and under his eyes. When he finally returned to the mansion, mansion security circulated photographs of him for everyone to see. One time the photos showed Governor Edwards sitting on horseback, looking like Ben Cartwright. Both he and his scout held high-powered rifles against their shoulders. No convict would really comment on the photos. We just said stuff like, "Gollee! That's a beautiful horse. That's some lovely countryside, Mr. Scott. That's a beautiful waterfall." When I received the pictures while sitting on the green stool by the coffeepot in the butler's station, I thought I had never seen any place in the United States that looked like this country—as if I had traveled the country.

That night when the rolling conference room pulled away from the mansion, I was on board, having taken a break from training. The trial began as soon as the four tires of the van were on the street. Phillip, the lead prosecuting attorney, immediately examined the evidence before passing it around to each juror. He looked at the governor in the eight-by-ten photograph and thoroughly checked out his scout. Then he examined the horses to see if they were real. He looked at every square inch of the photograph before giving his opening statement and argument all at once. "This ain't nothing but *Pops' proof tactic,* to get you to see, think, and believe he's been gone three weeks hunting in the wilderness. But what did he kill?"

"That man's fifty-two years old and don't have the stamina to be crossing all that country on horseback. Look at the mountains. Pops sits on his a-- all day playing governor."

"They probably dropped him down in a helicopter," Mason theorized. "He got out, got on a horse, they handed him his rifle, the photographer took the pictures, and Pops flew back to Lake Tahoe and laid out with four or five of them fine young white girls."

"What was he hunting?" Phillip asked. "Did he kill anything? Show me something. Show me something like a dead buck, a doe, a wild boar, a raccoon, a squirrel, a rabbit, a pigeon—*something!* I'll take a dead armadillo—a road kill—but show me *something dead.* When big-game hunters go hunting and make a kill, they take pictures standing over the quarry and holding its rack or horns, you know? What they killed be right in front or under them, laying on the ground, dead where it fell. Now, here is Pops sitting on a horse, toting a gun, and claiming he was out hunting. I don't believe that! This could be a studio or something. You know how rich white folks do. Where are the birds flying in the background? I don't see any. Pops, you give this to Moms and let her believe you been hunting, but don't come passing it around to me like you want to make me believe it."

"He was hunting two-leg dears," Sally said, laughing.

"That's right, Sally," Phillip agreed. His eyes were red from having hit a bottle that was being passed around. Slim made a daily liquor stop at Winn Bush, a store at the corner of Fuqua and North Twenty-Eighth streets.

The trial continued on another day as the Krewe of da Mansion drove to the barracks. When the governor went teal hunting, something he loved to do, he would be gone for days. He left for about ten days once and upon his return, the front desk called the kitchen for the butlers to come get the ducks he'd killed from the helicopter out front. We each grabbed from the helicopter a thick, frozen-solid, foam container that had *Governor's Ducks* written on it. Captain Jones got off the helicopter with a manila envelope of photographs and gave them to the front desk. Security knew what to do with them: disseminate them throughout the mansion. We all assembled at the dumbwaiter, looking at each other while sending the ducks down to the basement freezer. No one uttered a word while mansion security was around getting coffee, but the alleged ducks the governor allegedly killed on his alleged hunting trip would soon become evidence for the next trial of Governor Edwards in the rolling conference room.

"Boy, whoever cleaned those ducks must have been a sho-nuff professional," Roy Lee said in the van. He had inspected the containers inside and out. "Those containers were cleaner than a surgeon's scalpel."

"You ain't never lied," Devold said.

"They don't wrap stuff this good in Schwegmann's in New Orleans, huh, Frank?" Phillip asked, referring to the supermarket chain. "I look at the photos and I see Pops. I see his duck guide. I see his gun. I see the lake and Pops wearing knee-high rubber boots, but where's the dogs that go out in the water and fetch the ducks? If he was around duck hunting, where's the ducks in the background flying over the lake? Look like the wind ought to be blowing and moving the grass in different directions. I mean, you know, these supposed to be wild ducks he just went and kilt, right? Show me something wild. Where is the wild evidence? I wanna see some fresh wild blood in one container—just one wild feather stuck on the side. I'll take anything, a wild smell, a frozen quack, but don't come telling me these are wild ducks you killed on your hunting trip. I noticed a label on the bottom edge of one of the containers. Man, those were Winn-Dixie ducks. The tag said $4.49 a pound. A missed tag."

"I hope you took that tag off," Devold said, believing Phillip's jest. "You don't want Moms to get a hold of this. Pops a sho' get put in the doghouse. He'll have to sleep out there in that horse stable."

"Hey, Moms ain't no fool, now," Phillip said. "She got her little issue going on too when Pops be gone. You ever noticed every time Pops leaves out of town, Captain McCormick never fails to pop up over here to play tennis with Mrs. Elaine? *Every time!*" Phillip was introducing the next defendant to be placed on trial. We tried the first couple simultaneously.

"You know, every time Moms leaves and goes to Florida, Pops has Captain Jones drive her there," Mason said. "I walked in on her one morning in the bathroom when she got back. The door was open, and she was down on her hands and knees with a big ball of white paper towel, wiping the floor trying to pick up any fallen hairs from the blondes Pops been having over. Every time before she leaves, she tells me not to vacuum her room until after she gets back a day or two later. She searches and inspects everything—the shower, bathtub, the toilet, even the sink drain. She got this bright light and giant magnifying glass she used, looking for hairs in the bed and on the pillows. I had to put some luggage up and found that stuff in one of her suitcases. I didn't know what it was for until I saw her using it one time around the bed. I said, 'Damn! Your eyes that bad?'"

"Aw, you lying," Sugar Bear said. "You ain't asked Mrs. Elaine that."

"No, man," Mason admitted. "I was thinking that to myself."

Since it was open testimony time and I had something to add, I felt obligated to testify for the state penitentiary. "I'll tell you something y'all might not believe," I said. "I was riding around town with this Damon Robicheaux dude and on the rear floorboard was piles of little booklet-type magazines for clothing fashions addressed to Pops. They were all on the backseat and everywhere, so, when I see 'em, I'm asking myself, you know, like, what is Robicheaux doing with piles of the governor's magazines in his car? When I looked through 'em, all it had on each of the thirty pages was the finest white chicks you ever laid your eyes on. All of 'em in their late twenties, early thirties. It look like they were styling clothes when you first look at them wearing some good-looking, expensive threads, bro, I'm telling you."

"What'cha talking about, a Spiegel catalog? That's not admissible," Frank interjected.

"No, no, wait a minute. Let me finish, Two Times. It's a catalog all right, but different. On each page, it had a description of the woman, the chick's measurements, you know, her size, what she was wearing, and the pictures were so real, they looked like true-to-life professional photographs. They had a little write-up about them that talked about what was inside the clothing, man! It was a ho' menu. A menu of women. Each had an identification code under the picture and what she likes to do. I didn't know clothes like to do anything. You ever heard of that? Each chick had a separate page with just one full-body picture on it. They send Pops the booklet so he can order the ho' he wants, like ordering hamburgers off a restaurant menu."

"How you know that?" Phillip demanded.

"Robicheaux called it a menu. He said, 'Check this out, Saint,' he said, handing me a book. 'Would you believe those are menus back there in all those little books? The old man just places his orders well in advance of any trip he has planned. Now, I never told you that, okay?' They don't have names, just a number. You'd have to see it. It's just the way they describe the picture, and I know good and well they weren't talking about no dresses. The governor don't wear dresses, and why Robicheaux got all these magazines addressed to Pops in the backseat of his car? I heard the maid talking about cleaning up her sewing room the other day. Moms makes her own clothes. She don't need no magazines to order dresses. Sewing's her hobby, huh, Mason, Phillip? Y'all the only two house niggahs allowed up there to see her sewing room."

"Yeah, you right about that," Mason said.

We acted like we were the most ignorant niggahs on the planet when the good white folks told us anything they wanted us to believe. After we had given Moms and Pops a convict trial, we would all find them "guilty as charged" on all counts and then move on to something else to pass the time—anything that took the edge off of serving time and working at the mansion.

Chapter 19

Fifteen Months of Building Pressure

It was Friday, December 7, 1979, 2200 hours. Slim drove the van into the barracks complex slowly. Everyone exited, looking forward to some rest.

Bobby stopped at the office to pick up his mail. Roy Lee sat on the edge of Sally's bunk, talking to him. I stood in the aisle beside my bunk. My arms rested on the mattress and my head hung between my arms, looking down at the concrete floor. The double dormitory doors squeaked opening and footsteps approached.

"Say, Hammond, did you get your certified-stamp mail?" Mr. Williams asked.

"No, I haven't," I answered, lifting my head and turning to him. "I be so tired, I didn't feel like stopping and checking at the office."

"It's been in the office for a while. Come on. I don't know why the dayshift hasn't given it to you, but that's right—you guys are at the mansion all day."

I followed Mr. Williams to the office and signed for the envelope. "How long has this been here?" I asked. The envelope was dirty and worn as if it had been through weeks of circulation. It had several addresses—Hickory II, Spruce I, Governor's Mansion, and Police Barracks—written by different hands as the Department of Corrections tried to find me. Three locations had received it before it made it to the barracks. The black postmark was illegible, having been stamped so many times, and the post date was equally impossible to read. I sat at my favorite table in the activity room as Mr. Williams went back into the dormitory to make his nightly count.

Roy Lee and Sally were still talking when they heard it.

"Kiss my a--, mothaf---a!!"

Roy Lee came running through the double doors. "What's wrong, Saint? Who you talking to like that?" he asked. I was reading and snatching loose sheets of the magistrate's report, balling them up and throwing them across the room towards the wall with the phone. Roy Lee slowly approached me.

I continued reading the body of the report. "These white folks ain't playing by their own damn rules, man. Read this here. *Fifteen months and that b---- denied me!*" I yelled, looking at everyone.

"Who?" Roy Lee asked.

"Polozola! That b---- says the deal that I got was the deal that I bargained for." I considered every point of law in my favor that Polozola ruled against: no plea of guilty entered, not advised of my right to trial and my Sixth Amendment right to counsel, ineffective assistance of counsel, and the prosecutorial misconduct and misrepresentation of giving me a bargain that was not a bargain due to the protection against double jeopardy. Not to mention it was all in the five-page boykinization transcript.

"That's the best that b---- can do? Judge West dismissed my case because I failed to file an objection within fifteen days from when the magistrate's report was filed in October. S---, I'm just getting this s---. Why George K. Anding didn't file an objection? They act like they ain't knowin' where in the hell I was. They can't make a ruling unless they get a receipt showing I got my stamp mail. Polozola knew I was at the mansion. He came to the mansion and talked to Pops about my case!"

It was through all the cursing and rage that the revelation came. "I know the ramification—you gotta let me go, you rotten sons of b----es. The grand jury indicted me in April 1973. The state had three years to take me to trial, according to the statute of limitation for the commencement of trial for murder. I filed my first writ in 1975. That was the state's opportunity to bring me back to court and either get me to plead guilty or go to trial. But no, Judge Lear denied it the next day. He denied my second writ in April of 1976. The three-year statute of limitation expired in April of 1976. Since I was never convicted like Polozola said in court, and they refused to take me to trial after I filed the writ notifying them of their error that was no fault of mine, they had to release me after that date ever since. If Polozola granted me a new trial, I'd file a motion to quash the indictment due to prescription of the statute of limitation. By law, they got to let me go scott-free and clear my record. That's the damn underlying ramification of granting my writ of habeas corpus. Then I'll sue them dogs for sending me to Angola without convicting me."

I got my file, a pen, and legal pad from my breadbox and begin drafting a petition for rehearing and motion to vacate judgment. I fell asleep three-quarters of the way through. Mr. Williams woke me up at two thirty in the morning. I went to bed.

That weekend, my family visited the barracks. Everyone came except Michael. When I arrived at the barracks at 1300 hours, they were standing in the yard, waiting for me. They were glad to see me wearing my pinstripe black suit instead of prison clothes. I looked like a freeman. We embraced. I had never dreamed that I would end up like this. I was supposed to be playing professional football by now. I told Daddy about my upcoming fight at the Centroplex Coliseum in January. He just nodded. Daisy and Paul got excited.

"Where's Michael?" I asked while walking beneath a young sycamore tree. No one answered me. I noticed Daisy's reaction to my question, and everyone's eyes said something was wrong. Martin's eyes were covered with dark sunglasses. I wanted to tell Daddy about Polozola, but something kept saying, *Don't do it. Don't do it.* I talked as though I was still waiting to hear something from the courts.

Teresa was holding a baby. "This a newborn," I said to her.

She just smiled. "I named him Forest, after you," she said.

Paul was now going to Southern University. He acted as though I was still the brother he had grown up with, and he was awfully glad that I wasn't in Angola anymore. I was glad to see them, but

I still was troubled about Michael. At 1350 hours, my visit was almost over. I slowly walked my sisters and brother to the corner of the building. I watched them walk on a few steps before I turned back to Martin. Daisy half-turned, saying something to me I didn't quite catch. When I went back to the tree. Daddy didn't wait for me to ask him.

"Forest, let me tell

Paul at LSU's Bernie Moore Track Stadium for the 2003 High School State Track Meet.

you about Michael. Michael done cost me all kinds of money. He was taking money out of Mr. Howell's office there at General Credit Plan on Plank Road. He was the leader of a burglary ring. He had people working for him breaking in my offices and stealing. That boy kept money in his pockets. I heard him the other day on the steps telling Mary Blount how he had to keep a lot of cash on him so he could pay his men. He done caused me to lose Thrifty Finance, General Finance, American Thrift, and Commercial Securities. He took my van and the police stopped him on I-10 in Sunshine. I called the juvenile authorities and they came took him up the road. I'm tired. I've had enough of this."

When I heard that, I shut down. Everything was happening all over again. I looked back at the building. Then it hit me what Daisy was trying to say:

"Forest, Michael got 'ape . . . got 'aped . . . 'aped . . . 'aped . . . *raped!*"

I cringed and fell to my knees. I grabbed white shells with both hands, raised them above my head, and released the shells over my head and clothes. Other convicts and their visitors watched in confused silence.

"Oh, no, Daddy. Don't tell me they done raped my little brother," I cried.

"Well, Forest, I didn't know what else I could do," the old man said.

I stood up, in tears and filled with rage. I fought to not confront him. But I had to.

"Why you had my little brother locked up? What's *wrong* with you? You haven't learned your lesson yet?"

Martin was stunned. The son talking to him was not the son he knew. I was someone else, and he was afraid.

"All they gonna do in that damn place is lock him up so he could be f---ed in his butt. Then they gonna do it to him every night. That's what they gonna do to your son, but that's all right. You don't think he's your son anyway because of his light complexion, huh? Mommy looked like a white woman. She was Jewish and Indian! Why her son can't take on her skin-color traits? These people don't care nothin' about us. We're only numbers to these people. They abuse us in here."

Tears were running down our faces as we stood toe to toe. I saw how hurt he was. I was hurting too, but I knew no other way to tell him the unvarnished truth. It was the spoken word—one of those things Linkletter said couldn't be taken back.

"Go!" I shouted. "I don't ever want to see you, *no mo'!"*

Hearing those words crushed Martin. After all he had done to get me out, efforts that I was not privy to, he was confused. His lips quivered as he searched to understand a system that was broken. He looked as if he wanted to die right there. He groped for words but finally put his hat on and walked away, leaving me staring at the ground. I extended my arm, pointing him away. As much as I had been through—was still going through—I was outraged.

On the way back to the mansion, Slim drove through the 'hood. I saw people I knew. The thought kept running through my head that I was so close, yet so far away. I entertained thoughts of escaping. I felt really saddened by what I said to my daddy. I loved him, and it hurt me to have to use that language on him. I wished I hadn't talked to him like I did. Maybe there was another way I could have said it that would drive the point home. Memories of what I was dealing with tore at my mind. *Maybe I took the news of my writ denial out on him when I really want to take it out on the system.*

Writing my motion to vacate judgment and petition for rehearing took several days, but I finished and mailed it to the U.S. District Court, Middle District of Louisiana. While I was trying to secure my freedom, Governor Edwards pardoned BigOne, who had ridden shotgun with Slim. He was hired to work at the governor's new home, which was being built on Highland Road. I was so tired when I got in the van in the morning, I never missed him. I continued to sleep until Slim made his announcement like a Greyhound bus driver entering a destination city.

"All right, wake up in here! We have arrived at the plantation," Slim said as he turned into the mansion drive and moved the van over the first speed bump. "Master wants to see a--holes and elbows, so get you head on straight. We got ninety-nine days left."

As everyone showered and dressed for work, I dressed in training clothes. After running, I went into the boiler room and did my exercises: fifteen rounds on the heavy bag, ten on the canvas bag, ten on the speed bag, and thirty minutes of jumping rope. I'd been doing that routine so long, it was just a part of my life now. Mansion security always stuck their head in to see if I was working out or sleeping. They said nothing—just stood in the rear basement hall door, watching. I knew they were checking up on me. After workout, I would clean up and go topside to the butler's station.

Foreign tourists visited the mansion daily. One day they were out front, taking pictures of the flowerbeds and mansion.

"You, and you, come go with me," Damon said, pointing to Devold and then pretending to decide between Sugar Bear and me. He chose me. We followed him to the front door. On the way, he gave me a bag of greenery and a Christmas wreath and told Devold to bring the ladder. We passed Phillip and Mason in the foyer, setting up a tree. Devold got on the ladder and hung the wreath. I stood handing him greenery to decorate the wreath with. Two of the tourists walked over, taking pictures of us.

"What's your name?" one of them asked Devold.

"Richard Devold."

The skinny man wrote Devold's name down on a pocketsize tablet. *Why would a tourist write Devold's name down?* I wondered.

"And what's your name?" he asked me.

What you want my name for? I wondered. *Don't give him your real name,* something told me. "Saint!" I answered.

"I beg your pardon?" the man asked, turning his ear to me and watching my lips.

"Saint. *S-A-I-N-T,*" I said, spelling it for him.

"Could I have your true name, your actual name? Is there something wrong with your giving me your true name?" the man asked.

"Sir, Saint is my name. My mother named me Saint," I said.

He finally gave up and walked away. I handed Devold the remainder of the greenery and hurried back inside the mansion before the photographer could take another picture.

Slim came and got me at 11:00 P.M. as I waited for him in the back-desk lounge, watching TV. State police trooper Gary Vines was my competition in stealing and eating all of the pecan brownies Bobby made. He had a bowlful of them and a big glass of milk, and he was dunking those brownies in it like a heron swallowing a frog. Unlike his brother, Harold Vines was slim and trim. Both Vines brothers were friendly and easygoing.

The next morning when I was changing in the convict's locker room, Roy Lee rushed in with the *Morning Advocate* newspaper. He held the Metro page in my face, showing me a photo of me handing Devold greenery at the front door of the governor's mansion. It read:

MANSION DECORATED FOR CHRISTMAS—Workers put the finishing touches on a huge wreath over the door of the Governor's Mansion Monday. On the ladder is Richard Devold. The other man

Staff photo by Bob Kate

MANSION DECORATED FOR CHRISTMAS — Workers put the finishing touches on a huge wreath over the door of the Governor's Mansion Monday. On the ladder is Richard Devold. The other man identified himself only as "Saint." A Christmas tree was also put up at the Governor's Mansion Monday.

Saint stands handing greenery to Devold.

identified himself only as "Saint." A Christmas tree was also put up at the Governor's Mansion Monday.

"Boy, you better keep out of this newspaper," Roy Lee said. "It's a good thing you didn't give them reporters your real name. That man y'all killed got people here that will protest you away from here, and Mrs. Edwards will send you back to Angola."

"Something told me not go give him my name. I thought they were tourists."

Tuesday, December 18, 1979, marked the beginning of the Christmas party season. It was also the day I wrote a letter to the clerk of court inquiring about the status of my motion to vacate judgment and petition for rehearing. I gave the letter to Mrs. Clemons to mail for me.

We were doubling the number of times we were cleaning silverware. Phillip was bringing out silverware I had never seen before. All types of functions were being sponsored by civic groups. The social parties kicked off at night. The governor never attended any of these parties. The guests consisted primarily of lawyers, elected officials, doctors, businessmen, bankers, and plenty of fine, beautiful, white women in fabulous gowns like those worn at the Academy Awards.

The day groups were slow and boring. They were only tea drinkers who did not tip. Drinking tea didn't make you feel young, beautiful, and inclined to tipping black boys. As we all got dressed in the locker room on those mornings, Mason said he could make them give us tips. "I'll burn some more candles on everyone we take cups from. Y'all know it works. Just bring them to me. Don't take them to Sally. I'll handle it," Mason promised.

The evening party groups worked us hard. We began making it to bed at one o'clock in the morning. I would run for an hour, clean up, and hit the bomb shelter by two thirty. Roy Lee woke me three hours later so I could do my morning workout.

The Christmas season was especially grueling for the convicts. We lost track of time. Every day seemed identical. We worked from can't see to can't see. I would rather have been a field niggah. Slim drove the green suits and Bobby, Sally, and Francis back to the barracks daily. All the butlers slept in the bomb shelter in order to use what normally would have been travel time to get a few more minutes of sleep.

After dinner on Christmas Eve, mansion security officer Sidney Scott told the kitchen they could go, but he needed one butler to stay. Since I had to train, I volunteered. Everyone else left for the barracks. At nine o'clock, as I sat on the green stool in the butler's station, a new mansion security officer, Jake Segura, called the kitchen.

"Kitchen, Hammond speaking. May I help you?"

"Forest Hammond?" he asked.

"Yes sir."

"Come up front. You got a call in the office across from me," he said. "Hit line two blinking to get your party."

I wondered who in the world could be calling me here.

"Hello, this is Forest."

"Forest, this is Teresa. I'm so glad I could talk to you," she said. Teresa began crying and telling me Martin put her and her baby out of the house. He got Michael back home but threatened to kill him, and Daisy was the only one at home. Teresa was at our cousin Lucille Perry Toussaint's home, down on Washington and Twenty-Sixth. To console her, I said I would see what I could do. But I had no idea what to do. In fact, I needed help.

At eleven thirty that night, the entire first family was in the sitting room, opening Christmas presents: the first couple; Anna, John, and their two boys, Douglas and Scott; Stephen and Arlene; Victoria; and David and Jenny. I heard Anna say she spent $3,000 that day at Cortana Mall and she was tired.

"What are you going to do when you get out?"

When I opened my eyes, Governor Edwards was standing in front of me. I had been asleep on my feet against the doorframe with an empty tray in my hand, and his presence had not really registered until he spoke.

"Sugar Ray Leonard's trainer, Dave Jacobs, asked me to come to Maryland to box and go after the light-heavyweight championship," I answered.

Pops looked down, shook his head, and walked back to the sofa, where the first lady was.

"Hammond, you can leave now," she said.

"Thank you, ma'am," I replied and went down to the locker room. In my locker I kept a stash of pecan brownies, and I ate about three. I strapped on my gear, went out into the cold night, and ran for an hour in front of the mansion. It was Christmas morning.

Chapter 20

Listening to a Still Small Voice

It was Monday morning, New Year's Eve 1979. Slim had stopped the van after turning out of sight and was waiting as I ran to it. The door opened and I rushed in, shivering. "All right, Sally, who did it?"

"Did what?" Sally asked. "I don't know a t'ing." Bobby laughed from the backseat.

"I didn't go to sleep in the streets," I said, looking around.

"Put your clothes on before you catch pneumonia. You must t'ink we crazy. You da champ," Sally said, laughing.

"Okay, whoever put me in the streets, your mama and daddy is a ho'," I challenged, waiting for a reaction. Nobody said anything. Bobby and Sally laughed and picked at me all the way in.

The same day, BigOne let Governor Edwards' colt die because he didn't follow instructions. The first lady wanted him off her property immediately. Mr. Robicheaux told her he would go out and take him to the bus station. He drove out to the Highland Road property and got BigOne and all his possessions. But instead of going to the bus station, he drove him to the New Mississippi River Bridge and stopped at the top. He then told BigOne to get out, threw his luggage out, and drove off. Dodging traffic, BigOne attempted to get his important papers, but they blew over the rail and floated down to the Mississippi River. Phillip and Mason were sitting on milk crates in the basement, shining Governor Edwards' shoes, when they heard Robicheaux telling Sidney Scott, Mike Mix, Lieutenant Hart, and Butch what he had done. The security men all laughed.

That night, the state dining room, sitting and drawing rooms, and foyer were filled with doctors, bankers, businessmen, lawyers, and local and out-of-state politicians. Mason and Phillip set up a wet bar, and Mike Mix and Sidney Scott mixed drinks and sent them out with the butlers into the thick crowd.

"Mr. Mix, why are you in here mixing drinks? Is it because your name is Mr. Mix?" Mason asked, laughing and speaking louder than usual. Every butler laughed, but Mix didn't. He looked over his tinted-lens glasses at all of us.

"Yeah, just make sure you hurry and get these drinks and get back out there and mix with the crowd and serve them and pick up those empty glasses so Sally can wash and keep my stack from depleting," he replied.

As midnight drew near, everybody in the party was drunk or almost drunk, including Mason, but he hid it behind his big, bright, friendly smile. His eyes never turned red from the effect of the alcohol, as opposed to Phillip, who looked like a red-eyed vampire.

"Seven, six, five, four, three, two, one. Happy new year!" the mansion crowd cheered. Governor Edwards was present. He wore a gray suit with a black leather patch on the left side of the jacket. I considered it his ugliest suit. It just didn't make the Silver Fox look good. The patch destroyed the balance and was tacky!

Captain Jones opened the champagne, and Governor Edwards poured it in the glasses of the beautiful women surrounding him. Since he didn't drink, he didn't pour himself any. He waved at the crowd around him as he headed for the front door.

"I'll be back in four years, so don't spend all your money!" he yelled, making the party crowd laugh. He then followed Captain Jones and Butch out the front door.

By twelve thirty, the people were acting oddly. While serving guests, I watched the other butlers to see if I could get a reading, but they were all busy as usual. By now they were masters at carrying silver trays overloaded with orders and drinks through a crowd of drunk people. With our elbows tucked tight, we fascinated onlookers who waited for us to bump into someone and spill every drink on somebody or on the floor. The butlers always knew how certain crowds moved, and they calibrated their own movements accordingly. In and out of the crowds we moved. I could detect the butlers running their games for tips. The people who ran our state and city governments, courts, and businesses were just a bunch of older kids having a good time.

"Saint," Damon said, catching me by the armpit and quickly ushering me past the elevator to Mrs. Clemons' office. "I want you to spread the word around to all the butlers that Mrs. Edwards expects to see the epitome of courtesy and good behavior the remainder of the night. One more screw-up and everybody goes back to Angola tonight, understood?"

"What?" I asked, surprised. "What's going on? Why? For what? What happened?"

"Ol' Mason just tried to get him a little piece of white a-- tonight," Damon said.

"What?" I exclaimed, shocked.

"Yeah, he tried to get that doctor's girlfriend to come in here so he could have sex with her," he said. "He was trying to get her drunk. The doctor is a good friend of the family and Anna's guest. Mason got two drinks on his tray and walked up to that tall fine young girl in the bone-white sleeveless gown. Know who I'm talking about?"

"Yeah, yeah, the tall one. I've seen her," I answered.

"Well, he goes up to her and tells her there was someone over by the stairs that wanted to meet her. 'Please follow me, ma'am,' Mason says. When he gets to the stairs, he turns around with this pretty-boy smile on his face. Well, the girl had a few drinks, you know, and she was being super friendly with Mason. He'd evidently been counting her drinks and thought his little slick a-- had gotten her drunk. The girl then asks, 'Where is he?' Mason says, 'He's down the hall,' talking about the one we just came here through. She wouldn't go any further and asked him, 'Who is he?' He turned around and said, 'You're looking at him.' She thought it was a joke at first, but Mason was serious. He was evidently drunker than the girl was and probably thought she was as high as he was. When she didn't go along with his expectations, she told her boyfriend, the doctor who's a good friend of the Edwards family. Her leaving must have blown Mason's high."

"Where he's at now?" I asked.

"He's down in the bomb shelter right now."

"Okay, all right," I said.

"You don't have to worry about anything. Mrs. Edwards knows you didn't have anything to do with it. Go ahead and get back out there on the floor so Mrs. Elaine can see your face."

I worked my way back into the crowd, spreading the word around to all the butlers—except Roy Lee—without giving any details. I saw Roy Lee and started towards him when a white man I didn't know grabbed my hand as I passed the piano player. A white woman in her late thirties had begun singing "Send in the Clowns" as the pianist played. The man pulled me to the side, holding my hand down as he did so.

"Look," he said, "I'm a senator from Illinois. I want to tell you something. I like your style. I really like your style. I've been watching you all night and I like your style. Do you mind if I ask you something?" He still held his drink in his left hand. I automatically thought he was a ho' from the streets.

"No sir. I don't mind," I answered.

"Is it true that all of you guys waiting on us are convicted inmates that they have taken out of the state penitentiary to serve us?" he asked. He was six feet tall with clean-cut, sandy-brown hair and wore a three-piece pinstriped navy-blue suit. He reminded me of attorney Anding.

Still holding my sleeve, he placed his drink on the piano, caught my hand, and shoved it down between his legs with both hands. I stood there smiling, trying not to look traumatized—which I was. My uninvited invisible friend was right on the scene with me, with something to say.

Damn, Saint! What you got here? No, it's the other way around: what got him? I can see the rumors. 'Mason tried to get him some p----, but Hammond tried to get him some butt! Damn. It don't get any freakier than this!

The man was scaring me. He was off-balance as he manipulated my hand while staring at me, his face only inches from mine. I tried to resist his placing my hand where I thought he was trying to place it. I began thinking he was getting off on my facial expression amidst all these people. I didn't want to look down, because that would have attracted attention. He then attempted to place my fingers on something soft and tubular. *His penis!* I thought, frantic. He then pushed it, closed my fingers around it, and squeezed my fingers to hold it.

I looked around desperately for the other butlers. They were nowhere in sight. *Where's a butler when you need him?* Then I saw them, looking like African warriors wearing painted two-faced masks with a white zigzag separating the sides. One side of their faces was that of a clown crying red tears, endeavoring to make everyone happy. The other side was that of a warrior. I knew I was hallucinating.

The requirement that we be clean shaven gave the impression to gay men in the closet that we were homosexuals, I thought.

"Why, ya'suh, boss," I said. "We's all convicts from Angola, suh. They takes us out Angola and works us here in the government's house, the big house, suh. You wants another drink?"

Releasing my hand, he grabbed me by the shoulder. I whipped my hand behind my back as if a heavy spring had retracted it.

"You make sure you divide this with the rest of the guys, and no, I wouldn't take another drink of these Southern hypocrite bastards' liquor if it made me rich," the senator said. "I can't wait to get the hell out of here."

"I agree with you, suh. Ya'suh," I said. "I'll make sho' I divide it, suh. Thank ya, suh."

I made it to the men's room, locked the door, and counted $970. *Now, Saint, by right, the man, the Illinois senator, said divide the money.* I stood there looking at myself in the mirror, deliberating. "I'm going to divide it," I said to myself. I separated the money into three stacks of $240 each and $250 in a fourth and placed one stack into each of my four pants pockets. "It's divided," I whispered. I straightened my bowtie, checked my smile, picked up my tray, and exited.

News at the Barracks

At 0245 hours, we boarded the Krewe of da Mansion van and began our journey across town to the barracks. Nobody wanted to stay at the mansion. Nobody opened their mouths until the van rolled off of state property and was on the interstate.

"Man, what the hell got into Mason up there?" Slim asked. "What he did? I saw your boy Robicheaux punch him in the stomach and throw him in the back of a state police unit and one of them drove off with his a--."

Bobby sat silent in the backseat with his multicolor knit hat on, watching from behind his dark shades. Francis and Sally sat together, speechless. Vic was sitting with Ross. Phillip sat with Sugar Bear. Roy Lee and I sat together. Frank sat shotgun next to Slim.

"Man, too much liquor got in his a—," Roy Lee said. "I told him he better stop drinking them drinks he was taking out to the guest."

"That's all he did, was drink a drink?" Slim asked. "You see that Robicheaux? I can't stand him. He thinks he be a bad-a--. I'd hate to go back, but if he ever say the wrong thing to me, I'm-a gulf him in his face. That's messed up. They gonna send the man back because he took a drink?"

"Not just one drink, Slim," Roy Lee said. "Every time he got a tray of drinks from the bar, he'd drink at least one. He always does that when we have liquor functions. I told Mason, 'Man, them white folks gonna send you back up the river. You better cut that out.' But he wouldn't listen. Can't tell him nothing, because he then thinks you're getting in his business. So, I left him alone."

Bobby continued to listen, as everyone did. He liked all the butlers because they worked hard and he understood them. To him, losing Mason was like losing a soldier in a war.

"Man, Robicheaux said Mason was trying to get some doctor's girlfriend drunk and take her back to Mrs. Clemons' office and have sex with her in there," I explained. "Now, that's what he told me. If it was just about the drink, they wouldn't have sent him back, but trying to put the meat on one of them white gulls, man, that's a horse of a different color." The van had become dead silent. Slim drove slowly as we turned onto Fuqua Street.

"White obsession," Phillip said, casually. "That done got a lot of niggahs kilt."

Roy Lee turned around to look at Phillip. "Aw, niggah!" Roy Lee shouted. "You guilty of it too. You think nobody knows about you and Mason getting them two white girls drunk and f---in' 'em in that same office? You think a niggah don't know about that, huh? I know because Mason told me! You two niggahs been f---in' them old white women and taking their money at them tea functions too. That wasn't no voodoo s--- Mason was doin'! That's when Mason took a fifth of Beefeater's gin out his jacket and poured the whole fifth in the tea almost, then went to the bomb shelter to drink the rest so he could get his head right and come topside and hustle them old women. Don't act like, niggah, you don't know what I'm talking about. He did that to get 'em drunk and that's when you and him took them womens to Mrs. Clemons' office, so don't be acting like you don't know what I'm talking about."

"Oh, my goodness—Lord have mercy," Francis said. Those were the most words and the loudest anyone ever heard Francis speak. Sally began speaking in French, and it didn't sound good. Devold spoke to Sally in French, and it sounded like a question.

Roy Lee was mad as hell at Phillip for placing him in jeopardy of losing his freedom. "You two been doin' them white chicks at them, them, ah, debutante balls," Roy Lee continued. "You just lucky them white folks don't know about it. If them white folks ever find out about this, they gonna send every one of us back to Angola, and your a-- gonna get a rape charge."

"Awwww, s---," Bobby said.

"Damn, man!" Slim shouted.

Francis suddenly began speaking in tongues, as if he had experienced a spiritual revelation.

"I'm a green suit, a field niggah," Ross said. "We ain't allowed in y'all's parties, huh, Vic?" Ross rarely said a word to anyone. He was always loaded down with dry-cleaning clothes, so he worked all day alone. "I'm glad Pops never wears the same suit in a month. That keeps me busy. I was downstairs in the laundry working. I know they can't charge me with none of that up there." He was feeling safe.

Others tried to evaluate their potential exposure. Vic frowned at the thought so fiercely that he looked like a bulldog from all the wrinkles. Big, tall, and red, he always looked like Frankenstein anyway. "Thank the Lord," he finally said in his deep voice, releasing a long sigh.

"Let me tell you sumpin'," Sally began, speaking slowly with his French accent. Everyone became silent as the van coasted past Capitol High School's baseball diamond on Fuqua Street. "If ever dem white folks find out about this, they gonna t'ink every one of us niggahs in da mansion knew about it, and we wouldn't say nothing about it because all us done had us a white gal—one time or another. They's gonna get rid of all us a--es." He made the sign of the cross. "If that happens, I swear before God, Phillip, I'm gonna cut your throat. I swear before God, you better believe it." Those were the last English words Sally spoke in the van.

"Damn!" Slim exclaimed. "That's enough. Don't tell me no mo'! I don't wanna hear no mo'. I'm sorry I asked. Man, we gonna act like we ain't never had this conversation, all right? This damn van might be bugged. You never can tell."

"Slim, I thought you sweep this thing daily. That's what y'all told me day one, remember?" I asked.

"Them white folks. You never can tell, man," he answered.

Slim received his pardon later that week and was hired by Governor Edwards to work at his home. Slim came upstairs just before lunch as he always did and talked with Bobby in the rear dining room. They had been at the mansion a long time and had witnessed a lot of abuse in addition to what they experienced in Angola. His pardon surprised everyone and brought the hope of being free one step closer for the rest of us. Slim didn't want to eat at the mansion, so Bobby made him a to-go plate that Slim said he would eat in his stable office out at the governor's home. "I got my gold seal. I'm a free man," Slim said before he hit the stairs. They were the last words we heard from him.

Slim had served more than ten years of his sentence. He didn't like having to come in contact with state police at the mansion, and he didn't like what Robicheaux did to his friend Mason. Slim never made it to the governor's stable office to eat his lunch. That evening, when the van stopped on the street in front of the mansion, the plate Bobby fixed him was lying on the curb along with the plastic utensils.

The governor needed a man on his property to care for his expensive horses. Mansion security felt that a butler or house niggah would be the best choice, so as soon as the governor got back in town the second week of January 1980, he pardoned Frank. It made us even more hopeful when Frank, beaming, walked into the butler's station with his gold seal in the middle of lunch.

The attitude of most of mansion security towards the butlers had become hostile because of what Mason did. We knew they looked at each one of us as a potential Mason. The tension was palpable as all the convicts walked on eggshells. Mansion security seemed to be daring us to make a mistake.

The day before my fight, I was on the tennis court picking up sticks and clearing leaves with an electric blower. The first lady wanted to hit balls off the ball machine. "Hey, Champ!" somebody called. I looked up to see Governor Edwards standing in the doorway, waving for me to come to him. I put the blower down, ran to the door, and entered slowly.

"You wanna watch a fight, Champ?" the governor asked. I agreed before I noticed the first lady standing in front of his desk with her hands on her hips, obviously angry. Pops had his hands in his pockets, then grabbed his cup of coffee off his desk, took a sip, and set it down.

"Yes sir," I answered, looking at the world light-heavyweight champion fighting on the television. I sat on an ottoman and proceeded to watch the fight.

"Edwin!" Mrs. Edwards said. "How dare you call this convict in here when I'm talking to you. Get him out, now! I want him out!" She was shouting now.

Pops continued watching the fight on TV, as if the first lady wasn't even standing there. "You know who that is, Champ?" he asked.

"Yes sir," I answered. "That's Matthew Saad Muhammad fighting Johnson, a southpaw. Matthew is the light-heavyweight champion."

Pops was impressed that I knew without having been there to hear their names when the fight started. "What do you think about him?" he asked.

"He's a little too slow for me," I answered. "I can beat him, though."

The first lady walked between the governor and the TV, blocking his view. Pops punched a button on his stereo, and Cajun music filled the room. I was thinking, *Which fight was he talking about, the one on TV or the one building between him and Mrs. Edwards?*

"Well, that won't stop me," she said defiantly. "Why do you have to go hunting again this time? Oh, I know, because you're the governor of the state of Louisiana who loves to be in front of television cameras: the Silver Fox, the Gambler, the Don. Why don't you spend some time with me and the family?"

It sounded like an argument between my parents during the 1960s, I thought.

"You want to know why I'm going?" Pops asked. "You really want to know why, Elaine? Because I'm not going to tell you this again." Mrs. Edwards plopped down next to me on the ottoman. "Because it's caribou season, and because I need a break. Because all day long, all week long, all month long, all year long, I'm always asked to help people. There is not one time when I'm talking to anyone you see me talking to or that I have appointments with that they don't want me to do something for them. Honest people, dishonest people, rich people, poor people, crooked people, greedy people, prejudiced people, black people, white people, you name it; short, tall, fat, fine and skinny, males and females, sick and healthy, I've talked to all of them. That means I have to say yes to this one and no to that one. I have to judge. I have to play God. I am asked to do what people want and not what I think is right or not what I think is best for the majority of the state. People! When I go against the grain, the same people that asked me to help them call the attorney general's office crying foul play. I need to get away from all of these people for a while. I really do."

I was thinking, *Damn, I didn't know the governor went through all that, with all the money and power he has.*

The phone on his desk rang. He answered it. "This is Governor Edwards speaking," he said. He listened for two seconds and went off on the caller. "Clyde! You motherf----er, you! Let me tell you something. I appointed you to office. You've stole all the money you could steal and never gave me a f----ing penny. You've never invited me or my family to your house for breakfast, lunch, or dinner, for a cup of coffee, juice, or glass of water, or a piece of cake, a doughnut, not even a f----in' beignet, and you know I like them." He listened for a few seconds. "Oh, now you need me, you motherf---er. The feds are after your a-- and you want me to bail your f---ing a-- out." The governor listened for only another ten seconds, not giving Clyde a chance to run his game. "So what? So you owe somebody, Vidrine. I owe somebody. We're always gonna owe somebody. I ain't got no f---ing money." Pops gave little ear to what Clyde Vidrine had to say. "I don't wanna hear all that bulls---, and don't call my f---ing house anymore. You call my f---ing house again, you'll never make another f---ing call, comprendo?"

Governor Edwards slammed the phone down, sipped his coffee, and stared at the TV. Mrs. Edwards had gotten up and quietly exited. I figured if she knew when to leave, I should follow suit. I got up and was backing out of his office, watching the governor. "I'm going finish my work, sir." He was so angry, I doubted he even heard me. I turned and was exiting when he responded.

"Champ," he called.

I stepped back in. "Yes sir?"

"The local DA declined your weekend pass," he said. "You don't have long, so just stay out of trouble. You're a good man."

"Yes sir," I said. I closed the door and walked back to the tennis court, thinking about what he told me.

Bad news was awaiting my return to the police barracks. The clerk of court for the United States District Court, Middle District of Louisiana, sent back my motion to vacate judgment and petition for rehearing, along with my December 18, 1979, status request. The clerk didn't even bother to reply on official stationery but instead scribbled a note at the bottom of my letter.

YOUR DOCUMENTS CROSSED IN MAIL WITH MY LETTER RETURNING YOUR DOCUMENTS. YOUR CASE HAS BEEN DISMISSED. SIGNED: LAURENCE

The Fight

It was after lunch, and Sugar Bear headed for the bomb shelter to take his much-needed nap. Phillip and Devold followed him, leaving the first floor attended by just Roy Lee and me. Bobby sat on his stool in the kitchen, looking out the window. I stood next to the green stool with my back to the wall, fatigued but within reach of the service phone. I told Roy Lee to join Sally and Francis in the rear dining room; I had his back. Each man had his head on the dining table, sleeping.

Hearing someone clear his throat, I opened my eyes and saw Pops sipping his coffee, staring at me. I had been asleep on my feet during his whole ritual of getting a mug out of the cabinet, filling it with coffee, and stirring in three teaspoons of honey and one spoon of creamer.

"Champ!" he said. "You ready for the fight?" He patted my right shoulder with his left hand. "You're a good man." By the time I realized it was him, he was going out through the big oak elevator foyer door.

I was so tired that the one-minute standing nap had caused my throat and tongue to relax. I tried to answer but couldn't get my voice box to produce a sound. I cleared my throat for a second attempt, but the door was closing behind him by then. I wasn't sure if he heard me or not when I finally muttered, "Yes sir."

Frank was a free man, working for the governor and driving his blue pickup truck. He appeared to be trying to hide his intoxication when he visited us after lunch. Strangely, Frank never drank liquor when he was in the conference room. Now he looked like an alcoholic.

Phillip finished cleaning his assigned area in the elevator foyer and restrooms. Now he was polishing the brass doorknobs to a high sheen. He completed the ones for the men's room and was buffing the ones for the women's. Hearing Damon's voice and footsteps approaching from around the corner in the foyer, he hurried inside the ladies' room so as not to be seen, but he didn't have time to shut the door all the way. Since Mason was sent back, he had become leery of the police.

Another pair of footsteps met Robicheaux in the area just outside the restrooms. "Damon, you have a call holding from the DA's office on line two," said Jane Laborde, Governor Edwards' press secretary.

"Send the call to Mrs. Clemons' office," he replied and headed down the hall.

When Damon walked away, Phillip went straight to the butler's station. Hearing that it was the DA made him uneasy and curious. He went to the rear dining room and into the back hallway to Mrs. Clemons' office.

"The fights start at seven and his fight is the main event around nine or nine thirty, if every fight goes the distance," Damon said. "The guy he's fighting is a two-time national A.A.U. champion and a Southern regional and state-champion titleholder for two or three years straight, I believe. Well, I don't know. Do I think he can win? Let's say he has the potential. Hammond's a really good fighter and tough to beat if you ask me. Well, I don't know. He hasn't had much rest these last few days, so he will be fighting tired. Is the media ready? You bet."

Approaching footsteps didn't permit Phillip to hear the rest. When Damon hung up the phone and walked into the hall, Phillip was cleaning the doorknob brass in the hall. "Oh, good afternoon, Mr. Robicheaux," he said casually.

Damon was surprised to see Phillip. He hesitated and then kept walking to the front door.

Phillip rushed through the door and went to the cooler. Damon came in five seconds behind him. Knowing Phillip, I felt that his going to the cooler was to elude anybody following him. When Phillip came through the door, his eyes told me he had information for me.

Damon dismissed the mansion crew and they went down to the locker room to get changed to all whites. He kept me in a prefight conference there in the butler's station until I saw the Krewe of da Mansion van pass by the window, with Phillip in it. Damon said he had made arrangements for the crew to attend the fight.

I went down to the locker room and got dressed in my fight shorts. I wore my raggedy Capitol High gym shorts under the white-and-red striped boxer shorts. Instead of wearing new boxing shoes, I put on the old white boxing shoes Cheyenne had ordered for me. They were broken in and comfortable, and I wore them for good luck.

It was dark when we arrived at the Centroplex (now called the River Center) in Damon's unmarked unit. He parked illegally at the front door and talked to a city police officer, and we continued inside. A large crowd of people was buying tickets at the box office. I followed Damon to the ringside seating area where Governor Edwards, the first lady, the governor's bodyguards, Billy Wright, and a gang of what I suspected to be wealthy white folks were seated. I sat on the second row behind the governor, two seats away from him.

When the fights began, the first lady kept jumping in her seat as fighters got knocked out and fell to the canvas.

Across the ring from Governor Edwards was a short, fat, Italian man flanked by his own bodyguards. He and Governor Edwards were obviously waging bets on the fights. I tried to take a nap, but sitting at ringside seeing the fights got my adrenaline flowing. As my fight neared, I began to feel butterflies. Two fights before mine, Damon got a signal from Billy Roth to get me wrapped up. Damon led me to the locker room. I put on my headgear, which was optional, I was told. I needed all the help I could get. Strangely enough, the old Italian referee was the same one from my first fight in the police academy. He wrapped my hands perfectly. He put my gloves on and taped the strings around the wrist. I began to feel that maybe the boxing deal was still on the table, that I was still a commodity.

I warmed up for five minutes, stretching and trying to break a sweat, but was too tired. Someone came in and shouted, "Time to go!" I was still too tired to loosen up. I followed Damon to the ring and heard people calling my name—people from the 'hood who knew me from track and football at Capitol. As I climbed into the ring, all I heard was "Forest Hammond! Go get him, Forest. Get him!"

Ringside was in the shadows when I stepped through the ropes, but the lighting in the ring was bright. I saw the judges seated against the ring. *What kind of fighter did they like, and was I that kind of fighter?* I wondered.

I didn't bother to bounce up and down or throw combinations the way fighters traditionally do when they enter the ring. I was too tired. I turned and saw the apprehension in Damon's eyes. "Mr. Robicheaux, you look like you got to fight tonight," I said.

"No, I just, you know, I just want you to do good. Beat this guy. You have a lot of rich people looking at you. You beat this guy and you'll have a shot at the world title within a year, I guarantee. They got the money to push you up through the ranks. It's all about money."

My attention was drawn to the second level of the Centroplex seating. I couldn't believe Daddy and Daisy were there watching. The old man had on his tam cap, a green sweater, and baggy khakis, and the lights reflected off what I knew were his dirty, grease-smeared eyeglasses. He had the same posture as when he stood and watched me play football in Memorial Stadium—off to the side with his arms crossed. I waved and Daisy waved back. The old man either didn't see me or was still hurt from our last conversation.

My opponent climbed into the ring, escorted by a soldier wearing camouflage and one wearing khakis. The fighter was bulky, black, and solid. He moved with confidence, and I could tell he was very experienced and fluid. He began bouncing around in his corner and along the ropes, still wearing his robe. I perceived him to be a slugger. His chest and shoulders were wider than mine. His neck was thick, and I knew since he was in the military he was in excellent fighting condition. The U.S. government was backing this guy, and they made sure they were represented by the best.

"Well, let me go on over there and let him know this my mothaf---in' ring he's in," I said to Damon. It was now about getting down and dirty.

He nodded and laughed. "Go right ahead," he said.

I walked around the ring, feeling for weak spots or dips in the flooring that could throw you off. These were areas I would avoid during the fight. As I walked, I pulled on the ropes, testing their tension or looseness. I continued and invaded my opponent's corner as if it were mine, without making eye contact. I then walked through the middle of the ring and began dancing to feel how much spring was in the floor. It was solid and fast. The white canvas was an inch thick and pulled tightly over the floorboards underneath. I then walked back to my corner.

The ring announcer and referee entered the ring. The referee came to me and, with the back of his hand, tapped my groin to see if my cup was on. He then inspected my gloves and headgear and instructed Damon to stick my mouthpiece in. "Have a good fight, young man," the referee said and went to my opponent's corner to repeat the process. I was in the red corner and my opponent was in the blue corner.

The short Italian in the crowd was being updated by one of his assistants. "Sir, the blue corner is the champ, two times national, two times state, and two times Southern regional. He has a right that nobody ever sees coming. Forty-eight of his sixty-six fights were knockouts by his right hand. He's twenty-six, been fighting in the military for eight years. He's in excellent condition. The red corner is a no-name. I know absolutely nothing about the guy."

"Tell Eddie I got fifty grand the red corner goes down, KO, TKO, or eight count, any round."

"Sir, with all due respect, that's a no-name he's fighting. You're leaving a lot of dough on the table. A hundred grand is an easy win."

"Ladies and gentlemen," the announcer said. All the chatter ceased. I leaned back on the turnbuckle. A quick thirty-second nap wasn't a bad idea, I thought. "For the main event tonight, fighting out of the red corner, weighing 173 pounds, with no current fight record available, fighting unattached, Forest 'the Saint' Hammond. Hammond!" It looked as though the entire Centroplex stood up cheering. They knew me, but I didn't know them. I stood and raised my right hand to all four sides of the grandstand.

I knew what they were saying in the other corner after my introduction. *"Tank, I never heard of this guy, so don't play with his no-name, okay? Get it over with." "Looks like he's a boxer, so you know what you have to do from the start. Cut the ring on him. Cut his movement. Box him in and take him out."*

Tank was nodding as if to say, *"I got this, sir."*

The ring announcer continued. "And in the blue corner, weighing in at 178 pounds, fighting out of Fort Polk Military Base in Leesville, Louisiana, the two times national champion, the two times Southern regional champion, and two times Louisiana state champion, with a fight record of sixty-six fights, one loss and one draw, forty-eight by knockout, Larry 'the Tank' Strogen. Strogen!" The Tank bowed, and there were cheers from civilians all over the arena and from the large section of military personnel on the second level, where Martin and Daisy stood. It made his welcome equal to mine.

"He's all of that?" I asked. "This guy is the champ."

The governor never talked directly to anyone in public about

KISATCHIE GUARDIAN FT. POLK, LA. FRIDAY, MAY 13, 1977 PAGE 13

AAU light-heavyweight champion Larry Strogen gets advice on punching techniques from his coach, Rocky Romero during a workout Monday at the Post Fieldhouse.

Larry Strogen trains with his coach.

gambling. Tonight, he was using Captain Jones to communicate his bets to the Italian man's emissary.

Governor Edwards leaned forward with his head tilted. "Tell your boss that's a sissy bet," he said to the assistant who conveyed the wager. "Tell him I know the record behind his favorite's right hand. If he lands one, it's over. Tell him if he lands a right hand, just one, that's seventy-five Gs. Tell him my man goes the distance, 100,000 per round, and your man goes down in any round. Make it a 500 G-pack for the winner through a KO, TKO, or eight count." The man got up quickly and went over to his boss with the message.

"Well, Saint, the way the governor figures it, you're a champ that nobody knows about," Damon said. "That's giving him the edge. Who else out here knows there are two champions in the ring, one known and one unknown? Who would you put your money on?"

"Is that what the governor did?" I asked, speaking with my mouthpiece still in.

"They are putting a lot of money on you tonight," Damon said slowly. "They don't know I'm telling you this. You beat this guy and it's all gravy from here on out for you. You think you can take his guy with just bag work and the little sparring you had?"

"Ladies and gentlemen, we also have the honor to have present with us at ringside the governor of the state of Louisiana and the first lady, Mr. and Mrs. Edwin Edwards." The first couple stood and waved to the cheering crowd. Governor Edwards saw the Italian hold up one finger, but Edwards gave a thumbs-down and held up five fingers. The Italian held five fingers up and nodding, accepting the bet.

The referee called us to center ring to receive the fight instructions. "Young men, the three-knockdown rule is in effect. If one of you gets knocked down, I want the other fighter to go to a neutral corner. I will give you a standing eight count. No hitting behind the heads, below the belt. Protect yourselves at all times. When I say break, I want you to stop fighting at my command. Any questions?" he asked.

I wanted to ask him if he would get a school desk up here in the ring, put those instructions on paper, and let me define each word, as if I were taking an English test. *No sir. I don't understand,* I thought about saying. *Would you go over that again? What size ring is this? Why are the ropes red, white, and blue? What do you mean by standing eight count? Is there a sitting eight count?* I was so tired that I felt like doing anything to delay the fight. I didn't want to leave center ring and go to my corner. I knew that ten seconds later

I would hear a bell ring, which would mean I was in a fight.

The Tank had just as much confidence in himself as I had in myself. He stared into my eyes without blinking, searching for weaknesses. In return, I yawned in his face. I placed my glove in front of my mouth, then smiled, knowing that he did not find— would never find—what he was looking for: fear. I was too tired to be intimidated or afraid.

"Okay! Go to your corners," the referee instructed.

"Hey, Forest!" someone called at ringside. It was Billy Roth.

"Hey, Billy!" I shouted. He was all business. There was a lot of significant stuff going on that I didn't know about.

"Watch this boy's right hand! He has a right hand that nobody can stop. He'll box you in a corner where you can't run. He's good!" The people with Billy seemed surprised he knew me.

Phillip waved at me from the first level, shadowboxing and punching himself. He looked crazy. Roy Lee was shaking his head. I thought they were clowning and telling me what to do.

Ding! I leaned over, placed my nose at the top rope, and inhaled deeply to smell the sweat, the way I had always done while putting my helmet on before a football game, in order to trigger an attitude. It kind of woke me up. Tank tapped gloves with me at center ring, and I sprang away from a lethal right hand. He began stalking me immediately. I backpedaled around the ring, keeping my guard high and parrying and slipping every jab he was throwing as he tried to set me up with his right hand. I attempted to shut the ringside and grandstand chatter out of my mind. The only person who existed was the one stalking me in the ring. The judges knew the Tank's reputation but had no idea what to expect from me. The Mongoose was on the loose.

Tank didn't know it, but I was ready to run out of that ring, hit that exit door, and lose myself in the streets of Baton Rouge. I didn't have any fight strategy. I was a stick-and-move boxer. However, I knew that everything Cheyenne taught me worked, so whatever the Tank's strategy, I was ready.

He wasted no time. A by-the-books military fighter, he knew the exact measurements of the ring, the height of the ropes, the distances from each corner, and the size of the equilateral triangle in each corner where he planned to box me and go for the knockout. He was good—just as Billy Roth said.

Tank began cutting the ring off, forcing me along the ropes and boxing me in towards my corner. He thwarted my lateral moves by stepping left or right to cut me off. Again he stepped to my right, feigning to throw his right hand, but I danced to my left. *He's boxing you in.*

"Get out the corner!" the governor yelled as he stood watching. "Damon! His corner man is no help." Everyone around the ring stood up shouting. "Damon!" the governor repeated. "Tell him to stay out the corner. He's boxing him in! He's gonna throw a right. Oh my goodness gracious, s---! Can he hear me? If he loses my money, I'm-a kick his a--."

Tank backed me into my corner. My space was reduced to nine square feet. I knew that the red turnbuckle was a foot behind me. Instead of trying to escape, I went into the mongoose dance, springing back and forth, facing Tank as if I wanted to mix it up with him. Tank didn't expect that. He hesitated and bounced back a step. I danced a foot to the right, but Tank moved to his left, blocking my escape route. He tightened the box I was in and was ready to strike.

"Box him in! Box him! You got him, Champ!" the fat Italian yelled, standing.

Feign right, pivot left—use your space. During serious times like this, my inner voice blocked negative comments, as if raising an invisible shield. I lowered my guard to a position level with my neck. That exposed my chin and face, giving Tank an irresistible invitation to throw his bread-and-butter right hand.

"Move away from his power!" Governor Edwards yelled. "Go left; go left. Don't go right! Put your godd--- hands up. What is he doing, Gene? He's got to know better. Godd---!"

Larry Strogen had been set up from the word "go." The in-and-out, back-and-forth dancing motions of the Mongoose had hypnotized him. He took the bait. He thought he had figured me out. When he saw my upper body move right, he lunged, throwing his right hand, but my feet had never left the canvas. I had bent forward at my waist. As Larry's right hand shot out, I simply pivoted left, as Cheyenne taught me. I leaned back, pressing against the expandable ropes to avoid his right fist, which flew three inches from my face. He had invested so much energy into his setup that he almost went over the red turnbuckle when he missed me with his right hand.

Completing the slip-pivot and escaping the right hand had the whole arena standing and cheering, except for the judges. "That's it!" Governor Edwards yelled as I stood in the middle of the ring behind the Tank. "It's all over. That was his best shot! He invested his best and couldn't get him. That's my man! Tell him he's nothing, Champ!"

"A moving target is harrrrd to hit. That's what I think about your right hand!" I yelled as I bounced in the middle of the ring, pointing with my left glove.

Ding! The bell sounded, ending round one. *"Stop!"* the referee shouted, stepping between us as the Tank rushed towards me from my corner.

"Saint, Saint, all you did was run from this guy!" Damon yelled over the noise. "Why you didn't fight? You didn't do any fighting! He had to win the first round for just being aggressive."

"Cheyenne said boxing is 20 percent physical, 80 percent mental," I answered, barely able to speak. "Goodness gracious!" I exclaimed.

"What's wrong, Saint?" Damon asked, thinking I felt acute pain somewhere. I didn't answer him. Nothing was wrong with my eyes as they followed the milk-chocolate-toned round-card lady around every square inch of the ring until she bent over and stepped out.

"Ohhhh, my legs," I said. "They heavy. Can't pick 'em up. I can't dance no more. I thought I was in better shape. Pick my legs up. Pick 'em up. Take the pressure off them. I'm not scared. I had to run first. Mongoose frustrates Cobra, so he can't think. Become anxious. I never fought nobody like this. He's good. Water—give me water."

"Seconds out!" the referee shouted.

"That means you have to get out the ring. Round two starts in ten seconds," I explained. "Don't forget the stool." I felt I couldn't run any longer. I wasn't thinking about fighting—just surviving.

Ding! The bell sounded.

Tank ran to meet me and tried to corner me on the ropes again, but I jabbed two, three, and four times each time. That kept him at bay the first thirty seconds. I saw blood coming from his nose and he began respecting my jab. I could see he was rethinking his fight plan. When he realized I had a right and a left and was hard to hit, I saw his courage disappear from his eyes. Now it was time to introduce him to who *I* was. He had me against the ropes, pounding away at my head trying to find an opening, but two punches were all I allowed before I grabbed him and walked him back to the center of the ring. I pushed him off and sprang back out of reach. He set to throw his right hand. I feigned as I had done in the corner, leaving him thinking I was out of reach, but again, my feet had not moved. I leaned back from the waist up. He hesitated and then threw his right.

WITH EDWARDS IN THE GOVERNOR'S MANSION

Moja, mbili. I stepped in. *Tatu,* my left hook, clipped his chin. His arms fell to his sides. He leaned into my chest and went to sleep. I felt all his weight as if I were a human prop. I sidestepped and Tank fell flat on his face on the canvas. The coliseum thundered with screams and shouts.

Roy Lee and the Krewe of da Mansion sat together, cheering and going mad. Phillip, however, was cringing and shaking his head.

I walked to a neutral corner with both red gloves raised above my head in victory. Governor Edwards stood clapping with the fans. The Italian stood staring in despair as the champ lay flat on his face.

The referee began giving Tank the eight count. Tank managed to get up to his knees, then to his feet near the ropes.

"Box!" the referee yelled, Tank having survived the eight count. I ran to him as he backed closer to the ropes. Reaching my striking distance, I jackhammered five jabs, followed with my right hand to Tank's face, which knocked him on the ropes. I skipped in, repeating the attack. I landed my jab, right hand, two left hooks, then another right hand as Tank collapsed and got entangled in the ropes. The bell sounded. The referee grabbed me from behind and swung me around, pushing me into my corner. Two soldiers entered the ring, brought Tank to his blue corner, and sat him on the stool.

The fans were hysterical. I had never missed or wasted any punches on Tank. He was in la-la land. Damon was laughing and grinning in my corner.

"I'll kill that b----."

Damon couldn't hear me for the noise.

I did not sit during the one-minute break. Tank was seated and being doctored by his trainers. I wanted him to watch me stand and take his confidence. This fight was mine.

On the Run

"So, if Saint wins, it's an upset. His picture and name will be all over the sports section," Phillip explained to Roy Lee.

"You ain't lying," Roy Lee said. "You talk about a protest. The Tank's backers gonna put so much pressure on the Pops until Mrs. Elaine gonna *have* to send Saint back to Angola."

"Saint, you just won the governor a lot of money," Damon said. "Now, you got to go ahead and take this guy out. That will seal it up for you. Everybody knows you're the winner already. He can't take anymore. He hasn't hit you with one punch. Now, look, the only way you're going to win this fight is you're going to have to knock this guy out. He's a triple champion titleholder. All right, go knock him out!"

Ding! The bell sounded for the third and final round.

Tank came out revived and with his guard raised, with increased respect now. I came out as if the fight had just started. Tank began cutting the ring off again, keeping with the right hand that had made him a triple-crown champion. Halfway through the round, I was tired of dancing away from him. He kept pressuring me. This time I was being boxed into Tank's corner. I again lowered my hands to draw his right. Tank lunged desperately. His lightning-fast right hand was still threatening, but my left slip-pivot was still working.

Mbili.

Paralysis seized him. The crowd went mad as he tried to keep his balance. I had pivoted tightly, placing me directly behind the champ. He thought my pattern placed me in the center of the ring like the first time. As he turned around, my right clipped the butt of his chin. The crowd was again hysterical as I stood in front of Tank, able to take him out.

Don't do it, something told me. I'd heard that before. As Tank wobbled, the crowd sounded like the parish-prison thugs when they were screaming for my life. I threw a three-punch combination, but my arms wouldn't extend into full-blown punches. I felt overpowered. I could only taunt him childishly: "Nanny nanny pooh-pooh, you can't beat me."

Ding!

"Stop!" the referee yelled, stepping between us. I turned and walked to my corner with my hands raised high above my head in victory, grinning at the ecstatic crowd.

The judges tallied up their points. It was a split decision, but to my amazement, it went in favor of Tank. As I was exiting the ring, Tank ran up and embraced me. "Say, brother, they took your fight. You won this fight all night long. You're the best light heavyweight I ever fought," he said. He then pulled on the upper rope and stepped on the lower rope, giving me space to exit.

"I want to know who that fighter is," the Italian bettor said. "Where he comes from, his trainer, where he learned to move like that, side of the bed he was conceived on—*everything, damn it!*

That f---ing Silver Fox." He lit a cigar as he walked up to Governor Edwards and shook his hand.

I couldn't celebrate with all the free people. Damon was rushing me away through the crowd but not before someone called my name.

"Forest Hammond!"

I turned around and saw a beautiful woman. She ran up and hugged me. She told me her name was Julia and gave me her address.

Damon brought me back to the mansion and left to celebrate with Billy Wright and friends. I showered, got dressed, and hit the kitchen for my favorite pecan brownies and milk. I went to the back desk in the basement lounge to call Slim's replacement. Scott was as game as Slim but a little older, about forty-five, and drank a little heavier.

"Mr. Vine, can I use this phone to call my ride from the barracks?"

"Sure, go right ahead. Press line two," he said. He was my brownie competitor. He read the comic section of the newspaper as he devoured brownies and milk at the back desk.

Scott turned left out of the mansion driveway, passed the traffic light, and headed for the interstate overpass. A police car hidden in Capitol Park pulled out with its headlights off and came to a stop on the bridge near the mansion.

"I think it's a few more houses down," I directed Scott. "Keep going, keep—*stop!* This it." We arrived at an address behind Capitol High. He had stopped at Winn Bush and gotten a half-pint of Jack Daniel's. He took it out and broke the seal on the cap. "That b---- Ossie Brown denied my weekend pass," I told Scott. I couldn't go home like all the other convicts did. I was to the point of not giving a damn. They would have to catch me first. "Keep the engine running. I'll be right back, okay?"

"Go ahead; handle your business," Scott said and took a swig of Mr. Jack.

I ran up to the door and didn't have to knock. It just opened. Julia was standing there in a white robe. I lifted her up off the floor, kissing her as I walked towards the bedroom. I closed the door and set her down on her feet. Julia's robe fell off, exposing her naked body. I had never seen a live, beautiful, nude woman before like I was seeing now. I unbuttoned my shirt as she pulled the covers back and moved to get in the bed.

"Hold up," I said. "Not yet. Stand there for a minute, a second, a few seconds. I just wanna look at you first."

Julia giggled as if I was insane. She stretched her arms, twisting them above her head so that they blended with the curvatures of her beautiful, sexy, naked body.

"That's enough," I said, kissing her. "Let's hurry before the dogs come."

Meanwhile, Detectives Bob and Jimmy and a news photographer rode up to the van and got out of their unmarked city-police unit. "Baton Rouge city police! Back it up, park it, and turn the engine off," Detective Bob said, pointing at Scott. Scott thought he was seeing ghosts. He backed the van up slowly on the shoulder of Cherry Street.

Knock, knock, knock, knock, knock, knock, knock, knock, knock!

"Nine knocks. I heard that before," I said.

"Who is that? Is that your friend?" Julia asked.

"No. That's the dogs."

A marked unit arrived and parked behind Detective Bob's unit. Two motorcycle units were posted at the opposite end of the street. Jimmy and Bob had their weapons drawn. Jimmy stepped down from the porch and began moving towards the side of the house. The uniformed officer kicked the door in and entered with his weapon drawn. Bob entered Julia's bedroom as she was putting on her robe.

"What do you want? Why you in my house?" Julia yelled. "Get out of my house!"

"Where is he?" Bob asked. "Damn it!" He rushed to the open window. Bob stuck his head out and saw me hopping the back fence. I heard him tell Jimmy, "Put your gun up; he's unarmed. Y'all catch him! You got your radio?"

"Yeah, we got him; we got him!" Detective Jimmy shouted and carefully hopped the fence.

Detective Bob ran to his unit, got his handheld radio, and called other units in the area. "The suspect is on foot. Repeat, he's on foot and be on the lookout for a white fifteen-passenger van headed for the police barracks. Suspect might attempt to connect with the van in the area or run to the police barracks. That's about four miles away. That's nothing for this kid. Stay in position. Suspect is unarmed."

"Who y'all think y'all is kicking my door down for no reason?" Julia demanded. "You need to get my door fixed tonight, because it won't close and it's cold."

Scott kept backing slowly down Cherry Street until he swung around the corner onto North Twenty-Fifth Street. He then backed up to Lula Avenue, where he changed gears and sped forward to take the long way to the police barracks on South Foster Drive. *"I work for the state, not the city,"* Scott said to himself as he raced through the neighborhood.

Patrol cars and motorcycle units sped up and down Willow Street, illuminating yards with searchlights. Detective Jimmy ran down Willow and returned to run down North Twenty-Fifth towards Jefferson Avenue. Detective Bob and several other units drove onto the Bogan Walk Pasture Baseball Park complex, circling the diamonds and dugouts and searching with their lights before heading southwest on North Twenty-Eighth Street.

I dropped out of a tree after Detective Jimmy passed and ran the opposite direction to North Twenty-Third Street. Then something told me to go back. I came back to the corner, took some black plastic off a trash pile, folded it up, and ran east towards Jefferson Avenue. I was freezing with just my little warm-up suit on. At least I didn't wear the all whites that would have made me easy to spot.

Detective Jimmy picked up two young officers as they ran to Jefferson Avenue. I had made it to Jefferson, but dogs barking on North Twenty-Fifth told me that someone was approaching the corner of Jefferson and Twenty-Fifth. I jumped a fence and crossed a backyard, crouching to avoid clotheslines, and hit Twenty-Fifth behind them. I got on a trash pile and covered myself with the black plastic I had taken as a police unit with its lights off slowly trailed behind Jimmy and the two cops. From my trash pile, I could hear them as they communicated by radio.

"Ten to Sixty-Six, come in," Detective Jimmy said.

"Go ahead, Ten."

"I got Twenty-Four and Twenty-Five foot patrol with me and we haven't seen hide nor hair of him."

"What's your twenty?" Detective Bob asked.

"We're at, what's this?" Detective Jimmy asked.

"Twenty-Fourth at Jefferson Avenue," one cop said.

"No, hold up," the other advised as he jogged to the corner of Jefferson. "Twenty-Fifth!" he yelled. "This is Twenty-Fifth."

"On Twenty-Fifth—near the corner of Jefferson," Detective Jimmy said.

"Forty-Four, what's your twenty?"

"I'm at Acadian Thruway and Bogan Walk at a gas station. I'm working an accident. There's a Frank LeBlanc driving a blue pickup truck. Registration places ownership to Edwin W. Edwards, address listed on Highland Road, Baton Rouge. Driver is a black male. He has papers showing he was pardoned a few days ago."

"Naw. It's related, but nonrelated. It's been about ten minutes since we been in this manhunt.

"Ninety-Five, what's your twenty?" Detective Bob asked over the airwaves.

"I'm on Lula Avenue and Twenty-Ninth."

"Fourteen is freezing, hiding between two school buses over here at Capitol High across from the Department of Labor. If he comes this way, he'll have to climb a fence to I-110. We have to assume he's beyond your positions. Everybody move to the points across North Street."

The trash pile shifted and made noise. They stopped talking. I knew they heard it. I threw back the plastic. We couldn't see each other's faces for the crepe-myrtle limbs, but they saw my pants. I took off running on the sidewalk, moving southwest towards Bogan Walk. Detective Jimmy was behind a cop who was about seven feet behind me. The stiffness was just leaving my legs after being balled up on the trash pile, and the men were gaining on me. The third cop was in the street, keeping his angle on me. I approached a crepe myrtle and slowed down a bit. Hearing the cop behind me on my heels, I grabbed a branch and pulled and released it. There was a sudden grunt and then no more footsteps. He must have fallen.

A car was blocking the sidewalk, and I saw a tricycle next to it. I couldn't run into the street because the third cop was there, running parallel just a bit behind me but waiting for me. I hadn't broad-jumped in almost seven years, but I'd done it before. I knew how. I jumped, clearing the tricycle and trunk of the car.

"Owwww!" Detective Jimmy cried. I figured he had run into the car.

I ran off of the sidewalk onto Twenty-Fifth Street as I passed Cherry Street. The third cop was on my heels. He grunted as he reached to grab my clothes. At Willow Street, he began grunting louder and louder as I heard myself putting distance between us. I looked back and saw he had stopped under a streetlight, foaming at the mouth, coughing, crawling, and then lying on his side. Finally, he curled up in a ball. *Picking them up and laying them down,* as Edna once said. I ran in and out of the curve and down Bogan Walk.

I cut across Bogan Walk Pasture Baseball Park, adjacent to Capitol High, where I had played Little League baseball. Slowing to a jog to catch my breath, I envisioned Capitol's stadium alive with athletes practicing football and running track. I saw the 330 marker area where Boodie yelled at me to meet him on the basketball court at Fairfields on April 10, 1973.

As I approached Park Elementary, headlights flashed twice in the dark, secluded area behind the visitors' side of the stadium. I took off running for either the Park Elementary fence or Twenty-Eighth Street, but the car caught me immediately and cruised alongside me.

"I got more horses than you," a voice said over the car's public-address system. It was a cop, but I didn't see any markings on his dark car. "Looks like you could use some help. Get in. I'll give you a lift."

I'd heard that friendly voice before. I stopped and the car came to a halt next to me. I rested both hands on my knees, breathing hard. I was trying to see who it was, but the windows were tinted. The first thing that brought relief was recognizing that it was a blue unmarked state police unit and not city.

I know him, I thought. *He's all right. I think I know him.* The door opened. I looked inside and saw him. It was my old friend who first brought me to the mansion and to get a haircut, my driver's license, dress shoes and my Converse All-Star sneakers, and even my first McDonald's meal in years. Gasping for breath, I got in and closed the door. He drove across the field to North Twenty-Eighth Street and headed to the barracks.

"Boy, times are hard nowadays," he said. "A man can't even get himself a little coochie." I just looked at him and nodded, too tired to speak. "That was the best amateur fight tonight I have ever seen. You two fought like professionals. You were terrific. And what topped it all was how you ended it. That was great. Then I sat there listening on the city police channel frequency. They were camped out all around this area within a one-mile radius. They searched the ballpark and left. That's when I drove back in that dark hole and just waited. Something told me you would come this way. I was enjoying it. I figured you'd work your way through them. They knew you were going to be there because the lounge phone all the convicts use is tapped. They've been waiting for you to make a mistake. The governor knows who's working with him and against him at the mansion. He's no fool."

We took the back way to the barracks, using the street between Florida Boulevard and Government Street where McDonald's is located. Scott had just pulled up and gotten out. He had problems going to the barracks, because he had to avoid the police and took extended routes. I got out and joined him just as Detective Bob arrived. Scott and I were in the shadows on the walk that led to the barracks office when Detective Bob and a uniformed officer got out of the unit and walked towards us. More units arrived.

"Detective, I think right about when you turned into the front-entrance drive that you began to have a jurisdictional problem," the state trooper said.

Detective Bob stopped in his tracks. He thought about it and signaled to the uniformed officers to get back in their units. They drove off, and Scott and I entered the barracks office as if nothing ever happened. Mr. Williams met us and congratulated me on the fight.

No More Pardons?

You got to get out of here. You got to make a move on them before they move on you. The words kept swirling through my head that night as I sat cross-legged on my top bunk inside the darkened dormitory full of snoring convicts. Getting out of here was the only thing on my mind—the *only* thing! I felt alone in this whole infinite universe with this gigantic, impossible problem to solve. I continued sitting and nodding in and out of sleep.

Scenes from the entire period I'd been incarcerated recurred in my dreams.

"*What happened, Champ?*" the governor asked. "*I'm all right.*" "*You're a good man.*" "*You wanna watch a fight, Champ?*" "*Boxer. Come get behind the wheel. When was the last time you drove?*" "*What are you going to do when you get out? When you get out? When you get out?*"

There had to be a reason for all this going through my mind. What could I do? What should I do?

Just ask the governor if he needs a good man to work for him.

"Huh?" I responded, surprised. I looked to my right, expecting to see someone sitting on the top bunk next to mine. I saw nothing but darkness between me and the light peeking through a pinhole at the rear of the barracks. It never dawned on me that my eyes were closed when I heard the voice. It came from the confines of my mind as I sat nodding in and out of sleep.

Seeing no one sitting there, I pondered what I thought I'd heard.

Oh, no, I can't ask the governor that, I thought. I remembered the first lady made it clear during my interview that we were forbidden to initiate any conversation with the governor. I knew that the governor had already pardoned three convicts. Slim and BigOne were both gone and he already had Frank working for him. He probably did not need anyone else. If I ask him that, he might ask what problems I have in store for him.

If you approach him like he's a businessman, he'll respect you. If you approach him like a foolish nigger boy, then you'll be treated like a foolish nigger boy.

What in the world is going on here?

Clear dialog was taking place in my head. I was being spoken to by something or someone else, something spiritual-like. I'd had nothing to drink and had taken no drugs, so I wasn't tripping. *I'm imagining voices*, I told myself. *Ain't nobody else experiencing this.*

By three o'clock, I realized that it or he was keeping me awake. I tried forcing myself to think of something else. Unable to sleep despite my fatigue from the fight and all the running, I figured I'd just go ahead and give an answer. Maybe then I could sleep.

If I'm suppose to do this and my mind isn't playing tricks on me, then let Governor Edwards be wearing that gray suit with the ugly-looking black patch on the left side of the jacket. If that's what he has on in the morning, then I'll do it. With that, I got under the cover and went to sleep, remembering what Ross said New Year's morning about the governor's suit rotation. He never wears the same suit twice within a month. Ross had been dry-cleaning the governor's suits for years and definitely knew his dress habits. I'd been seeing him wearing suits for eleven months, and this was the ugliest one I ever saw him wear. I wondered why he even wore it.

The white van turned into the mansion driveway and slowly approached the first speed hump. The Krewe of da Mansion driver assumed the responsibility of narrator, giving us the time remaining to labor and slave at the good white folks' plantation big house. Everyone was accustomed to hearing it and in fact anticipated it. It put the day in perspective.

"Wake up! We have just arrived on the plantation. We got sixty-four days left. Mrs. Elaine just peeked out her second-story window and saw five thirty on her watch and said, 'Now, that's what I'm talking 'bout!'"

We entered the back-desk door past Lieutenant Hart. Devold went straight upstairs and got the first batch of Community coffee brewing. In the locker room, everybody was showering, shaving, brushing teeth, or getting dressed. Roy Lee moved aside as Phillip stepped up to the mirror. He put his bowtie on, adjusted it to perfection, patted down his curly hair that had grown too long, smiled, and headed out the door.

I sat on the bench in front of my locker, working my feet into my crusty, worn, leather work shoes that I began running in four years earlier. They were misshapen, yet I was attached to them, because for four years I ran five miles in them five days a week. They had seen a lot of steps.

"One of these days, Bobby, gonna be my last day I put this stuff on," I said. Bobby was looking in the mirror, adjusting his chef's hat. He chuckled as he headed for the first floor.

After getting dressed, I hit the cooler in the butler's station and drank a half a quart of orange juice, dripping it on the front of my gray plastic running suit.

"Say, Saint, why don't you take that newspaper there on the salad bar and drop it at the back desk for Mr. Hart, would you please, sir?" Bobby asked, tauntingly. He knew how I felt. He was taking out his first tray of bacon and putting a fresh batch of homemade biscuits in the oven. A bowl containing all the eggs he'd scrambled was covered with a paper towel. He stirred his grits on the back burner.

"Going to hit it again, huh?" Lieutenant Hart asked when he saw me dressed for the cold. A thick towel was draped around my neck, and I had a ski-mask ready to pull down over my face. I held the newspaper an inch above the desk and let it drop—the closest I could get to throwing it. I walked outside, pulling the ski-mask down without answering him. As I headed up the incline I looked back and saw Bobby. He was saluting me and grinning.

"Going hit it again, huh? Going hit it again, huh?" I said, mimicking Hart. "Hell, no, Lieutenant Hart. I'm going out here in this freezing-cold weather to bake your mama a cake. What on earth do you think I'm going do? Asking me a stupid question like that. No! I'm going out here to pray." Given my anger at the moment, that was not such a bad idea. So I did.

"Yahshua, God of my mind, whoever you are, if you be for real, help me," I said.

The front lawn was covered with thick white frost. My footsteps crunched as I walked across it. With my hands wrapped under my winter gloves, I tried to jumpstart my roadwork by skipping to the left while jabbing, then repeating to the right. I bobbed and weaved, threw slow combinations of ten or twelve punches, then took off in an ice-crushing jog across the front lawn of the governor's mansion on January 15, 1979. It was 0600 hours.

Thirty minutes of running was enough. My entire body was sore. I went to the boiler room and only worked on the speed bag for a few minutes because I started feeling butterflies. I picked up a freshly dry-cleaned butler's uniform and went to the locker room to shower.

At 0715 hours, Ossie Brown, Detectives Bob and Jimmy, two foot-patrol officers, and an East Baton Rouge sheriff's deputy arrived at the mansion. I was so tired when Mr. Williams woke me up at the barracks that I didn't notice the absence of Ross. Nobody made any commotion about it. He was reported as AWOL. He had escaped.

Governor Edwards was in his office, meeting with the district attorney and police officers. The first lady was also present. Robicheaux and Butch were talking to the sheriff's deputy in an effort to locate Ross. They were having his photo shown to the Continental Trailways and Greyhound bus stations to see if such a man had bought a ticket to New Orleans, Ross's hometown.

"Hammond's appeal has been dismissed in federal court and he's a threat to society," Brown said. "If he stays here at the mansion another day, my office will be the platform for the most massive public protest that this state has ever known." Although it was early, people were already in the sitting room waiting to see the governor. "I'd also like to point out that his weekend application was denied by my office. He doesn't have a right to go into the community."

"I understand that, Mr. Brown," the governor replied. "In that case, if it was Hammond, he's in the custody of the state. That's the state's responsibility and they will have to take appropriate action and deal with him."

"Yes sir," Brown answered.

"So, what I'm understanding is that you all are claiming that this young man was in a neighborhood last night and went to a young woman's house. You saw the van parked in front of her house, and you went inside and didn't find him in the house, and at all times you said you had a photographer, but you have no pictures, is that right?" the governor asked.

"That was because he got out through the window when he heard us knocking," Detective Jimmy said.

"That's right, Governor, sir," Detective Bob confirmed.

"Next, a couple of your local police officers got into a foot chase after him through the neighborhood, and you say it was dark and you didn't get a clear look at his face, but you came within inches of grabbing him. But you, one of you, didn't see a tree branch hit you in the face, but you saw him and you know it was him, is that correct?"

"Yes, Governor, sir. That's correct," Detective Bob said.

"You further said a state trooper in an unmarked car drove him to the barracks, right?"

"Yes sir. That's right," Detective Bob said.

"That's strange. I wonder what a twelve-man jury would believe about this story."

"I know it was him, Governor," Detective Jimmy insisted. "I know it was him we were chasing. Look at the officer's face. It's swollen from the branch hitting him."

"Are you saying Hammond hit the officer with the branch?" the governor asked.

"No sir," the officer replied. "It happened so fast. I was about to, I was right—we were running and I was right on him about to grab him when we passed this tree on the sidewalk and it hit me in the face across my nose and I went down."

"If you ask me, Edwin, I don't think you should sign another pardon except for Bobby and Sally," the first lady said. "All the others are better off incarcerated. As soon as you release them, they will get in trouble again, like LeBlanc did last night wrecking our truck."

"That's Frank LeBlanc, correct?" Brown asked.

"Yes, Frank LeBlanc," the first lady answered. "Bobby and Sally have been with us for eight years. Hammond hasn't been here a year yet. He can stay here and help transition through training the next group of butlers for Governor-Elect Treen."

"Will this young woman come forth whose door you kicked down? Will she come forth and say Hammond was at her house last night?" Governor Edwards asked Detective Bob.

"I don't know, Governor, sir. We thought we had him."

"Did you get a license plate on the unmarked state police car you say picked Hammond up and drove him to the barracks?"

Detective Bob looked at the other officers, who shook their heads. "No sir."

"Well, did you get a name or description of the person driving the van and the license plate of it? Did you get any of that?" the governor asked. "I mean, I was at the fight last night and he fought a great fight. He actually won. That's a whole lot of running you say he did after having fought a very rigorous fight like he did. I'm just wondering if you have the right person, because you certainly don't have any evidence that he actually, well, I don't know what you are attempting to charge him with, or what makes him such a violent person that you don't want him in your city, Mr. Brown.

"I know a lot of innocent people have been convicted and sent to prison for life and they did nothing wrong. I am concerned with whether or not you have the right person. Sending him back to Angola is like convicting him of a crime he hasn't committed. Just as I told Polozola, he does his work here at the mansion and nobody, including Elaine, she will tell you, has had any problem with him. Never once do you say he responded to your calling his name, or that you told him to stop at your command, that he was under arrest and he didn't respond. I'm trying to see what the real allegations are here. I'm just wondering what you all were trying to do. I have a lot of unanswered questions and so far, a jury would want those questions answered.

"And as for the fact that his appeal has been dismissed in federal court, I talked to Polozola here in this office and at the dining table about Hammond. I did tell him one thing I remember clearly and that was a man shouldn't serve time in a penitentiary if he has never been convicted, but I respect your concerns and, well, that's fair enough for me."

Phillip left after serving the visitors coffee and couldn't wait to get out and report what he heard.

When I arrived on the second floor, I went straight to the coffeepot. Phillip, Roy Lee, Devold, Sugar Bear, and Sally were all gathered around Bobby in his corner at the stove and sink. I could sense that something was wrong and knew I would soon find out what it was. After I made my coffee I joined them.

"What's going on?" I asked.

"Moms is on a rampage. Frank wrecked the governor's truck last night. Pops had to pay $10,000 to keep it out of the newspaper and off the television news. Ross done escaped. Robicheaux and them checking bus stations right now, and Moms said if she could, she'd send us all back to Africa today," Roy Lee told me.

"What?" I exclaimed. "Are you serious?"

"Moms just told Pops if he were to pardon anybody else, it should be Bobby and Sally," Phillip said. "You ain't been locked up long enough. The DA Brown just told Pops he's gonna protest if you here for one more day. It's all messed up. Did you get it?" Phillip grinned.

"Damn! Did I get what?" I asked.

"Man, them people that arrested you and a cop you hit in the face with a tree limb, he all red and blue—they said they was chasing you all over Baton Rouge last night after the fight. They kicked your girlfriend's door in but you escaped out the bedroom window. They had a dragnet set to catch you but you slipped through it. They even said a state trooper helped you."

"Man, are you serious? Why don't you get serious sometime, man? Don't y'all look at me. I don't have no idea what you are talking about," I said. "That is messed up. That sound like, aw, hell, I don't know what."

Guardian Angel

I sat on the green stool sipping my coffee. The elevator-foyer door cracked open and then closed. The soft thud caused me to turn. Then the door cracked open again. I thought someone was snooping around, but then I saw four little fingers near the bottom of the door. It was John Todd, trying to push the huge door open to come through. I rushed off the stool to open the door before it crushed his fingers but was too late. His scream went through the entire mansion. I pulled the door open, picked him up, and rubbed his hands as I walked back to the stool.

Butch and Damon, along with front-desk mansion security, came running into the butler's station to see what the trouble was.

"What did you do to him?" Butch yelled, as if I'd injured the baby.

Damon was right with him. "Now what have you done?" he asked.

"What did I do to him?" I repeated. "Y'all still don't get it. The governor wouldn't have me here if I were a threat to his grandson! The door pinched his hand. He was trying to get through to come in here."

Governor Edwards entered behind Butch and Damon. Three businessmen followed him to the coffeepot like obedient lapdogs.

"Come on, John Todd," I said, playing with the baby to stop him from crying. "You're tough. That old mean door bit your hand, huh?"

I glared at Butch and Damon. I was tired of this. I couldn't take their falsely accusing me, trying to build a case against me any way they could. Because of my attitude, Butch always went on the offensive, protecting the governor from clear and present danger. Damon couldn't hide his contempt of me for being a bit smarter and wiser than he thought.

I set John Todd down and stood in front of the green stool. Governor Edwards was a foot from me, holding the pot's lever down as coffee poured into his mug. He and the three men were talking in French. Butch and Damon stood in the open area behind the governor, watching me.

The governor grabbed the honey bear, filled a spoon, and stirred it in his coffee. I observed his neatly groomed hair and the snow-white collar of his dress shirt. I was looking at him to keep from seeing Butch and Damon glaring at me. I saw the collar of his suit coat. I had a life sentence and this was the place to be to get help. I didn't want to go back to Angola, but I was tired of these people. I couldn't take it anymore—not to mention what the courts had done to me.

Then, strangely, my mind was invaded by memories of a dream I'd had. The governor was connected in some way, but it wasn't clear. *Am I dreaming now?* I wondered. *This ain't for real! This can't be for real. Is this the suit he wore New Year's Eve? Maybe he has two identical suits and he's wearing the twin.*

Roy Lee was in the background, mouthing to me, "Be cool!"

While watching the honey slowly fill the second spoon, I leaned forward to see if the ugly black patch was there. I stared in shock, as if seeing my mother rise from her grave. The intensity of my gaze heightened Butch's concern for the governor's safety. I realized that I was too close to the governor to be acting strange and nervous. I straightened up and pressed my thumb and index finger on my eyes. Maybe my vision was blurred. Maybe it was all the stress I was under. When I looked again, the suit hadn't changed. It was what I asked for as a sign, an omen.

Governor Edwards began pouring his third and last spoon of honey. His guests responded to him in French. The chime from the spoon hitting the mug and the foreign dialog were the only sounds in the butler's station.

Sally stood in front of his dishwasher with his legs crossed and toothpick in his mouth—the same as I remembered seeing him on my first day at the mansion. Bobby was busy in his corner, moving around quiet as a mouse. He'd heard and seen my interaction with Butch and Damon. Bobby saw half of my body to the left. The wall blocked out the governor.

"Phan-tas-ma-go-ri-a: A changing group of figures or images, seen as if in a dream.

"That's the still small voice of your guardian angel. If you listen and obey his voice, it'll keep you out of trouble," I said through Edna. "Lean

*forward," I told you when Skookie shot at you, grazing your neck.
"Don't go back. Don't go back," I said the night Pee Wee called you to
go inside the drugstore to get Boodie. "Look, you have been arrested for
murder and gave a statement of your involvement. You are in the police
station. Isn't it strange that you don't have any handcuffs on after giving
a statement? They handcuffed you at home before knowing anything
definite about your involvement. What they are trying to do now is kill
you," I warned you, remember? "Heads up, heads up!" I said, warning
you that Boodie was about to attack you with the mop wringer. "Drop
to your knees," I told you when Boodie threw salt in your eyes. "Go to
the dorm," I said, to get you out of the testing office before Leonard and
Black came back to kill you. "If one can do it, two can do it," I told you
when Cheyenne said he trained the only fighter to leave Angola through
the boxing club. "Don't trust nobody," I said, through the convict you
call Mississippi and the state trooper you call your friend.*

*Now, Saint. There are four things that come not back: the spoken
word, a spent arrow, time past, and a neglected opportunity.*

I simply had to rely on pure faith in something I alone perceived.
The evidence had just been presented in this phantasmagoria.

*If this don't work, Mrs. Elaine is for sure going to send me back
to Angola,* I thought. One last image arose in my mind.

"Aunt Daisy!"

"Deputy, may I speak to my nephew for a moment, please?"

"Make it snappy, lady."

*"Forest, boy, you listen to me and you listen to me good. You pray
to Yahweh, God of the Hebrews, and whatever you ask him for, at
the end of your prayer, you say, 'Yahweh, I ask you this in the name
of your son, Yahshua.' Now, you trust what you hear in your heart
and he'll walk you right out this mess you done got yourself into,
boy. He is the good Lord and he loves hard cases."*

At that moment, the first lady pushed open the door and stood
there looking at us. Butch, noting my peculiar behavior, swung
back the right half of his sports coat, to get either his weapon or
handcuffs. My mind was made up. This could not end. Governor
Edwards could not leave this room without my saying something to
him—even if it was the wrong thing!

"Governor, I need to talk to you."

"Edwin, I'm leaving with Jake."

"Governor, sir, I need you to . . . "

The first lady, Butch, and I spoke simultaneously. Governor

Edwards opened a dish, got a spoon of creamer, and stirred it into his coffee. Things were really messed up now. I hadn't greeted the governor by saying, "Good morning, sir." I had compounded my violation by interrupting his conversation with mansion guests. Then I had tried to initiate a conversation with him and did it in front of the first lady—probably the worst offense of all. If she'd been there earlier, I doubt I would have said anything. She just popped in.

The chimes were ringing. Butch turned around to face the first lady and cringed. "You heard that? Did you see him?"

"Yes, I did," the first lady said, stepping into the room and allowing the door to close behind her. John Todd began crying and walked up to her. She picked him up while staring at me.

Governor Edwards acted as if he didn't hear any of us, especially me. *S---! I knew I shouldn't have believed it.* I could see the front gates of Angola. *It's all over with now! She's coming after you. Call the Angola patrol!*

"Go ahead, talk," Governor Edwards said as he continued to stir his coffee.

The clique beat the hell out of you, making you think you hearing all kinds of stuff you can't trust!

Pops heard all of them, but he only answered you, a still small voice said.

He answered me! He answered me! I cried inside. *But I don't know what to say. I don't want to talk to him in here. What do I tell him?*

Tell him it's business.

That's gonna sound like you being smart and . . .

Bobby, unable to see around the wall, couldn't take the suspense any longer. He grabbed a big pot and rushed to the dumbwaiter. He pushed the button and turned, watching.

"It's business, sir," I said, staring at Edwards like a hungry lion. I ignored everyone in the butler's station. Two front-desk security stood in the dining-room doorway. The butlers stood on either side of the salad bar. Bobby, with his tall chef's hat on, stood holding the pot, opening the dumbwaiter. The three Cajun guests mutely observed the tension. Sally moved closer to the doorway to observe the action. Francis leaned against the ice machine, a clean white kitchen towel over his right shoulder. Butch, Damon, and the first lady all had their eyes fixed on me, but the governor did not.

Governor Edwards placed the spoon on a napkin on the counter, then faced me. He stared me in the eye while holding the mug to his lower lip and blowing on his coffee.

I stared back. I had placed all my chips on the table and he knew it. I was all in. I was tired. I was hungry for freedom. The governor saw it in a strange, intense meeting of the minds.

"Go to my office and wait for me in there," Governor Edwards ordered.

I turned, looking at the door leading out of the butler's station, into the elevator foyer, and to the governor's office. It looked like a long row to hoe. I led off with my right foot, ignoring Butch and Damon. I stopped as I faced the gawking first lady. She fixed her eyes on me as she approached me. She was fuming.

"Well, well, well! What kind of business is this?" she asked, expecting me to answer her.

I adjusted my bowtie and straightened my maroon butler's jacket. *I was talking to your man*, I thought as I stared at her. I walked past the first lady, turned my head, and brushed my left shoulder off with my right hand, as if brushing lint and dandruff in her face. I kept walking without verbally answering her.

"Edwin? Edwin! What kind of business is this he's talking about?" the first lady demanded. "I want to know what is this business."

"Sir, Hammond's not allowed according to mansion policy to speak or talk to . . . "

"How many governors we got in here? How many we got? Tell me! Oh, I thought I heard him say he wanted to talk to the governor about business. That's my business!" Governor Edwards shouted, raising his voice for the first time. The butler's station fell dead silent. Even John Todd stopped whining.

As the elevator foyer door closed behind me, the only sound came from the kitchen. It was Sally's patented, *"Pooool!"* It meant, "Good God Almighty!"

Burying the Hatchet

When Governor Edwards entered his office, he found me standing by a chair in front of his desk. He placed his coffee on a coaster on his desk and punched a button on his desk stereo, which played Cajun music.

He's recording this conversation. The music is just for background, the still small voice said.

The governor then sat behind his desk and reached for his coffee. "Okay, what is this business that you wanted to talk to me about?"

he asked, taking a sip of coffee as he looked at me. He held the coffee mug to his lips with both hands as he listened.

"Sir, on Christmas Eve, you asked me in the sitting room what I was going to do when I get out. At that time, I told you I had Sugar Ray Leonard's trainer's address, who wanted me to come and box for him up there in Palmer Park, Maryland. I have made some drastic changes to my plans. My family lives here and I need to stay here and try to help my sisters and brothers because they are going through some hard times and need my help. I will need a job when I get out and I know you need somebody to work for you out at your home on Highland Road and I just wanted to know if you need a good man to work for you," I said in a single breath.

The governor seemed impressed that I stated my business without a stumbling word while maintaining direct eye contact. "Well, let me ask you two questions," he said.

I knew whatever he asked I had to be truthful with him. "Yes sir," I answered.

"I pardoned one inmate and he let my valuable horse die and was never on time so Elaine fired him. I pardoned a second inmate, Slim, and he never showed up to my house to work. I pardoned a third inmate, Frank LeBlanc, and he got drunk and wrecked my pickup truck." Any other time, what he was saying would have been funny. "So, now here you come. What, now, do you have in store for me?" he asked. "Are you going to kill all of my valuable horses? Are you going to burn down my new house? Are you going to destroy my stables and barn, wreck my tractor, knock my fence down, and run off with my wife? What? I want to know. I need to know."

I knew I could only answer him according to what he already knew about me. "Well, Governor, sir," I said, smiling, "all I can say is, I'll work for you with the same dedication and commitment that I employ when I train for boxing." The answer was short, sweet, and to the point.

Governor Edwards nodded. He believed I was telling him the truth. I was.

"My next question is this: I am very informed about your case and your record in penitentiary. I've gotten calls all the way from Washington, D.C., from congressmen asking me not to grant you any clemency. This man you are charged with killing was well known and liked. A lot of people don't want me to release you. My decision is not based on who the man was, or who you were then, but who you are now. I need to know before I pardon you, have you buried the hatchet?"

His eyes bored into my very soul. I respected his question and again would tell him the truth. In view of his question, I knew I had to eradicate any plans for revenge. I bowed my head only briefly. I didn't want him to think I was having a problem with my answer. I looked back into his eyes and nodded. "Yes sir. I've buried the hatchet," I answered.

"Okay, good!" he said. "I need a good man to work for me. How does $1,000 a month sound for starters? That's $500 every two weeks."

"That sounds good, sir. I can live with that."

"Capt. Gene Jones will get in touch with you and tell you when to come to work. I know you need a few days to be back home. You know, regardless of what people say or think, I think you're a good man. You come from a good family background. You made a mistake when you were young and I think you deserve a second chance. You lost a lot. You've suffered a lot and paid for your mistakes."

Governor Edwards then opened a file on his desk. He took his pen out and signed the executive clemency document. He then opened a box and took out a golden state seal and a stamp tool to affix the seal to the document. The document had already been filled out to a certain extent. The governor then stood up, handed me the pardon document with his left hand, and extended his right hand to shake. I grabbed the pardon and shook his hand vigorously.

"All right," he said. "It's a done deal. You're free to go. Good luck. You can go on home to your family." He walked me to the front door of his office. "Oh, one other thing, and don't forget this. The city police detectives and undercover agents are going to try to set you up to be arrested on a rape charge of a white woman, or somebody is going to try to sell you something hot, then you get arrested for receiving stolen goods, so be mindful of that. You know how it works. You were an inmate lawyer. Just watch your back. Okay?"

"Yes sir. Thank you, sir."

I now understood what I saw on the day I entered Angola. I recalled the faces of the two old convicts at the front gate and the demeanor of the convicts in the lobby when I tried to envision the heartwrenching agonies and mental beatings they had suffered over the years that had left them still incarcerated in Angola.

I didn't bother to change clothes. I walked straight through the foyer. When I passed the double dining-room doors, the first lady stood watching with Butch and Damon, unable to say a word to me. Behind them I saw Bobby, Phillip, Devold, and Sally waving and smiling. When the first lady turned around, they disappeared fast, like in a cartoon.

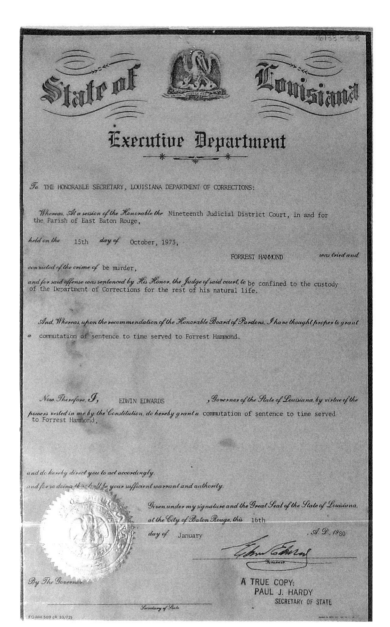

Executive clemency document signed by Gov. Edwin W. Edwards, commuting Forest Hammond's sentence from natural life to time served.

As I walked past the sitting room, where Detectives Bob and Jimmy, Ossie Brown, and a uniformed police officer were, I stopped momentarily. While looking at the front door of the mansion, I could see them in my peripheral vision. *"Kufyanza mbawa nguruwe."*

"What did you say?" Detective Bob asked. Governor Edwards stood in his office, watching.

"I said, 'I like your hat.'" I never turned to look at him.

As I headed towards the front door, two front-desk mansion security officers walked out of the office—one from either side—as if to intercept me. I flashed my golden seal in their faces. They saw it and backed off me, as if they were vampires who feared the color of gold. Roy Lee rushed to the front door and opened it for me.

"Have a nice life, sir," he said, smiling and flashing all of his dentures.

"Thank you, Roy Lee. Thank you, man. Take care."

"For sho', Saint. Be cool," Roy Lee said.

I walked out and turned back to look at him. "Take care, brother. Take care. I'm going home."

I stood on the front steps, rolling my freedom papers up like a diploma. Like a fighter who has defeated his opponent or a graduate who has earned his intended degree, I lifted my arms up high towards the sky. My gold-seal master's degree was in my right hand.

As I walked down the steps, there was another surprise waiting for me. My friend in his blue unmarked state police unit was there to take me to the barracks to get my breadbox. After all he did for me, I never once thought to ask him his name. But I didn't need to know his name. I saw him as a righteous angel in the flesh. He had taken care of me like a guardian.

I called my cousin Lucille Perry Toussaint, at whose house Teresa was staying when she called me at the mansion. She came and got me. As I placed my breadbox in her station wagon, it began to rain on us. We looked up at the blue sky and saw not one cloud.

"You know, Mrs. Lucille, it rained on me the day I was being locked up. Now it's raining on me the day I'm freed."

Lucille smiled and was joyous. As she drove me home, she kept asking, "How did you get out to be a free man?"

"Mrs. Lucille, you'd never believe me if I told you," I answered repeatedly.

I got out, took my breadbox from the backseat, and watched as she drove off. Daddy's new Chrysler New Yorker was in the driveway. It was trash day and two full trashcans sat in front of the house on the curb. As I stood in the driveway, I couldn't stop the tears from running down my cheeks as memories rushed over me. Everyone had gone to work or school and the streets and sidewalks were empty. I studied the surrounding houses to see how much they had changed. I then ran up the platform steps, opened the glass door, and looked around. I stood halfway in the door with a foot on the slab, holding my breadbox. The handle had nearly torn off when I ran up the steps.

All the boxing trophies I had sent home were on a new table in the living room. The old showcase with my track and football trophies had been moved into the corner. The glass front was cracked and taped up with masking tape.

Daddy's desk was as junky as ever. The house was dirty and not kept up and the smell was different from what I had become accustomed to the past eleven months. The sound of a blender came from the kitchen. It was too much for my heart. I felt so happy and hurt at the same time that I didn't feel I could make a sound. My throat seemed to close.

"Daddeeee!" I screamed. The handle of the breadbox broke and all the contents poured out in the doorway and on the slab, like groceries from a burst paper bag. In my right hand was the knife Vietnam had given me. I hid it in the handle of the breadbox and threw it down. Then I crumpled onto the threshold, crying.

"Who in the world is that yelling in my house this time of day?" Martin demanded. I must have startled him because he dropped something and I heard glass break in the kitchen. He was getting old and his nerves were not as good as they used to be. He walked up behind me. I hugged my legs and rocked back and forth while crying with both sorrow and joy.

I could only whisper. "I'm home, Daddy. I'm home for good. I made it home, Daddy. I'm sorry, Daddy. I still love you. I didn't mean what I told you. I do love you, Daddy."

"Forest, is that you?" Martin asked, confused. "What are you doing home?" He stood behind me looking up and down the street for police cars.

I wiped my face and tried to stop crying. Then I stood up and hugged him.

"See, well, I told you I was gonna make you happy again. I do love you, Daddy."

Epilogue

The *Baton Rouge Advocate* printed a small article the next day with a headline that said: "Youth Gets Pardoned in Druggist Murder." Baton Rouge television station WBRZ, on its evening news, displayed the mug shot taken of me November 8, 1973, the day I entered Angola. Governor Edwards was interviewed explaining the circumstances that led to my receiving executive clemency. My siblings and Martin were all in the living room, their eyes and ears glued to the television.

"Daddy, none of that happened," I said. "See how the system really works?"

Shortly after the news went off, the telephone rang. It was Mr. Williams calling from the police barracks. "Say, Saint, I heard your Robicheaux talking to some other troopers," he began. "They said there was a contract out to kill you. You better be careful and watch your back. They don't like you. Don't let nobody fool you." Hearing that made me think about getting me some "fireworks." I told Governor Edwards. He said, "Don't worry about it. Just don't react."

In the following days, the *Advocate* published longer and longer news articles about the case, and for the next few months it even ran huge editorials. The media continued to sensationalize my release. Carloads of young white males and females drove past 2929 screaming, cursing, and yelling, *"Murderer!"* They threw bags of trash, bricks, and beer bottles in the front yard and at the house. I called the governor and he said District Attorney Ossie Brown was using the media to incite the public because he believed I might go after him.

The brown wrecked Plymouth Duster I was driving coasted on Silverleaf Avenue towards the traffic light at Mickens Road. Bright lights in the rearview mirror blinded me as a new white Corvette caught up, passed, and got in front of me, stopping at the red light. It was approximately midnight. The passenger door opened. A white woman with fabulous legs, wearing shiny black dress shoes, pantyhose, a short black skirt, and red blouse, got out. I thought, *Damn, she's fine!* Her hair was dark and long. It was cold. Exhaust was billowing from the Corvette tailpipe. I had my windows up, and the heater of the Duster was barely keeping me warm. The lady walked towards the back of the Corvette. I expected the driver's door to open. *They're changing drivers,* I thought. The woman turned and passed between the Duster and 'Vette. She carried a black handbag. The driver's door never opened. I was surprised when she turned and walked up to my door. I looked at her momentarily and rolled the window down three inches.

"Can I get in and ride with you?" she asked. Her breasts were standing out like soldiers at attention, exposing enough sensuous cleavage to demand my attention. I was disoriented for a brief second. I then looked her up and down, examining her body. *Damn, you fine,* I thought. From head to toe she was a dream girl. I looked at the car she just got out of.

The male driver must have pissed her off and she got out not caring who she could catch a ride with, I first thought, with momentary sympathy. But then a voice audible only to me spoke. *You're looking at a rape charge of a young fine white woman. Tell her no.*

"No," I politely said. I quickly rolled my window up and sped around the Corvette, turning right on Mickens Road and flooring the Duster. From all the cases I had read in the *Southern* and *Federal Reporter* law books, I knew the good white folks had me under surveillance, just as Governor Edwards said.

At a 7-Eleven store on Florida Boulevard, I paid the cashier twenty dollars for gas. I walked back outside and noticed several people around the gas pumps. A young white male was holding a big radio/tape player. He appeared antsy as he approached me. I read him like a book. The trained eyes I possessed from living in Angola had now become tools I used to interpret body language.

"Say, brother, you can have this for fifty dollars. It's a boombox. It's brand new." He said they cost over two hundred at New Generations, a local electronics store.

Before I said anything, my innate defense system kicked in, and I mentally replayed my steps as I exited the store. I realized that he had bypassed others, blacks and whites, in the parking lot. I remembered seeing his face as he watched me leave the store. He had intentionally waited for me.

"I don't want it," I said. He came down to thirty-five dollars, then twenty-five, and finally ten as I pumped gas into the Duster. Reading all those law books had me looking around for a van or vans, undercover police vehicles, or even an old pickup truck. I realized that they had been following me and knew I was going to Teresa's apartment in her car. "Back off me!" I said forcibly. Reading my eyes, he backed off, got in an old car, and drove away. *Receiving stolen goods,* I thought. It was just like Pops said they would do. For all I knew, the boom-box was also loaded with drugs.

I worked faithfully for Governor Edwards until March 22, 1980, the day after he pardoned the remainder of the Krewe of da Mansion. I then informed him that I had to leave town and go get this boxing out of my system. He knew I was going to Sugar Ray Leonard's fighting camp. Shaking my hand, he said he understood and, if the boxing didn't work out, I could always come back and work for him.

I fought for the Maryland National Capital Park and Planning Commission, the sponsor for Sugar Ray Leonard's fight training club and gym. I won the district championship at the Washington, D.C. Armory. Many of my fellow boxers and I soon became discouraged about training for the Olympics. Pres. Jimmy Carter was boycotting the 1980 Moscow Games because of the Soviet invasion of Afghanistan. At Carter's urging, more than fifty nations turned their backs on the 1980 Olympics. *Damn, just when I get out and would be seen on national TV, in comes a godd---ed boycott,* I thought. I managed, however, to come within one fight of the 1980 Olympic trials in the light-heavyweight division despite not training. In West Virginia, I lost my last fight by a split decision, to a fighter named Buford Spenser. He went to Las Vegas and got slaughtered.

Dave Jacobs, Sugar Ray's trainer, only allowed me to do three rounds on all of the bags. In fights, I would be out of breath while the referee gave my opponents the eight count. Something wasn't right. I couldn't fight anymore, I told Jacobs. The Mongoose had retired. I no longer possessed the killer instinct that's needed to win fights. I was thinking, *Well, maybe I've won the fight of fights I was fighting for, and that was freedom.*

I went to live in Chicago for two months, trying to find a chef's job. I knew how to cook everything that I watched Bobby Turner cook in the mansion.

I returned to Baton Rouge on July 4, 1980, and worked for

Kentucky Fried Chicken, where I met Marilyn Jones, a young Southern University student who also worked there. Marilyn invited me to visit her Bible class at the Institute of Divine Metaphysical Research on July 30, 1980.

Today I am a minister in the I.D.M.R. and dean of the Alexandria branch. I was married January 28, 1982, to Karen Denise Thomas, a member of the New Orleans branch since 1976. Together we've had four children, Misty, Forest, Jr., Neal Nassor, and Miranda. All my children's names have meanings. For example, the name Miranda is a memorial to my father's objection to my arrest, because the police didn't read me my Miranda rights. From 1983 to 2005 I owned a successful janitorial business in Baton Rouge and Alexandria, employing many people.

I have also worked for the Baton Rouge Public Defender's Office. A judge allowed me to represent an African student who attended Southern University. Our attorney was late that day and the judge permitted me to sit at the counsel table to help her question the state's witnesses. The student was found not guilty. Ossie Brown called my boss and told him I was practicing law without a license.

William Shakespeare wrote, "All the world's a stage, And all the men and women merely players; They have their exits and their entrances, And one man in his time plays many parts, His acts being seven ages." It was a voice only audible to me that guided me to my freedom.

Many of the figures in this book have exited the stage.

My brother Michael exited in 1990, dying of AIDS complications.

Aunt Daisy exited in 2008 while being prepped for knee surgery. Although she was in a coma, I stood beside her hospital bed, talking and thanking her for being a wonderful Aunt Daisy and my good friend. I'll always love and will never forget you, Aunt Daisy.

On July 21, 1982, as Damon Robicheaux was leaving his home, his service weapon fell on the floor and fired a shot into his chest. He called in on his radio and exited the stage two hours later, dying in surgery. He was thirty years old.

Judge Elmo E. Lear exited the stage in 1987.

Ossie Brown left the stage in 2008.

Walkie-Talkie was using an outside telephone at a motel on Jefferson Avenue in the Fairfields neighborhood and was gunned down by an unknown black suspect who was eating a hotdog while he shot him.

Boodie exited the stage in 2012 following a long illness.

On the other hand, John L. "Vietnam" Hardy has a beautiful wife and son. He owns an auto-mechanic shop in Baton Rouge.

Daniel R. Pugh had pled guilty to rape and was given a life sentence. I filed a writ and got him released on parole from Angola. He is an electrician living in Baton Rouge.

Larry Smith is retired after making significant changes in the Department of Corrections at Angola. He is currently a minister at Rose of Sharon Baptist Church in Alexandria.

Gov. Edwin Edwards lives in the Gonzales, Louisiana, area and is married to his third wife, Trina, whom he met while serving a ten-year racketeering sentence in federal prison imposed on him by United States District Judge Frank J. Polozola. One must wonder if Edwards received that sentence as a result of the bad blood established between him and Polozola in 1979, when Edwards refused Polozola's demand that I be sent back to Angola.

My son, Forest, Jr., was charged with and went to trial for armed robbery of a night depositor at a bank. I was arrested and charged with accessory after the fact because I visited the codefendant at the Grant Parish Detention Center and told him his Miranda rights had been violated when he was interrogated by three white police detectives. They actually got angry because I advised the codefendant to recant what the police made him say without advising him of his right to have an attorney present. I told him, while looking into the video camera, not to talk to any police detectives if they came back and tried to get him to recant what he had recanted. I obtained Forest Jr.'s seventy-seven-page district attorney file through discovery. I read it and red-lined it in four hours. He was acquitted by the unanimous verdict of a jury of six blacks and six whites. The Grant Parish district attorney offered me a plea bargain if I pled guilty to criminal mischief. I demanded a full trial. The charge was dismissed. I've gotten police reports of over a dozen young men and women in the last few years, and after studying them and comparing them with the law, I advised them not to plead guilty. All charges were dismissed.

And so, "He that fights or runs away shall live to fight another day." Now, I see that the fight is definitely spiritual.

That *still small voice* warns us. It's our spiritual indicator switch, like the "check engine" light in a vehicle. When the light comes on, we may not know what the problem is, but we do know that if we continue in that direction without stopping and checking something, we will suffer loss. Some losses are great. Some are minor. The point is we suffer whenever we go against the commands of the *still small voice*. Like a concerned parent who talks to a child for his own good, *the still small voice* is that of our spiritual parent, our Heavenly Father (1 Kings 19:12 KJV).

Not long ago, I borrowed Daddy's new blue Chrysler New Yorker and drove to Zion City. I parked in front of Bea's Café and got out, looking down the black asphalt of Kissel Street, which was covered with a thick bed of gravel the last time I saw it. I envisioned a little boy running with a bag of groceries, chased by John Henry. I could see the little boy sprinting down the dusty dirt trail barefooted, with John Henry reaching out and scratching at his shoulder. The new resident at 5035 Packard Street allowed me to walk around the house to the back steps. "What's wrong?" she asked as I stood there. "Are you crying?"

"Ah, nothing," I said. "I was just thinking, ah, nothing."

My final stop was at the old red church on Ford Street, where my crawfish hole was. I squatted, looking at the dried-up hole. I got back in the car and turned around, heading for Plank Road. As I passed the crawfish hole, I looked; a shadowy figure of something or someone was running low to the ground as if to avoid detection. It was caped, giving it the appearance of a desperado.

"Damn!" I then sped off, heading for home.

I believe now that, this time, the home I am running to is the kingdom of Heaven. With that villain, the devil, on my track, it's a race to the finish line—a bell-to-bell fight. I look for my Heavenly Father to say, "Come, ye blessed of my Father, inherit the kingdom prepared for you from the foundation of the world" (Matthew 25:34 KJV).